Online and Social Networking Communities

Online and Social Networking Communities is a professional guide written for educational practitioners and trainers who wish to use online communication tools effectively in their teaching. Focusing on the student experience of learning in online communities, it addresses 'web 2.0' and other 'social software' tools and considers the role these technologies play in supporting student learning and building learning communities.

The guide offers:

- real-world case studies and quality research
- must-have lists of useful resources
- guidance on building and supporting online learning communities
- discussion of how collaborative learning can be assessed
- coverage of wikis, forums, blogging, instant messaging, Second Life, Twitter, desktop videoconferencing and social networking sites such as Facebook.

Online and Social Networking Communities helps educators and trainers develop a critical approach by exploring online learning from both the student's and educator's perspective. This practical guide provides the tools to help develop confident and thoughtful online educators, able to create successful and enjoyable learning experiences for their students.

Karen Kear is a Senior Lecturer in the Communication and Systems Department, Faculty of Mathematics, Computing and Technology, The Open University, UK.

Open and Flexible Learning Series

Series Editors: Fred Lockwood, A.W. (Tony) Bates and Som Naidu

Online and Social Networking Communities

A Best Practice Guide for Educators

Karen Kear

Routledge
Taylor & Francis Group

NEW YORK AND LONDON

First published 2011
by Routledge
270 Madison Avenue, New York, NY 10016

Simultaneously published in the UK
by Routledge
2 Park Square, Milton Park, Abingdon, Oxon OX14 4RN

Routledge is an imprint of the Taylor & Francis Group, an informa business

Typeset in Minion by
RefineCatch Limited, Bungay, Suffolk
Printed and bound in the United States of America on acid-free paper by
Walsworth Publishing Company, Marceline, MO

Library of Congress Cataloging in Publication Data
Kear, Karen Lesley, 1957–
  Online and social networking communities : a best practice guide for
  educators / Karen Kear.
    p. cm.
  Includes bibliographical references and index.
  1. Online social networks.   2. Communication in learning and
  scholarship—Technological innovations.   I. Title.
  HM742.K43 2011
  303.48′33—dc22   2010015934

ISBN13: 978–0–415–87246–1 (hbk)
ISBN13: 978–0–415–87247–8 (pbk)
ISBN13: 978–0–203–84273–7 (ebk)

SUSTAINABLE
FORESTRY
INITIATIVE

Certified Chain of Custody
Promoting Sustainable
Forest Management
www.sfiprogram.org

NSF-SFI-COC-C0004285
The SFI label applies to the text stock.

To my parents

Contents

List of Figures

List of Tables

List of Case Studies

Series Editor's Foreword

Twenty years ago online learning, 'computer-based learning' or 'computer mediated communication' as it was called, was the province of the *innovators* – as described by Moore in his book *Inside the Tornado* (1995). The allure of actual interaction between isolated students and between students and a remote tutor was a driving force. Even cumbersome and slow hardware and primitive software could not dim their enthusiasm. However, for the majority of teachers and trainers at that time Second Generation Distance Education techniques were providing outstanding results. Impersonal computer-based learning, with all its frustrations, was regarded as peripheral at best – a distraction at worse. How things change. Today I suspect there is not a school, college or university in the UK – let alone a commercial, industrial or public service training centre that does not employ some degree of online learning. The same will be true for many countries around the world.

Several recent books in the Series have focused on the contribution that online learning is making at all levels of education. Sir John Daniel's book *Mega-Schools, Technology and Teachers* (2010) challenges our long-held assumptions about the exclusivity of small group teaching of children rather than mass education, the primacy of pre-service teacher training compared to in-service training and, of course, the role that Communication and Information Technology (C&IT) can play. The book *Distance and Blended Learning in Asia* (2010) by Colin Latchem and Insung Jung provides an insight into development and innovation across Asia and reveals it to be a dynamic and rapidly developing region. It reveals advances in C&IT and its pervasive nature at all levels of learning and teaching. *Students' Experiences of E-Learning in Higher Education* (2010) by Rob Ellis and Peter Goodyear focuses upon students' experience of learning, the challenges they face, and how their conceptions of learning and approach to learning impact their learning.

However, to date no book has refined its focus to offer a critical approach to online collaborative learning and associated communication tools. This book, *Online and Social Networking Communities: A Best Practice Guide for Educators* by Karen Kear, marks a quantum leap in our thinking – from isolated to collaborative learning. Karen addresses our aspiration to create learning communities and reveals how concepts of *social presence* and *belonging* impact on learning. She methodically presents the available social software – discussion forums, chat rooms, wikis, blogs, instant messaging, virtual worlds – and discusses their potential benefits to members of learning communities. She also acknowledges the associated drawbacks emanating from

xx • Series Editor's Foreword

these technologies; from technical/access demands to information overload, from low participation rates to the perceived impersonal nature of online learning.

Fifteen years ago Tony Bates, in his book *Technology, Open Learning and Distance Education* (1995) warned us that 'technology will never save bad teaching; usually it makes it worse' (p. 12). This book is not about technology, seductive as it is. Its primary focus is on learning and teaching – and our role as teacher or trainer in equipping learners with those tools and skills that will build a sense of community and help students to experience enhanced levels of learning.

I wish I had this book twenty years ago; I would have been a better educator. I hope you and your learners benefit from it now.

Fred Lockwood
Yelvertoft,
March 2010

Acknowledgements

I would like to express my sincere thanks to all my colleagues at the UK Open University. They have given me their time, ideas and encouragement while I have been writing this book, and also their valued friendship over many years.

I am grateful to the many practitioners and researchers from across the world who have contributed case studies to this book. Collaborating with the case study authors, who are all innovators in online learning, has been a fascinating experience.

I would also like to thank Fred Lockwood, the series editor, for his encouragement and advice, and the editorial team at Routledge for all their help.

I am grateful to my partner Allan, who has encouraged me throughout the period of writing, and whose help was invaluable. His skills, practical help and thoughtfulness made all the difference.

Finally, I would like to thank my family for their constant support in everything I do.

1
Introduction

This chapter explains the purpose of the book and provides a brief introduction to online collaborative learning. It considers the concept of community, and how this can apply in an online setting. A brief commentary is given on the communication tools that can be used to support online learning communities. The chapter then explains how the book is organized, and how the subsequent chapters will use: case studies from around the world; summaries of key points for practitioners; suggestions for further reading.

This book is aimed at educators who want to use online communication to support learning and build community among learners. This includes lecturers at universities and colleges, school teachers, and staff developers in business and public organizations. The book discusses the benefits of learning in online communities, the communication tools that can be used, and the issues that arise. Particular attention is paid to 'web 2.0' or 'social software' tools, and the role these technologies can play in supporting learning and building community.

The primary focus of the book is the practice of online learning and teaching, but this is grounded in a discussion of research in this area. The aim is to enable readers to develop an informed and critical approach to online collaborative learning, and to the communication tools that can support this. The book builds on many years of experience and practice at my own institution, the UK Open University, which has been a leader in online learning and online communication for many years.

Learning in Social Networks

The educational experiences of learners are being changed by new approaches to education. In these new approaches, learners are active – they learn by working with each other and communicating with each other. Studying is no longer an individual activity, with hours spent alone, reading books or lecture notes. Instead, there is an increased focus on collaborative learning, with students working in teams, sharing ideas and resources, and creating things together.

In parallel with these developments in learning, there has been a rapid adoption of the web in education. Until relatively recently, use of the web in education was largely based on the delivery of course content, but the focus has now changed to communication. This is in line with wider changes in how the web is used in society. The web is no longer just a transmission medium, presenting content to passive recipients. Instead, the web enables users to interact with what they find, and to communicate with each other, directly or indirectly. Through social network sites, such as Facebook and MySpace, users can maintain social networks beyond their immediate location. These new developments in web use have been characterized by the much-debated term 'web 2.0' (O'Reilly, 2005).

Although face-to-face education has adopted online communication only relatively recently, the educational use of this kind of technology is not new in itself. There is a long history of its use in distance education. What made this technology attractive to distance educators also applies to face-to-face education. Online communication technology can provide flexible settings, where learners can keep in regular contact with each other and with their teachers, and can also make use of the wide range of resources available via the web. Through online communication, learners can gain support from their peers, and feel part of a learning group, or a course cohort, or their institution as a whole. The increased sense of belonging that can arise from regular online interaction perhaps explains why the term 'online community' is often used in this context. The development of a sense of community is an important aim for educators, and for many students it is a key factor in promoting motivation, confidence and enjoyment of their learning.

By using online networking tools such as discussion forums, social network sites, wikis, blogs and instant messaging, learners can carry out activities together. They can be members of online learning communities, able to support each other wherever they are. However, simply giving learners communication tools will not automatically create a learning community. It requires a teacher with skill, knowledge and imagination. The remainder of this book is an exploration of how online communication can be used to foster collaborative learning and a sense of community. In this chapter, I give a brief overview of some of the concepts that will be examined in greater depth later in the book.

Collaborative Learning Online

Collaborative learning involves interaction and dialogue. This interaction is not simply the one-way transmission of information from teacher to student. It is the exploration of ideas with other people, asking and answering questions, and solving problems with others. When students meet with their teachers and peers, there are many opportunities for learning through communication and interaction. However, face-to-face interaction is not always feasible for students, so an alternative is to 'meet' online. This kind of meeting can be done synchronously, where all participants are online at the same time (for example, via instant messaging or videoconferencing), or asynchronously, where contributions can be made at one time and then viewed by others later (for example via forums and wikis). This distinction between synchronous (real-time) and asynchronous communication is a basic organising principle of the material in this book.

Online communication tools, whether real-time or asynchronous, address constraints created by spatial separation: learners who are in different locations can nevertheless communicate online. In addition, asynchronous communication tools address separation in time: learners can communicate even if they are not available at the same time. Using real-time and asynchronous tools, learners can jointly carry out activities, share ideas, and support each other. Teachers can be in more regular and convenient contact with their students, and can keep track of their needs and progress.

The use of online communication in education is not without difficulties. Learners can feel overwhelmed and confused when taking part in very active online communities, where there may be large numbers of contributions. A further problem, particularly with asynchronous communication, is that it can seem impersonal, particularly if there are long delays between contributions. These issues, and others, can result in low participation, and therefore less effective learning. Later chapters of this book will explore these issues in more detail, and consider how to address them.

Concepts of Community

I have already mentioned 'community' and the scope for using online technology to develop a sense of community. However, although we are all familiar with the idea of a community, it is a difficult concept to pin down. A community is often associated with a geographical locality, perhaps a town or village, where people interact with neighbours, and may be involved with local schools, societies or religious groups. But in the modern world some people interact with others online more than they do locally face-to-face. So the concept of community has been broadened to encompass the online world. However, the issue of whether community can develop online has been much debated (Rheingold, 1993; Jones, 1995; Haythornthwaite, 2007). Some argue that people cannot truly get to know each other without meeting face-to-face. Others argue that the face-to-face element is not essential. For example, Wellman (2001, p. 228) has described community as:

> networks of interpersonal ties that provide sociability, support, information, a sense of belonging, and social identity

This definition emphasises the connections, or 'ties' between members of a community, but does not preclude the possibility that these ties might be created and maintained through communication technology.

Other common features in definitions of community are:

- a shared purpose or purposes;
- shared values or beliefs;
- shared practices or ways of interacting.

None of these features implies that being a member of a community is always a comfortable experience, but they do imply that community members are connected to each other, and interact on some kind of common, shared basis. There is therefore the potential for mutual support, shared working and shared learning.

These ideas have led educators to consider how the concept of community could apply in a learning context (Palloff & Pratt, 2007). In this context, what would be shared? On what would the sense of community be based? Lave and Wenger (1991) have developed the idea of a 'community of practice', where a group of people share and develop a set of practices, and hence learn together. Garrison and Anderson (2003) described an online 'community of inquiry' where learners and teachers work together online to develop shared understanding and learning. Thus 'community' is an important concept for learning, whether online or not. It lends a social dimension to learning.

Tools for Online Communities

Online learning communities can be supported by many different communication tools. For example, a simple email list allows a group of students to contact each other easily, and discussion forums provide more structured environments for group communication. For real-time communication there are chat rooms, instant messaging and videoconferencing. To help a group of learners work together on a shared document, and keep track of progress, a wiki can be used. To support reflective learning, students can keep a blog, and others can comment on the blog entries. All these tools, together with ways of using them for learning, will be discussed at greater length later in the book.

Over the years, a number of educational institutions have created their own online learning environments, to support group discussion and collaborative work. Examples include: the Virtual-U for adult learners (Harasim, 1999); and CSILE (computer-supported intentional learning environments), aimed at younger students (Scardamalia & Bereiter, 1996a). There are also numerous commercial and open source products, known variously as virtual learning environments, course management systems, or learning management systems. These include Blackboard (www.blackboard.com) and Moodle (moodle.org). Virtual learning environments are widely used by educational institutions, and typically include:

- facilities for delivering course materials online;
- tools for managing assessment;
- discussion forums;
- other communication tools, such as chat rooms, wikis and blogs.

Wikis and blogs are examples of the range of relatively recent communication technologies described variously as 'web 2.0', 'social software', 'social media' or 'social interaction technologies'. Other examples include microblogging tools such as Twitter (twitter.com), real-time communication facilities such as Skype (www.skype.com), and social network sites such as Facebook (www.facebook.com).

In view of the range of communication tools available, either within virtual learning environments or on the web, educators need to consider carefully which tools to use for supporting online learning communities. How should educators choose or create suitable online environments? Which characteristics of communication tools will support the learning process, and which might inhibit it? To answer questions like these, it is useful to understand how the features of different tools make them suited to different purposes. For example:

- discussion forums and wikis are of practical value for collaborative tasks;
- real-time chat and instant messaging tools can enhance social contact and a sense of 'presence';
- videoconferencing, together with a shared whiteboard, can mimic the experience of a face-to-face lesson or tutorial;
- social network sites can connect students' learning activities with their everyday online interactions.

Teachers need to suit the tools to the context and to the learning activities that students will undertake. This requires thought, a degree of experimentation, and a willingness to evaluate, iterate and change.

Terminology

It is helpful at this point to clarify some common terms that are used in this book and elsewhere in relation to online communication and learning. An important place to start is with the learner – who may also be described as a student, pupil, trainee and so on. Although the term 'learner' is generic, it can sound clumsy when used together with the word 'learning'. For this reason 'student' is used interchangeably with 'learner' in this book.

Unless the learner is entirely autonomous, or entirely engaged in peer learning, there is likely to be an instructor, teacher, lecturer, trainer and so on. In this book the term 'teacher' is used. This is because it is an inclusive term that does not imply a model of learning based on transfer of information.

Moving on to the technology, over the years many terms have been used for online communication, and for the software used to support it. Terms such as 'computer conferencing' and 'computer-mediated communication' (CMC) were once widespread, but are now used less often. This book uses 'online communication' for the process, and 'tools', 'technologies' or 'facilities' for the software involved.

There are several terms in use for online environments that are designed for learning and equipped with a range of tools. In the UK these are described as 'virtual learning environments' (VLE), and this is the term I use in this book. These environments are also described elsewhere as learning management systems or course management systems.

Finally, we come to the newer communication tools such as social network sites, blogs and wikis. These facilities are variously described as web 2.0 tools, social media, social technologies and so on. The category is not well defined, but has the common theme of facilitating online connections between people. The term 'social software', which I have already used in this chapter, seems to match this category of tools most closely.

Overview of the Book

A feature of this book is the use of case studies. These are used to illustrate the ideas introduced in the main text of Chapters 2 to 9, and to demonstrate how the ideas apply in a practical context. There are two case studies per chapter, and they are drawn from the USA, China, Canada, Africa, Australia, Europe and the United Arab Emirates. Some of the case studies are based on practice and research at the UK Open University. The book also includes other examples of practice, learning resources and research findings from The Open University.

Each chapter except the first and last ends with a list of key points for practitioners, and a list of suggestions for further reading. The key points provide a quick overview of important issues, findings, techniques and recommendations from the chapter. The suggestions for further reading highlight several sources, mentioned in the chapter, which will prove of value to readers who wish to follow up the topic.

The topic areas of the remaining chapters of the book are as follows.

Chapter 2: Theories of Learning in Online Communities discusses theories of collaborative learning, online communication and community. It introduces theoretical concepts such as constructivist learning, communities of practice, social presence and online community. It also considers a number of frameworks that have been proposed for learning and teaching in online communities.

Chapter 3: Tools for Online Learning Communities discusses online communication tools that can be used for supporting learning communities. It considers the range of 'social software' tools being adopted in education, for example: instant messaging; wikis; blogs; social network sites; podcasts; and virtual worlds. The chapter also presents the views of students who have used online communication tools for learning.

Chapter 4: Benefits and Problems of Online Learning Communities discusses the benefits of online communication for learning, and also the problems that can arise. Problems such as information overload, low participation, and perceptions of impersonality are considered. The chapter discusses how online communication can be used in ways that increase the benefits and reduce the problems.

Chapter 5: Too Much Information considers the problem of information overload that can arise in active online communities. It relates overload issues to the user interfaces of discussion forums, and to web-based facilities such as social bookmarking. The chapter discusses how members of an online learning community can share ideas and resources without overwhelming each other.

Chapter 6: Feeling Connected focuses on ideas of community among online learners. It considers the concept of social presence, which relates to whether online communication feels 'real' to the participants. The chapter discusses whether online learners feel a sense of community, and how this varies between individuals. It also considers the steps that educators can take to build community.

Chapter 7: In Real Time looks at the role of synchronous technologies for learning and for enhancing social presence. The chapter considers research and practice in using tools such as instant messaging, audio-conferencing, and virtual worlds. It considers these technologies from the perspectives of learners and of teachers.

Chapter 8: Assessment for Learning in Online Communities concentrates on the role of assessment for supporting learning and encouraging participation. It discusses the benefits and problems of peer assessment, and considers how online group work can be assessed fairly. The chapter discusses how online tools can help teachers to assess the process, as well as the product, of students' collaborative work.

Chapter 9: Supporting Online Learning Communities brings the book to a close by focusing on the role of the teacher. The chapter discusses factors that need to be considered when designing and facilitating online learning activities, and when choosing tools to support them. It includes the perspectives of teachers who have made the move from face-to-face teaching to using a blend of face-to-face and online learning activities.

2
Theories of Learning in Online Communities

This chapter introduces some theoretical ideas that are helpful for understanding online learning communities. The main part of the chapter covers theories of learning, with a focus on learning as a social activity. Theoretical ideas related to online communication and community are also introduced. The chapter moves on to consider several frameworks for understanding and supporting online learning communities.

In this chapter, I will introduce a range of theoretical ideas that are useful for practitioners of community-based online learning. Many of these ideas come from educational research, but some are from the social sciences more generally, and from theories of communication in particular. I shall start this brief tour of theoretical ideas within the discipline of education by looking at theories of learning.

Theories of Learning

In education, as in other social sciences, it is rare to find a theory being claimed as 'true' or being dismissed as 'false', as we expect to happen in the physical sciences. Instead, theories are developed and used as ways of helping to understand how people interact and how they learn.

Theories in education tend to evolve, rather than replacing each other. So, as time passes we are faced with a choice of many different theoretical ideas. These theoretical ideas, even if they do not make a grand claim to be 'theories', may be described as 'models', 'frameworks' or 'perspectives'. Because learning encompasses such a wide range of activities, different theoretical perspectives can be used to interpret different aspects of learning. Mayes and de Freitas (2007, pp. 14–15) comment:

> Although learning theory is often presented as though there is a large set of competing accounts for the same phenomena, it is more accurate to think of theory as a set of quite compatible explanations for a large range of different phenomena.

A particular difficulty when studying the literature on theories of learning is the terminology. Learning theories are described using a range of terms, such as 'associative', cognitive' and 'constructivist'. There are also different interpretations of how the theories relate to each other, and where key researchers and practitioners should be positioned. This confusing situation reflects the complexity of research in learning, which defies attempts at categorization and labelling.

The remainder of this section introduces three theoretical perspectives on learning, and presents a view of the relationships between them. These perspectives are behaviourism, cognitivism and constructivism.

The Behaviourist Perspective

Early ideas about learning were based on behaviourism, where learning is seen as the forming of a connection between a stimulus and a response. This perspective, also described as 'associationist' (Mayes & De Freitas, 2007), has its roots in the work of experimental psychologists such as Pavlov, who investigated learning in animals. It was found that animals learned from the repeated use of rewards when a stimulus produced the desired response – a process described as 'conditioning'. Skinner (1954) developed similar ideas in relation to human learning and to teaching. He advocated breaking learning activities into clearly specified sequences of small steps, where the learner masters one step before moving on to the next. In this approach, frequent positive reinforcement is provided via feedback to the learner.

Skinner's ideas were further developed by Gagne (1985) into the 'Information Systems Design' (ISD) teaching approach. Here complex tasks are broken down into hierarchies and sequences of smaller tasks. Through practice and feedback, each element is learned and joined with others before the learner moves up to the higher level. The ISD approach has been popular for training, and for certain uses of learning technology.

Some educators have been very critical of the behaviourist perspective, partly because it is seen as too teacher-centred, giving the learner little control over their learning. Behaviourism has been associated with 'transmissive' approaches to teaching, where students are expected to memorize material. However, Skinner was actually against such rote-learning approaches, and his aim was to improve the quality of teaching. Another criticism of behaviourism is that it takes no account of the mental processes involved in learning, or the internal representations resulting from it.

The Cognitive Perspective

In contrast to extreme behaviourist views, the cognitive perspective argues that the mental processes of the learner can be investigated and taken into account. There is a focus on aspects such as perception, memory and the forming of concepts. This perspective developed in the context of increased interest in computer processing and storage, so models from each domain influenced the other.

In the cognitive perspective, learning is a process of internalizing new knowledge so that it integrates with the learner's existing knowledge, and builds on it. For example, learners are considered to have mental 'schema', which are structures for representing what is already known. As learning takes place, these schema are extended to encompass the new experiences.

When compared with behaviourism, the cognitive perspective has more focus on the learner as actively involved in learning and in control of the process. There is an emphasis on thinking, problem-solving and exploratory activity. However, this perspective takes little account of the context in which learning takes place, or of social factors such as the role of other people.

The Constructivist Perspective

The term 'constructivism' arises from the premise that learners construct their own knowledge and understanding through the intellectual and physical activities that they carry out. Constructivist learning theories focus on learners' own personal understanding, as opposed to any externally imposed view. As in the cognitive perspective, learning is seen as a change in the learner's conceptual frameworks that arises from new activities and experiences.

The main focus of constructivism is learning based on activity. This may be individual activity or activities involving other people. When the focus is on individual activity, the term 'cognitive constructivism' is sometimes used. When the focus is on interacting with others within a social context, a term often used is 'social constructivism'.

Cognitive constructivism is based on the work of Piaget, who carried out studies of learning in young children (for example, Piaget, 1952). He investigated how children learn through play and activity. Piaget observed that children learn by trying out new things, and fitting the results with their current understanding. If the new experiences do not fit with existing mental frameworks, then these frameworks are changed to accommodate the new experiences.

An example of this perspective is provided by Kolb's experiential learning cycle (Kolb, 1984). As shown in Figure 2.1, this model has four stages. Learners move through these stages in turn, repeating the cycle as many times as they need to. Experiential learning is an iterative process of reflecting on experience and forming tentative concepts, then experimenting in order to investigate these concepts. This investigation results in further experience, and so the cycle can continue.

Social constructivism is based on the work of researchers such as Vygotsky (1962, 1978) and Bruner (1975, 1984), which emphasized social contexts and the role of language in learning. The focus is on learning as a social process,

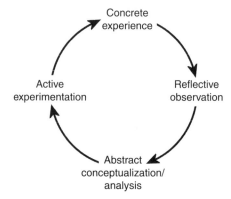

Figure 2.1 Kolb's experiential learning cycle.

Source: Reproduced with permission from The Open University.

where communication with others plays a key role. For example, children learn by interacting with parents, teachers, other adults and other children. University students learn through communication with their teachers and with their peers.

Social constructivism is an important framework for considering how students learn from their teachers and from each other. For example, a key concept from the work of Vygotsky (1978) is the 'zone of proximal development' (ZPD). This rather cumbersome term expresses the idea that learners can operate beyond their current level of competence, provided they are helped. In the ZPD, learners will feel challenged, but can cope if they have support. This support is often described as 'scaffolding', a term used by Bruner and his co-researchers (Wood et al., 1976). Vygotsky claimed that operating within the ZPD was important for further development.

Social constructivism encapsulates the importance of other people, whether teachers or peers, in learning. It is the basis for learning approaches focused on communication and collaboration, and is therefore a major theoretical perspective for learning in online communities.

Situated and Authentic Learning

Some educators have strongly advocated teaching and learning approaches based on social constructivism (Scardamalia et al., 1989; Jonassen et al., 1995). In particular, social constructivists highlight the importance of the context in which learning takes place, and the culture of the learning setting. These ideas of context and culture are characterized by the term 'situated cognition', as presented by Brown et al. (1989). The viewpoint presented by Brown et al. is that learning takes place through social interaction and authentic activities, and cannot be abstracted from its context. Brown et al. (p. 32) claimed that 'knowledge is situated, being in part a product of the activity, context and culture in which it is developed and used'.

From this perspective, it is important that the contexts and activities provided for learning are representative of a practice-based culture, rather than a school-based culture. In order to have meaning and value, the learning activities should be as close as possible to the activities of actual practitioners. If this authenticity is not achieved, students will only learn how to operate in a school culture, and will not be able to transfer their skills beyond that setting into the real world. For example, students of science should not simply be asked to memorize scientific facts and theories. They should carry out experiments, analyse data and discover things for themselves. Problem-based learning approaches, where students work in groups to carry out investigations, are an example of authentic learning activities.

The case study 'Canadian border crossing in a virtual world' gives an example of a learning activity modelled on actual practice in a real-world context. In this example, because students could not gain access to the real physical setting, their experiential learning took place using a simulation in a 'virtual world'.

CASE STUDY

CANADIAN BORDER CROSSING IN A VIRTUAL WORLD: A SIMULATION IN SECOND LIFE

Ken Hudson and Kathryn deGast-Kennedy, Loyalist College, Canada

Loyalist College is a modestly sized rural college located in South Eastern Ontario, between Toronto and Ottawa. In late 2006 the college became the first Canadian post-secondary institution to build a campus in Second Life – a public 'virtual world' where users can interact with each other in simulated environments. Then, early in 2007, Loyalist College became the first Canadian college to begin teaching classes in Second Life.

It was always the intention of the college to find suitable instructional uses for Second Life as a blended component of in-class instruction. The Virtual World Design Centre (the group at the college responsible for the Second Life campus) therefore surveyed relevant curriculum areas that could benefit from the inclusion of a virtual world experience.

Authentic Learning for Border Control

The Customs and Immigration stream in the Justice Studies department of Loyalist College teaches border control process as part of its curriculum. Prior to 2001, students in the program experienced a post-instructional placement at a real border crossing. However, recent security restrictions at the border forced the cancellation of these placements, and faculty were left with little alternative but to attempt to cover this material using in-class role-play scenarios. These were not very effective because they lacked realism and did not provide first-hand experience for learners.

A consultation and development process was therefore initiated to create an authentic replica of a border crossing in Second Life, for use in classroom instruction. The development included border officer uniforms, traveller identification, and vehicles with various licence plates and contraband. An instructional process was also developed in which a student, taking on the role of a border officer, interviewed travellers while the class observed. The roles of travellers were played by a team of students in a separate location, in order to create an unknown quality to each crossing. After-action review involved all students in discussion of the elements of port of entry processes they had experienced or witnessed.

Outcomes for Learners

Although students had initially been sceptical of the value of this experience, they soon found expression for the skills they were required to learn, and were able to apply these skills in a contextually relevant setting. Student opinion radically shifted during the exercise, and, once the activity was complete, students felt that they had a valuable experience that supported learning outcomes.

The final grade results for students using the Second Life simulation increased dramatically compared with previous results based on live action role-play. Prior to using the simulation, students had received an average grade

Figure 2.2 Simulated Canadian border in Second Life.

Figure 2.3 Students as border officers in Second Life.

of 58 per cent for their interview skills. For the first group who used the virtual border, the grades increased to a final average of 86 per cent (Hudson & deGast-Kennedy, 2009).

For the second group to use the simulation there was an additional average gain of 9 per cent, possibly because of the increased confidence of the facilitators in the value of the simulation. This second group of students showed no resistance to taking part in the simulation, largely, it is believed, due to positive peer feedback on the experience.

Training Professionals in Border Control

The success of the Loyalist College use of Second Life caught the attention of the Canadian Border Services Agency (CBSA), who then partnered with the college's Virtual World Design Centre to pilot the border simulation with new CBSA recruits. Those hired by CBSA are required to participate in an online pre-training course to help them prepare for face-to-face training. The Second

Life experience was offered to new recruits on a voluntary basis, and about half of the participants opted to try the virtual border.

The CBSA use of the border simulation was distributed rather than in-class, but the results were comparable to those from Loyalist College. CBSA found that the group of recruits who practised port of entry interviews using Second Life were 39 per cent more successful at the first testing milestone than those who did not participate. The group also exhibited, in addition to better core competency, a higher level of confidence (Hudson & Nowosielski, 2009). Both the Loyalist College and the CBSA experiences point to significant gains in retention and performance from using the Second Life border simulation.

Developing the Simulation

As this simulation matures, more detailed elements and streamlined interfaces have been added to facilitate its success. Loyalist College has added both an immigration office and an airport crossing into the simulation, so that students may experience a range of port of entry procedures. Additionally, a self-guided automobile search experience has been created to train students in effective search techniques. For travellers, an advanced traveller HUD (Head Up Display) has been incorporated to help the traveller participants quickly change citizenship, licence plates, and contraband.

Conclusion

The Canadian border simulation in Second Life demonstrates the successful use of a virtual environment for applied, situated learning. It allows learners to experience the port of entry environment in a realistic but controlled manner, and gives them the opportunity to practice interview processes in a relevant context.

The simulation continues to garner attention as one of the only virtual world educational experiences, to date, which demonstrates successful metrics. Philip Rosedale, founder of Second Life, described the simulation as:

> an incredible example of using virtual worlds in general and Second Life specifically to do something that is pretty compelling and simply cannot be done in the real world.
>
> (Rosedale, 2009)

The techniques used to develop this simulation extend beyond the specific border process to any context where successful interaction with other people is paramount. For training applications, this could include sales and customer service applications, new employee orientation, working in dangerous or remote locations, and so forth. Loyalist College has shown a path through all the possible usages for virtual worlds to find a specific use that has significant real world benefits.

Communities of Practice

The paper on situated cognition discussed earlier (Brown et al., 1989) points to the work of Lave and Wenger, where learning is seen as increasing participation in a 'community of practice' (Lave and Wenger, 1991). Wenger et al. (2002) explain this concept as follows:

> communities of practice are groups of people who share a concern, a set of problems, or a passion about a topic, and who deepen their knowledge and expertise in this area by interacting on an ongoing basis.
>
> (Wenger et al., 2002, p. 4, quoted in Ramage, 2010)

Based on studies of practice-based communities, Lave and Wenger claimed that novices in the community start their learning process by observing others, and then gradually become more active – a process they described as 'legitimate peripheral participation'. Wenger (1998) took these ideas further and claimed that learning is a process of developing an identity as a member of a community of practice. Through taking part in the activities and practices of the community, members learn and change. Wenger characterized this as follows:

> Such learning has to do with the development of our practices and our ability to negotiate meaning. It is not just the acquisition of memories, habits and skills, but the formation of an identity.
>
> (Wenger, 1998, p. 96)

In his (1998) book, Wenger identified three key aspects of a community of practice: 'mutual engagement'; 'joint enterprise'; and 'shared repertoire'. These reflect the fact that members are involved with each other, have a common purpose, and have shared ways of working. More recently, communities of practice have been characterized using the concepts 'community', 'domain' and 'practice' (Ramage, 2010).

There has been some debate as to whether a community of practice can exist online (Kimble and Hildreth, 2004). The views for and against the concept of a 'virtual community of practice' are similar to the debates about online communities more generally, as discussed in Chapter 1. In the following section these ideas are considered further, with a focus on communities of learners.

Social Aspects of Online Learning Communities

The above material has made a case for learning as a social activity. In an online environment, the social side of learning is potentially problematic. For example:

- Can online learners get to know each other?
- Do online learners feel that they are communicating with real people?
- Can a sense of community develop among online learners?

These issues affect levels of participation, interaction and engagement, and therefore influence learning. Unless students feel comfortable in an online environment, they may not participate openly, and so may not gain the benefits of discussion, collaboration, questioning and help that an online group can provide. If students feel uncomfortable or disengaged, they may withdraw from the online environment or even from the course as a whole.

In the literature on online learning, these social aspects tend to be related to one or other of two general themes: 'online community'; and 'social presence'. In a community, people feel a sense of belonging, even if their interactions are mainly or entirely online. If there is social presence, people feel that they are interacting with real people, even though the communication is mediated by technology.

Online Community

As discussed in Chapter 1, the concept of 'community' originally related to a local area (Wellman, 1999). However, as online communication tools were developed and used, the concept of community was extended to groups of people who were geographically dispersed but connected online (Baym, 1997; Wellman & Gulia, 1999). This raised the question of whether a community can exist solely online.

Rheingold (1993) used the expression 'virtual community' when he wrote about his experiences of using the 'WELL' online communication system. This was a text-based online discussion environment. Rheingold gave an explanation of what he called a 'virtual community':

> Virtual communities are social aggregations that emerge from the Net when enough people carry on [...] public discussions long enough, with sufficient human feeling, to form webs of personal relationships in cyberspace.
>
> (Rheingold, 1993, p. xx)

Preece (2000, p. 10) has defined an online community as consisting of:

- *people* who interact socially;
- a shared *purpose*, such as an interest or need;
- *policies*, such as tacit assumptions or rules to guide the interactions;
- *computer systems* to support the interactions.

Preece's definition adds the ideas of shared purpose and shared ways of interacting to Rheingold's focus on personal relationships.

The concept of an online or virtual community has been applied by many researchers and practitioners in educational settings (Palloff & Pratt, 1999; Renningar & Shumar, 2002; McConnell, 2006). Educators see a range of benefits when a sense of community is developed among learners. This is particularly important, and particularly challenging, in the context of online and distance learning, when students rarely meet face-to-face and have little social contact with each other. If a course cohort can evolve into an online community, students will feel more comfortable exchanging ideas and sharing problems with each other. Online activities will be more enjoyable, so students will engage more actively, and will deepen their learning as a result.

Social Presence

The concept of social presence has been used by many researchers in relation to online communities (Rourke et al., 1999; Preece, 2000). The term originated with Short et al.'s (1976) analysis of interpersonal communication via different media. Different definitions of social presence can be found in the research literature, but Gunawardena and Zittle's description (1997, p. 8) seems to express the idea clearly and succinctly. They define social presence as 'the degree to which a person is perceived as "real" in mediated communication'.

Social presence is influenced by the characteristics of the communication medium. From this perspective, the telephone offers higher social presence than email because participants can hear each other's voices, and are communicating in real-time. A video link would offer yet higher social presence. Low social presence can be a particular problem in text-based asynchronous communication, for example online discussion forums, because of the lack of body language, and the delays between messages.

More recent research (Swan, 2002) considers the behaviours of the communicators as a contributor to social presence. For example, when communication is via text, where there are no additional communication cues (such as tone of voice or facial expression) some people tailor their communications to compensate. They might, for example, post a purely social message to a discussion forum, or add an 'emoticon' such as ;-)) to indicate the tone and meaning of a message. In this 'equilibrium model' of social presence, learners in an online community increase social presence by communicating in ways which are perceived as 'warm' or 'sociable', and which therefore compensate for the lack of richness of the medium.

The Community of Inquiry Framework

In the previous section, I introduced the concept of social presence, and briefly considered its role in online learning communities. Garrison et al. (2000) have built on this concept to develop the *community of inquiry* framework for online learning communities. This framework adds the two concepts of *cognitive presence* and *teaching presence* to that of social presence (see Garrison & Anderson, 2003, for a detailed account). The result is a model that identifies three interacting aspects of a learning community, as shown in Figure 2.4. The three circles represent three concepts of presence: social, cognitive, and teaching. These concepts are discussed briefly below.

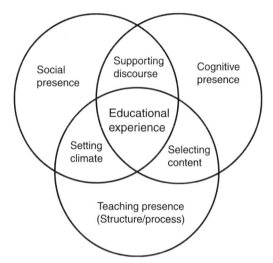

Figure 2.4 The community of inquiry framework.

Source: Based on Figure 1, Garrison and Arbaugh, 2007. Reproduced with permission.

Garrison et al. (2000) define social presence in much the same way as Gunawardena and Zittle (1997), quoted earlier:

> The ability of participants to project themselves socially and emotionally as 'real' people (i.e., their full personality), through the medium of communication being used.
>
> (Garrison et al., 2000, p. 94)

In the community of inquiry framework, social presence is characterized by:

- open communication;
- group cohesion;
- affective responses.

Open communication means that learners are freely interacting with each other, for example by replying to postings, expressing appreciation of others' input or asking questions. Group cohesion means that participants start to develop a sense of belonging. Indicators of group cohesion might include greetings, referring to other participants by name, and using 'we' or 'us'. Affective responses are those that express emotion. This is difficult when using a text-based medium, but can be achieved using punctuation, emoticons, etc. Self-disclosure and expressions of empathy are also affective responses.

Cognitive presence, another of the circles in the framework, describes how participants construct meaning together through their communication and interactions. It is described using a model of 'practical inquiry' (Garrison et al., 2000) derived from earlier work by Dewey (1933) on reflective thinking. Cognitive presence is characterized by four stages:

- triggering event;
- exploration;
- integration;
- resolution.

A triggering event could be when learners are given a problem to solve. The exploration stage involves finding and sharing relevant information. The integration stage requires connecting ideas together to come to a provisional solution. The resolution stage means applying and checking these ideas. This final stage may reveal further issues to investigate, and so the stages would become a cycle. The four stages of the practical inquiry model are reminiscent of Kolb's experiential learning cycle (see Figure 2.1).

The third circle in the framework, teaching presence, describes the process of structuring and supporting learning activities. Structuring is normally the responsibility of a teacher, but contributions to supporting learning can also be made by students. Teaching presence is broken down into:

- design and organization;
- facilitating discussion;
- direct instruction.

However, on the basis of different research studies, there is debate over the extent to which the latter two activities are separable. For a discussion of this issue, see Garrison and Arbaugh (2007).

Design and organization refers to the planning and structuring of learning activities for students, for example, selecting learning materials and specifying collaborative tasks. Facilitating discussion relates to the online support teachers provide for students, for example encouraging participation and drawing together students' contributions. Direct instruction emphasizes the teacher's knowledge of the specific curriculum subject. It refers to contributions made by the teacher in order to develop students' knowledge of the course topic.

Although the above description of the community of inquiry framework treats social presence, cognitive presence and teaching presence separately, an important aspect of the framework is the interaction between them. For example, teaching presence is important for developing students' cognitive presence, and also for encouraging the social presence that will support this: 'the element of teaching presence is a means to an end – to support and enhance social and cognitive presence for the purpose of realizing educational outcomes' (Garrison et al., 2000, p. 90).

The case study 'Hope this helps' applies the community of inquiry framework to peer learning and support in large-scale discussion forums. Here teaching presence was provided by students as well as by teachers.

CASE STUDY

HOPE THIS HELPS: PEER LEARNING USING DISCUSSION FORUMS

Chris Bissell, David Chapman and Karen Kear, The Open University, UK

The Level 3 course 'Digital communications' (600 study hours) was offered by the UK Open University from 1999 until 2008. It attracted up to 1,200 students per year, most of whom were employed full time in technological professions. Students, who were distributed throughout the UK, and to a lesser extent beyond, studied the course part time at a distance for nine months. The course materials were mainly delivered in print, with a number of computer-assisted learning packages. The course also provided a suite of discussion forums, so that students could communicate online and support each other's learning.

Teaching Presence

Members of the course team moderated (facilitated) the forums, but the interactions in the forums were largely student-led. At the start of each course presentation, the forum moderators engaged the students in discussion, and modelled an appropriate style of online interaction. But as the course progressed, the moderators consciously took a step back, intervening as little as possible. This was partly because prior experience had shown that contributions from staff tended to inhibit further discussion of a topic. In terms of the community of inquiry framework (Garrison & Anderson, 2003), the moderators tried to encourage students to provide much of the 'teaching presence' in the forums.

This peer-learning approach seemed to work well, with only a few occasions when a moderator needed to intervene because discussions became misleading, or a student had behaved inappropriately. In general, students were willing to trust each other for help, and largely did not seek direct answers from a moderator. They seemed to internalize the teaching role, particularly when responding to each other's questions about course assignments. It was rare for a response to give too much away. Instead students offered hints, help with terminology or pointers to resources, providing scaffolding just as an instructor might. For example, in response to a request for support with a technical assignment question, a fellow student wrote:

Read carefully Block 1 book page 98. Remember that a 32-bit word is 4 octets.

Cognitive Presence

The messages in the forums clearly showed that there were many helpful online exchanges taking place among the students. Difficulties were resolved, questions answered and explanations given. Students questioned each other's contributions, to ensure that the explanations given were consistent with their own understanding. Where this was not the case, they engaged in further discussion to resolve the differences. These activities are consistent with the community of inquiry's concept of 'cognitive presence'.

Students' messages used a combination of advice, explanations and resources to develop their shared understanding of course concepts. The forums included evidence that these learning dialogues helped to overcome conceptual difficulties. One such exchange was triggered by a posting from a frustrated student. It related to an assignment question on a technical specification language (SDL). The student's message began:

> I have reached a point where I don't know what I am doing. SDL is getting on my nerves, I don't get it!!!!! . . .

There followed an exchange of messages involving three other students, where an approach to resolving the problem was suggested by one student, queried by another and then confirmed. Following this, the original student posted:

> I had another look last week and I followed your instructions and I did see the light then. Thanks so much.

In the forums there were a number of these discussions, where students explored ways of understanding difficult ideas in the course. They offered each other different kinds of explanations, sometimes sharing analogies that they found helpful. An explanation was often presented as simply one of a number of ways of understanding a concept. For example, one student described an analogy of posting an assignment to a course tutor, which helped him to understand Internet protocols:

> I've come up with the following which is how I understand TCP/IP. It may not be totally correct but it's the way I think about it. Suppose you write your [assignment] and it covers a number of pages . . .

The interactions among students are in line with social constructivist ideas about learning. Students were trying to fit new material with what they already knew, either from their work experience or from previous study. Having the forums available meant that this could take place collaboratively.

Although a relatively small proportion of students (typically less than 30 per cent) actively contributed to the forums, many more students (over 80 per cent) read the messages. This relates to Lave and Wenger's (1991) concept of legitimate peripheral participation in a community of practice. The value of this passive mode of interaction (sometimes called 'lurking') was confirmed by results from a survey of students at the end of the first course presentation, where 77 per cent of the respondents reported finding the online forums useful. Students felt that the messages in the forums contained useful information and helped their understanding.

Social Presence

Students' discussions were largely carried out with tact and consideration, in a spirit of mutual support. For example, at the end of a message a student might add:

> Please check this – I'm quite willing to be wrong!

This is an example of how students acted (perhaps subconsciously) to build feelings of community and to enhance social presence. They paid attention to the social and affective aspects of the interactions, in both the tone and content of their messages. However, there were sometimes disagreements and heated exchanges. Interactions of this kind are not, in themselves, counter to the idea of a community, but they can be difficult to deal with online.

In spite of these occasional problems, the general level of helpfulness shown in the forums gave a strong sense of a learning community. Students' messages were sympathetic and tactful, and the friendly responses helped to encourage openness and build confidence. This is important if students are to reveal their difficulties and ask questions. In an online forum, communication 'cues', such as tone of voice or body language, are absent, and students can feel uncomfortable at the prospect of making a contribution (Wegerif, 1998). This is why the development of social presence is so important.

In the forums, students and moderators made use of friendly or self-deprecatory phrases to convey a sense of solidarity. For example, at the end of an explanation, a student added:

> P.S. Sorry about spelling mistakes.

In a similar vein, a forum moderator wrote:

> I hope this has helped and that I haven't made too many spelling mistakes.

The phrase 'Hope this helps' was used at the end of several messages, and illustrates the supportive ethos of the forums. Small touches such as these helped to create an online community for where members were working collaboratively to help each other learn.

Laurillard's Conversational Framework

In the previous section and the 'Hope this helps' case study, we have been considering the 'community of inquiry' framework. Other frameworks have also been developed for online learning or, more broadly, for learning using

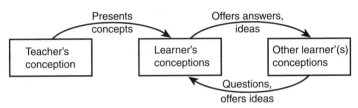

Figure 2.5 Laurillard's conversational framework applied to peer discussion.

Source: Based on Figure 3, Laurillard, 2009. Reproduced with permission.

technology. To end this chapter I will look at two further frameworks that are relevant for learning in online communities. The first of these, which we will consider in this section, is Laurillard's 'conversational framework' (Laurillard, 2002). Then in the following section we will look at Salmon's 'five-stage model' (Salmon, 2004).

Laurillard's conversational framework considers how ideas of dialogue, interaction and feedback can be applied to learning using technology. In this framework, a dialogue can be between: the learner and the teacher; the learner and other learners; the learner and his or herself (reflection). In effect, the conversational framework gives a model for the mechanism of social learning.

The framework takes into account the conceptions and practices (actions) of learners and teachers. It expresses how these conceptions and practices interact with each other in the process of learning. Laurillard developed the framework in order to consider how learning technologies can support different types of learning. The framework can therefore be used to help choose suitable technologies for particular learning purposes.

Originally Laurillard's framework was concerned only with the interactions between the teacher and an individual learner. But it has now been extended to take into account collaborative learning. For example, Figure 2.5 shows the interactions for peer learning where the teacher has provided an initial topic for discussion. The learning here is discursive, so the interactions are between the conceptions of learners. In other learning activities there would also be interactions between learners' and teachers' conceptions and their practices.

Salmon's Five-Stage Model

A further framework that has been particularly influential among practitioners is Salmon's 'five-stage model' (Salmon, 2004). This model applies to learning through group communication, in particular via discussion forums. It describes how learners progress through stages of development in their online interactions. Using the model, teachers or 'e-moderators' can provide support for students as they progress through the stages, in order to build knowledge and understanding together. E-moderators can also provide appropriate learning activities for students to carry out together (Salmon, 2002).

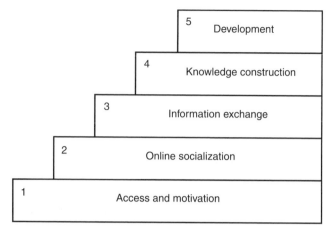

Figure 2.6 Salmon's five-stage model.

Source: Based on Figure 2.1, Salmon, 2004. Reproduced with permission.

The five stages, shown in Figure 2.6 to represent a flight of steps, are explained below.

- In Stage 1, learners become familiar with the online environment and begin to feel comfortable interacting online.
- In Stage 2, learners interact socially with fellow learners and begin to feel part of a community online.
- In Stage 3, learners access course resources online, as well as locating and sharing other sources of relevant information.
- In Stage 4, learners engage in course-related discussion and collaboration.
- In Stage 5, learners reflect on their experiences and consider how online interaction can help them achieve their goals.

Stages 3, 4 and 5 are the most productive in terms of learning, but stages 1 and 2 are important in order for learners to reach the higher levels. For each stage, Salmon identifies the skills that students need to develop and the support that e-moderators should provide.

Summary

A range of theoretical perspectives can help our understanding of online learning communities. The central theoretical ideas stem from social constructivist viewpoints of education. Here, learning is seen as arising from interactions between people. From the perspective of situated learning, these interactions should be as authentic as possible in relation to the field of study. Students will then gain something of the experience of working within a community of practice.

Theories of community can be applied to an online context, although this is subject to debate. Some researchers hold that students can be members of a virtual community with the shared purpose of learning. In this context, the roles students play, and the norms of the community, have an important influence on students' interactions, and therefore on their learning.

Social presence expresses how 'real' the online interactions feel to learners. It represents learners' sense of each other as actual people, even though they are interacting at a distance. Social presence depends partly on the medium of communication, and also on how students and teachers communicate via the medium. Even a text-based communication environment, such as a discussion forum, can provide high levels of social presence if participants take care about the style and content of their messages.

Several models or frameworks have been developed which can guide practitioners in supporting online learning communities. The community of inquiry framework builds on the idea of social presence by adding the concepts of cognitive presence and teaching presence. Laurillard's conversational framework applies ideas of dialogue and interaction to technology-supported learning. Salmon's five-stage model identifies a series of stages through which members of an online learning community progress as they interact with each other and with their teachers.

Key Points for Practitioners

- There are a number of theoretical perspectives on learning, including: behaviourist; cognitive; and constructivist.
- The constructivist perspective emphasizes the importance of activity and interaction with others in building understanding.
- For the concept of community to transfer to an online context, learners need to experience social presence – to feel that the communication is 'real'.
- Social presence, cognitive presence and teaching presence are brought together in the community of inquiry framework for online learning communities.
- Other frameworks include: Laurillard's conversational framework, which considers interactions; and Salmon's five-stage model, which considers development over time.

Further Reading

Brown, J.S., Collins, A. and Duguid, P. (1989) 'Situated cognition and the culture of learning', *Educational Researcher*, 18(1), pp. 32–42.

This classic paper explores ideas based on constructivist learning theory. Using a range of examples, it argues that learning is always situated in a specific physical and social context, and that this context influences what is learned and how it is learned.

Garrison, D. R. and Anderson, T. (2003) *E-learning in the 21st century*, Abingdon, UK & New York: Routledge-Falmer.

This book discusses the community of inquiry framework, where online learning is described in terms of social presence, cognitive presence and teaching presence. These ideas are also covered in a range of journal papers (for example, Garrison, Anderson & Archer, 2000; Garrison & Arbaugh, 2007).

Lave, J. and Wenger, E. (1991) *Situated learning: legitimate peripheral participation*, Cambridge: Cambridge University Press.

This book considers learning as membership of a community, where newcomers are helped by more expert, longer-standing members. The expression 'legitimate peripheral participation' refers to the early stages of membership, where learning occurs primarily through observing others (as in an apprenticeship). Wenger went on to develop these ideas further in his (1998) book *Communities of practice: learning, meaning and identity*.

3
Tools for Online Learning Communities

This chapter discusses tools for supporting online learning communities. It considers a range of social software tools such as wikis, blogs, instant messaging, virtual worlds and social network sites. The tools, categorized as either synchronous or asynchronous, are discussed in terms of the facilities they provide and the ways in which they can be used for learning. The chapter ends by presenting the views of students who have used online communication for learning.

Recent years have seen a significant increase in the number and range of tools available for supporting online communities. There are tools for discussion, resource sharing, collaborative writing and many other activities that learning communities might engage in. Some of these tools have been developed and used by individual educators or research groups, some are provided within virtual learning environments, and some are available via the open web.

In the early years of online communities, the choice of communication tools was more limited, and educational use tended to focus on what we now describe as discussion forums. At that time (around the 1980s) these online environments were typically called computer conferencing systems or bulletin boards. They were often extensive systems with a range of features (Rapaport, 1991). Based on experience of these early communication tools, educational practitioners began to design and evaluate online communication systems for use in learning contexts (Mason & Kaye, 1989; Harasim, 1990). For example, Hiltz (1994) discusses the Virtual Classroom, an asynchronous discussion environment with additional features for learning and teaching. Barab et al. (2001, 2003) comment extensively on the development of the Inquiry Learning Forum (ILF), an online environment for teacher education based on a community of practice model.

More recently, the focus of attention has been on the communication facilities within virtual learning environments (VLEs) such as Blackboard and

Moodle (Weller, 2007). Many educational institutions use a virtual learning environment to provide a range of online facilities, such as:

- areas for delivery of teaching materials;
- areas for notices to students;
- tools for online assessment;
- calendars;
- email;
- discussion forums;
- synchronous communication tools;
- wikis;
- blogs.

At the time of writing the main interest among e-learning practitioners lies in the possibilities of social software or 'web 2.0' tools, such as social network sites, blogs and wikis (Mason & Rennie, 2008; Redecker, 2009). These newer tools are generating considerable interest among educators, and research into their use is appearing in the published literature. Social software tools are discussed in more detail later in this chapter, and their possibilities for learning are considered throughout this book.

Categorizing Communication Tools

In this chapter I will be looking at a number of different kinds of communication tool that can be used for supporting learning communities. In view of the wide range of tools that exists, it is helpful to have a framework by which to categorize the tools. A classic framework for online communication was developed in the field of computer-supported collaborative work (Ellis et al., 1991). This framework, illustrated in Figure 3.1, provides a two-dimensional time/space grid for communication tools.

When the framework in Figure 3.1 was developed, there was considerable interest in technical support systems for co-located meetings. However, in this

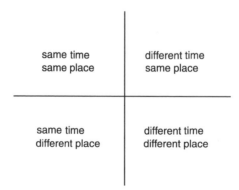

Figure 3.1 A time-space grid for communication tools.

book we will not be considering systems specifically designed for co-located communication. Our categorization of communication tools will therefore simply be 'synchronous' (same time) or 'asynchronous' (different time).

Synchronous tools require those communicating to be online at the same time as each other. There is no delay (or minimal delay) between one person sending a communication and another person receiving it, and possibly responding. Examples of synchronous tools include chat rooms, instant messaging and videoconferencing systems. In contrast, asynchronous tools do not require those communicating to be online simultaneously, because the communications are stored for later use. One person can submit a contribution, and others can access it later. Examples of asynchronous tools include email, discussion forums, blogs and wikis.

In practice, the boundary between these categories is not as rigid as it might first appear. Many communication tools can be used either synchronously or asynchronously. One example is the microblogging tool Twitter, which is a facility for people to post short messages or updates for other users to read. It can be used much like an instant messaging system, enabling people who are online together to have a rapid exchange of messages. In this mode, Twitter is used as a synchronous communication tool. However, because the messages are stored and can be accessed later, Twitter can also be used asynchronously.

For the purposes of clarity, when categorizing communication tools I will define an asynchronous communication system as one where the contributions are stored, so that they can be accessed at any time. Although synchronous tools may have facilities for users to record a session (for example a chat transcript or a recording of an audio-conference), the communications in themselves are transient, rather than being stored centrally. Using this definition, Twitter is categorized as an asynchronous tool.

I will now look at a range of tools that can be used to support communities of learners. My discussions will be of an introductory nature, in order to give an overview of the tools. Later chapters of this book will include more detailed analyses of the various tools, together with examples of how they can be used for learning. Many of the tools I discuss are available in combination as parts of larger systems, such as virtual learning environments. Many are also freely available as 'social software' via the web. The set of tools discussed here is not exhaustive, and new tools will no doubt become available. Moreover, online communication tools are constantly evolving and blending. Over time, the features of one type of tool often appear as part of another. My discussion starts with asynchronous tools, and then I move on to synchronous tools.

Asynchronous Communication Tools

Asynchronous communication tools have been used in education for some time. Their main advantage is that they provide flexibility in terms of the time of communication as well as the location. The most widespread asynchronous communication tool is email, which can be used for group communication via mailing lists (also called listservers). A long-standing form of group communication is the Internet newsgroup (Preece, 2000). Other systems for asynchronous group communication have been described using a variety of names, for example bulletin boards, computer conferencing systems, web boards or web forums. Recently terminology has converged, and these systems are now typically described as 'discussion forums'.

All the above tools are based on a conversational model, where participants interact online mainly through text-based messages. However, more recent developments have broadened the scope of asynchronous communication to include, for example: collaborative writing via wikis; blogs where the author shares their reflections; podcasts where audio resources are created for others to listen to. In this section I will discuss these social software tools, together with the other tools shown in Table 3.1. I will begin with discussion forums, as these are still the most widespread communication tool in educational use.

Discussion Forums

A discussion forum is an online space for text-based group discussion. Members of the forum can post messages for other members to read and reply to. Typically, a forum is dedicated to a particular topic, or a particular set of participants. Within a forum, messages may be grouped further into discussion threads on different subjects. The central features of a discussion forum are a means of posting messages, a repository for storing them, and an interface for navigating through the threads of messages and replies.

Discussion forums of different kinds have been used in education for many years. Originally, forums were used mainly in distance learning contexts (Mason & Kaye, 1989) but they are now used more widely. Their wider user is partly because forums are a key feature of virtual learning environments, which are now used by many educational institutions. Examples of discussion forum software used in education include: FirstClass (www.firstclass.com); Lotus Notes (www-01.ibm.com/software/lotus/products/notes); and the

Table 3.1 Asynchronous Communication

Discussion forums
Blogging
Microblogging
Wikis
Podcasting
E-portfolios
Social bookmarking sites
Media sharing sites
Social network sites

discussion forums within the Blackboard and Moodle virtual learning environments. Web-based software for hosting forums is widely available, and forums also form part of social network sites such as Facebook. There has been a considerable amount of research into the educational value of discussion forums, as you will see in later chapters of this book. Several of the case studies in the book relate to learning activities within discussion forums.

Blogging

Blogging (short for weblogging) is like keeping a log or diary on the web. The blogger writes entries describing things they have done, or simply shares their thoughts. These entries are automatically given the current date, and published on the user's blog site. Blogs are typically written by one person, though it is also possible to have a group blog where many people can contribute postings. Normally a blog can be viewed by anyone on the web, so it can be seen as a form of online publishing. However, it is possible to have a blog that is only open to a named set of users. Most blogging tools have commenting facilities, so that readers can add their responses to blog entries. This enables a blog to support discussion between readers and the blog author, and among readers.

In recent years there has been considerable exploration of blogging for educational purposes. For example, students can use a blog as a reflective journal, or to share thoughts with others and gain feedback (Kerawalla et al., 2009). Some educators argue for blogs to be public, as the potentially global audience could increase students' motivation to produce high-quality entries. Besides being used for individual reflection, blogs can be used collaboratively by communities of learners. This could be via a group blog, where all students can create entries, or by students using the commenting facility to discuss entries posted by other students or by the teacher. Blogging facilities can be provided via an institutional VLE, or by using one of the many blogging tools available via the web, for example Wordpress (wordpress.org) or Blogger (www.blogger.com). Chapter 4, *Benefits and Problems of Online Learning Communities*, includes a case study illustrating the benefits of blogging for learners.

Following someone's blog (that is, being a regular reader) is made easier by using an 'aggregator', also known as a feed reader or RSS (really simple syndication) reader. RSS readers aggregate material from websites that are regularly updated. An aggregator runs on the reader's computer and is set to 'subscribe' to one or more blogs or websites. It checks these periodically for new material, and, if there is any, displays it. Web browsers such as Internet Explorer or Firefox now incorporate aggregators. If a website is capable of supplying RSS feeds to an aggregator, it usually carries the icon (in orange) shown in Figure 3.2.

Figure 3.2 Icon indicating that an RSS feed is available.

Microblogging

Microblogging is a form of group blogging, where the blog entries are very short (typically fewer than 140 characters). It was originally based on mobile phone text messages, hence the size limit. Microblogging is really a blend of blogging and social networking. Each participant's entries are read by their 'followers', and each participant 'follows' a set of other users by reading their entries. These two sets of users are not necessarily the same, though typically there will be considerable overlap.

The dominant microblogging service at the time of writing is Twitter. It can be used via a range of websites and client software, on computers or mobile phones and devices. Twitter's flexibility of access gives it the feel of an instant messaging facility, where users are 'always-on'. There are also other microblogging facilities, for example Plurk (www.plurk.com). Social network sites such as Facebook also include microblogging, and it is possible to forward updates from some microblogging facilities to others (e.g. from Twitter to Facebook).

Microblogging is a very flexible facility that can be used to keep in touch with other users, and to build communities or networks. Its social networking aspects make it useful for finding new contacts, and for sharing information and experiences. Because the entries are short and informal, users tend to see it as a 'flow' to dip into, and this can help to alleviate any feelings of overload. To date, there are few studies of the use of microblogging in education, though it is potentially a valuable tool for connecting communities of learners or practitioners. Chapter 6, *Feeling Connected*, includes a case study discussing the use of Twitter for peer support among learners.

Wikis

Wikis enable many users to collaborate in the development of a web resource. The best-known example is Wikipedia (wikipedia.org), which has been developed by web users into a large repository of information on a very wide range of topics. Wikis allow users to combine text, links to other websites, images, and possibly also audio and video. With a completely open wiki, any web user can make contributions or modify the contributions of others, but wikis can also be made private to a group of users. Wikis are provided in some virtual learning environments, and a range of wiki tools are available via the web, including MediaWiki (www.mediawiki.org) – the software used for Wikipedia. An alternative technology that allows students to work together on shared documents is Google Docs (docs.google.com).

A key feature of a wiki is that it maintains a history of all the changes made. This is a very powerful facility, enabling current and past versions of a wiki document to be compared, and edits to be removed if necessary. The wiki's history facility provides a record of each student's contribution, and can therefore be a useful tool for assessed group work (see Chapter 8, *Assessment for Learning in Online Communities*).

Wikis can provide shared workspaces for large communities of learners or for small project groups. They can be structured by the teacher or it can be left to students to create the structure via the wiki's page linking facilities. Wikis can be used in many different ways. For example, they can enable students to create an online glossary for their field of study, or to collaboratively write a story. By providing a shared, editable online workspace, wikis have fulfilled a longstanding requirement for collaborative learning (West & West, 2009). However, some students feel uncomfortable about editing others' contributions, or having their own material modified, so editing protocols need to be discussed and agreed in advance (Wheeler et al., 2008; Hemmi et al, 2009).

Podcasting

Strictly speaking, a podcast is an audio file made available via the web for automatic downloading. Users can download podcasts as they became available using a 'podcatcher' utility, which is similar in function to an RSS aggregator (mentioned above in relation to following blogs). Podcatching utilities include Juice (juicereceiver.sourceforge.net), which was formerly called iPodder, and Apple's iTunes (www.apple.com/itunes) – which does much more than collect podcasts. The term 'podcast' is now used generally to mean any kind of audio file made available for download via the web, whether collected automatically or not. Another type of audio delivery is streaming, where the user clicks a link on a website to initiate immediate playing of the audio.

Podcasts are usually supplied as MP3 files, or other widely used audio formats, and can be listened to on computers, iPods or small portable MP3 players. Podcasts can be created by anyone with access to fairly simple computer-based recording and editing tools, for example Audacity (audacity.sourceforge.net). Web space is also needed in order to make the results available for download. Creators of podcasts range from individuals to large broadcasting organizations such as the BBC. There are also video versions of podcasts – called 'vodcasts'.

It may not be apparent how podcasts could be valuable for a learning community, where the focus is on interaction among members. However, podcasts have been used successfully in this context (Richardson, 2006; McLoughlin & Lee, 2010). One mode of use is for the teacher to provide podcasts for students to listen to and discuss. The podcast might be a pre-recorded resource, such as a radio programme, or a recording of the teacher discussing a topic, or perhaps giving generic feedback on an assignment. A quite different mode of use is for students to work together in groups to create a podcast. This can be motivating for students who do not often have the opportunity to create resources in a medium other than text. Creating a podcast can help to develop students' skills in a range of activities, such as presenting, interviewing, editing, and using sound creatively, as well as developing their skills in group working.

E-portfolios

An e-portfolio is an online environment where students can create, manage and store resources related to their studies and to their learning. For example, students might use an e-portfolio environment to store samples of their work, their CV or entries for a learning journal. E-portfolios can be private to individual learners or can be shared with teachers and fellow students. Ideally, e-portfolios should allow students to carry their portfolio of online resources from one course module to another, and even beyond the end of their studies. A number of e-portfolio systems are available, for example Mahara (mahara.org) and PebblePad (www.pebblepad.co.uk).

E-portfolios are flexible tools that can be used in a variety of ways (Cotterill et al., 2006). Making students' resources available to others in their learning community can help to build connections among learners. Students can give feedback on each other's work, and help to improve it. They can also gain ideas and encouragement from seeing fellow learners' work, which is not possible in most learning contexts. Teachers can gain a better sense of how students are progressing, and what their current needs might be. E-portfolios can be used for formative or summative assessment, in addition to supporting reflection and learning (see Chapter 8).

Social Bookmarking Sites

Social bookmarking sites provide an online storage area for bookmarks to favourite websites. They also enable users to share bookmarks with other people. Each user has their own area where they can create bookmarks to sites, add descriptions for them and assign to them keywords, known as 'tags'. Other people can use the site's tagging and searching facilities to find resources of interest to them. With some systems, bookmarked sites can be rated by users, so that the most highly rated ones become prominent. It may also be possible to add comments and reviews, as another way of helping others to find resources that will be of value. At the time of writing, the best-known social bookmarking site is Delicious (delicious.com). Other similar facilities include CiteULike (www.citeulike.org), which is focused on scholarly resources, and Digg (digg.com) for recommending news items.

Members of learning communities have always shared and recommended resources, but previously this was done in an ad hoc manner, for example within the text of a forum message. Social bookmarking sites provide a more focused way for learners to share useful resources that they have found, and also to keep them in a single place on the web (Hammond et al., 2005). Tagging helps to group resources by topic, and is more flexible than a scheme of categories, because a single resource can have any number of tags. By using the tagging facilities, resources can be linked to a particular module or project, so that they can easily be found by fellow students. Social bookmarking is discussed in more detail in Chapter 5, *Too Much Information*, which also includes a case study where students used the social bookmarking site Diigo (www.diigo.com).

Media Sharing Sites

Media sharing sites allow users to upload images, video or audio resources, and to make them available to other users. The sites typically include a range of facilities for tagging, grouping and searching the resources. Some sites also have facilities for building communities around the resources, and in this respect media sharing sites can have much in common with social network sites (see below). For example, groups can be formed around a shared style of photography or type of music. Members can gain reputation by posting high-quality material, and receiving favourable comments and ratings from other users.

The best-known media sharing sites are Flickr (www.flickr.com) for photographs and still images, and YouTube (www.youtube.com) for video. Flickr contains powerful features for community building, so is potentially valuable for groups of learners in subjects such as photography or design. YouTube is used in education, but mainly as a source of pre-existing video resources. YouTube has videos on a wide range of topics, and includes videos of lectures and other educational resources.

Because of their specialized nature, media sharing sites have not, to date, been widely used for communities of learners. However, they have potential for subjects where visual resources are of interest. The widespread availability of mobile phones with integrated cameras has opened up many opportunities. For example, students on field trips can upload photos and videos to a media sharing site, allowing the teacher and other students to comment on them. One of the case studies in Chapter 6, *Feeling Connected*, describes how students on a photography course share and comment on each other's photos via a media sharing site.

Social Network Sites

Social network sites provide a way for users to make and maintain online connections with other people (boyd & Ellison, 2007). These sites have their basis in the concept of a 'social network', which is the mesh of connections each person has with others, either directly or via 'friends of friends'. Social network sites provide a range of facilities, including different kinds of messaging and updating tools, and facilities for uploading photographs, music and video. A key element is the individual's profile, which typically contains a photograph and a range of social and personal information.

Popular social network sites at the time of writing include Facebook (www. facebook.com), MySpace (www.myspace.com) and Bebo (www.bebo.com). These sites have different characteristics, and hence different memberships. For example, MySpace is often used by those whose main focus is music, and Bebo is popular with younger people. Other social network sites are more locally based, for example Mixi (www.mixi.jp) in Japan and Cyworld (www. cyworld.com) in Korea. There are also sites that focus on social networking for career purposes, such as LinkedIn (www.linkedin.com). Facilities such as Ning (www.ning.com) and Elgg (elgg.org) allow new social network sites to be designed and made available to users. These facilities are of particular interest to educators and institutions that wish to experiment with social software, whether on a large or small scale. Chapter 6, *Feeling Connected*, includes further discussion of the use of social network sites for learning.

Because of the popularity of social network sites in recent years, especially among young people, there has been considerable interest in their possibilities for learning. However, to date there have been only a few studies evaluating their use in education. The case study below discusses one such initiative – an educational social network site developed using the Elgg open source software.

CASE STUDY

EKADEMIA: A LEARNING ENVIRONMENT USING ELGG SOCIAL SOFTWARE

Thomas Ryberg and Helle Wentzer, Aalborg University, Denmark

In the autumn of 2007, an online environment called Ekademia was opened to the new undergraduate cohort studying Humanistic Informatics at Aalborg University. Ekademia is based on the *Elgg* social networking software (www.elgg.org). This is an open source product which contains 'web 2.0' features such as blogs, personal profiles, podcasting facilities, widgets, RSS-integration and tagging.

Elgg was offered to students as an addition to the pre-existing learning platform QuickPlace, built on the IBM Lotus QuickPlace/Quickr platform (www-01.ibm.com/software/lotus/products/quickr/), which has been available to students since 2001. QuickPlace has various areas divided into semesters and courses, in order to provide learning resources and communication facilities.

Educational Aims

The aims in developing Ekademia for students, in line with those expressed in Dalsgaard (2006) were to:

- provide students with tools for construction, presentation, reflection and collaboration;
- facilitate networks between students within the same course;
- facilitate networks between students and other people working within the same academic field.

It was hoped that students would develop a stronger sense of professional identity and would share resources and ideas that would inspire their fellow students. The intention was to support exchange and sharing across the three different levels of aggregation presented by Dron and Anderson (2007): the group; the network; and the collective. An online community can be used for communication and collaboration within a *group* of students (e.g. a project group). It can equally act as a support for a more loosely connected *network* of students (e.g. a student cohort). The level of the *collective* can be supported by, for example, facilities for importing and sharing bookmarks, blog posts, photos and videos from external sources.

Aalborg University uses a problem-based approach to learning (Dirckinck-Holmfeld, 2002). In each semester (4–5 months) students spend roughly half their time in lectures, workshops and so on, and the other half working on group projects. The project work takes place in parallel with the other course activities. In this context, it was hoped that Ekademia would encourage communication between different project groups, as well as across the whole student body.

The Ekademia Online Environment

In Ekademia each student has a blog, a file-space, an overview of their network, a private messaging tool, an RSS aggregator, a profile, and access to a forum (see Figure 3.3). On the front page there is a text area with a few links and the ten latest blog postings. There is also an overview of the student's activities, a list of their 'friends' and a list of the Ekademia 'communities' the student belongs to.

Elgg communities (now called 'groups') work in a similar way to an individual's profile. A community has a group blog, a file space, resources and a community profile page. All users have permissions to create new

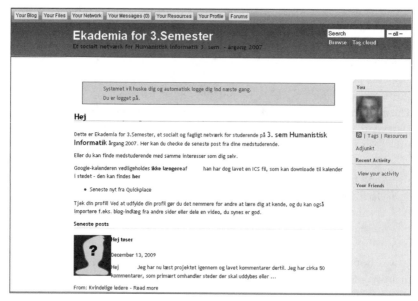

Figure 3.3 A page from Ekademia.

Source: Reproduced with permission.

communities. Communities can be open or can be restricted to a specific set of users.

Users can create a number of 'widgets', by filling out information and keywords in their profile. For example, widgets could be added to import external RSS feeds or to show friends who had recently logged on.

Students' Use of Ekademia

Data was gathered on the use of Ekademia by following one year of students' interactions, and from a questionnaire to students (Clausen & Jacobsen, 2008). The questionnaire was given to 162 students, but only 36 (22 per cent) responded fully. Most of the respondents were active users of Ekademia (logging in typically once a day) but use across the cohort as a whole was lower than this.

The primary use of the environment seemed to be communication between students, carried out via blog postings and within Ekademia 'communities'. Students mainly used the community facility for their semester project groups. This was somewhat surprising, because one of the aims had been to increase communication between project groups rather than within them.

It was hoped that students would gradually populate their profiles with links, files and resources that might be of interest to other students. However, there does not seem to have been much use of these features. Even though some students linked their profile to their private (external) blog, they did not use the facility to import the blog posts directly. Similarly, not many students imported RSS feeds.

Ekademia was also used for a variety of social purposes. For example, students posted invitations to parties or sports events on their blogs. These posts appeared for a time as one of the recent messages on the front page, where other students could see them. Students also created open communities for organizing social events and for other purposes (for example, a self-help group for users of Apple Mac computers).

As part of the evaluation, students were asked for their thoughts on the role of Ekademia as compared with QuickPlace (the more longstanding learning platform). Most students saw Ekademia as their own platform for group work and social interactions, whereas QuickPlace (QP) was seen as a more formal environment, where teachers put up materials for their courses. One student commented:

> QP is the knowledge database for us, that is where we get our information. But it does happen that I look at Ekademia first. Ekademia is more of a social forum in my opinion
>
> (quoted in Ryberg et al., 2010)

Social and Academic Spaces

Research and experience with Ekademia suggests that it is a mixed social and academic space, defined by its users' shared identity. Students personalize their profiles, but they do so within the norms of an academic community. Although no rules or guidelines for content have been provided, students have adopted conventions for themselves, and there have been no problems with content or online behaviour.

However, the environment was not used as much as, or in the ways that, the designers had anticipated. Academic use of Ekademia was focused on communication within project groups, rather than more widely, and students did not use the 'web 2.0' features of RSS, tagging and so on. This suggests that current students are not as comfortable using these kinds of facilities as we are led to believe, and current students may not all be 'digital natives' (Ryberg et al., 2010).

An issue for further investigation is whether students prefer to keep academic spaces and social spaces separate. Would they be uncomfortable if the boundaries were blurred? This is an important issue to consider in the current era when there is considerable interest in the potential uses of social network sites for learning.

Synchronous Communication Tools

So far in this chapter I have discussed asynchronous communication tools, which allow users to communicate when they are separated in distance and time. In this section I will move on to consider a range of synchronous (real-time) tools, as shown in Table 3.2. These facilities are discussed further in Chapter 7, *In Real Time*, which considers their role in supporting online learning communities.

Compared with asynchronous tools, synchronous communication tools are, in the main, a relatively recent introduction to education. There is increasing interest in the educational use of tools such as desktop videoconferencing, partly because of the widespread availability of inexpensive, high bandwidth data connections. Synchronous tools offer possibilities for different kinds of interaction among learners and teachers. The real-time nature of the communication can make the interactions seem more spontaneous and natural than with asynchronous tools. The use of audio, video and tools such as shared whiteboards allows for a wider range of activities, and enables rapid feedback. Synchronous tools are good for 'brainstorming' ideas, and can be useful for planning and decision-making (which are slow processes when carried out asynchronously).

Synchronous communication has disadvantages as well as advantages, when compared to asynchronous communication. With synchronous tools, participants need to be available at the same time as each other. This can be difficult to achieve, except as a scheduled part of a course. Another consideration is that synchronous communication allows little time for participants to reflect on contributions before responding. Finally, when using synchronous facilities such as chat and audio-conferencing, turn-taking can be tricky. If it is not managed sensitively, quieter students may be left out of the interactions. Overall, with synchronous tools, it is necessary to balance the advantages of an increase in social presence against the practical problems of interacting in real time.

Chat Tools

Chat tools, unlike many other synchronous tools, have a long history, beginning with command-based facilities such as Internet Relay Chat (IRC), which preceded the development of the web. When using a chat tool, each user has a

Table 3.2 Synchronous Communication

Chat tools
Instant messaging
Internet telephony
Audio- and videoconferencing
Virtual worlds

'nickname', which could be their own name or could be one they have invented. Users 'chat' by typing messages and comments, and these appear in a sequence, one beneath the other, interspersed with the messages and comments of other participants. Chat tools are often used for group communication, hence the metaphor of a 'chat room' where users can go to find others to chat with. However, one-to-one chat sessions can also be very useful. Chat facilities are often included in virtual learning environments. Other chat tools that are available via the web include the IRC client mIRC (www.mirc.com).

In a learning setting, a chat tool can be a good way for a group to have a live debate or to carry out planning or decision-making. The informal nature of chat tools means they can help students to get to know each other better. However, because of the rapid nature of the interactions, they can be confusing to use. Contributions from different users often arrive 'out of synch' and can be interspersed with different topics of conversation. Taking part in chat sessions requires reasonably fast typing, which is difficult for learners who are not working in their first language, or who have problems with motor skills. Because of the focus on brief and rapid interaction, chat tools are less appropriate for reflective discussions, where participants need more time to think about their own, and others' contributions (Honeycutt, 2001). Increasingly, synchronous chat tools are being recast as 'instant messaging' systems. The boundary between these two types of tool is rather fuzzy, but I will try to make a distinction, as discussed below.

Instant Messaging

Instant messaging (IM) is similar to chat, in that the communications are typically short pieces of text exchanged in real time. IM tools are primarily used for one-to-one interactions, but some systems also support group conversations. A distinguishing feature of an IM tool is the 'buddy' or 'contact' list. A user creates a list of contacts, and is then notified when any of these users come online. In addition to text-based facilities, some modern IM systems offer voice or video interaction. Widely available IM tools include: Windows Live Messenger (http://download.live.com/messenger), also known as Windows Messenger or MSN; AOL Instant Messenger (products.aim.com); and Google Talk (www.google.com/talk). Some social network sites also include facilities for instant messaging.

Instant messaging tools enable learners to share their thoughts or ask for help whenever they are online together, without the need to make special arrangements beforehand (Rutter, 2009). They encourage impromptu contact and informal conversations, which can be helpful for increasing a sense of community. The ability to see when others are online can provide an enhanced sense of presence and belonging for students, even if they do not feel the need to communicate at that time. Instant messaging tools play a role in two of the case studies in this book. These are in Chapter 7, *In Real Time*, and Chapter 9, *Supporting Online Learning Communities*.

Internet Telephony

Internet telephony (also known as Voice over IP or VoIP) allows users to have voice conversations over the Internet using their computers. VoIP users can connect to other VoIP users over the Internet, and can also connect into the normal telephone system. In the Internet-only mode, the system is usually free of cost, regardless of the locations of the participants. Some VoIP systems allow conversations among more than two people, which is useful for group working. VoIP systems can also support communication via media other than voice, for example text chat, webcam and shared whiteboard. It may also be possible to transfer files and share applications.

The most widely known VoIP system at the time of writing is Skype (www.skype.com). Other VoIP systems include Vonage (www.vonage.com) and Gizmo5, acquired in 2009 by Google (www.google.com/gizmo5). Some VoIP networks use proprietary protocols and do not readily work with other networks.

The cost-free nature of VoIP is one of its major benefits for learning. Conversations can be held at any time, and can take place internationally. The broad range of facilities that are available in VoIP systems means that they are approaching the capabilities of desktop videoconferencing systems (see below), while being freely available to any Internet user.

Audio- and Videoconferencing

Desktop synchronous conferencing systems (audio- and videoconferencing) generally include a range of tools for communication among a group. Live voice communication is a standard inclusion, and live video communication via webcams is common. Typically, systems also include text chat, shared whiteboards and polling facilities. At the time of writing, most synchronous conferencing tools are commercial products, for example Microsoft Office Live meeting and Cisco Webex. Elluminate (www.elluminate.com) is becoming popular in education.

The range of tools and facilities in synchronous conferencing systems makes them very rich learning environments (de Freitas & Neumann, 2009). However, synchronous conferencing sessions need to be carefully managed to enable all participants to contribute and play an active part. It is advisable that participants have headsets with earphones and microphones, otherwise there can be problems with background noise, echo and feedback (the noise when a microphone picks up its own sound from a loudspeaker). The difficulties of managing turn-taking, particularly in audio-only systems, mean that there can be a tendency for the teacher to dominate the interactions. Sometimes this is appropriate, but it is not ideal for collaborative learning.

Virtual Worlds

A virtual world is a graphical online environment that represents a 3D physical space (real or imagined). Each user has an 'avatar' to represent them and to enable them to move around within the virtual world. Users can choose their avatars to look like their real-world selves or to be quite different (perhaps not even human). Virtual worlds had their origins in the older text-based systems known as MUDs (multi-user dungeons), and also have precedents in virtual reality systems, chat rooms and online games. Originally, the primary mode of communication in virtual worlds was text chat, but voice communication is now available in some systems.

A number of virtual worlds have been used for learning (Moshell & Hughes, 2002). For example, there has been considerable use of the Active-Worlds virtual environment (www.activeworlds.com) in education (Dickey, 2005). The best-known virtual world at the time of writing is Second Life (www.secondlife.com), which has caused significant interest among educators. The many users of Second Life have created a large and varied online environment, which learners and teachers can explore and develop. An alternative is provided by the open source product OpenSim (opensimulator.org), which enables the development of virtual environments free from commercial interests.

The graphical and spatial aspects of virtual worlds make them suitable for simulations, role-play, and representing real-world contexts, as illustrated by the first case study in this book (page 13). These same aspects, together with the representation of users by avatars, can help to enhance feelings of presence, connection and enjoyment. However, current systems can be difficult to use, and the environments may seem strange, and perhaps unsettling, to some learners.

Students' Views of Online Communication Tools

The tools described so far in this chapter are discussed at greater length later in the book. In the remainder of this chapter I want to look at some research relating to students' perceptions of online tools. This research suggests how students might respond to the use of tools of the sort I have discussed, and suggests factors educators should bear in mind when adopting these tools. The bias of this research is towards older tools such as discussion forums, partly because of the time it takes for newer tools to be adopted in the educational world and for research activity to begin.

The research project involved interviews and observations with ten students at the UK Open University who were studying a course that used online communication. The students were asked for their views on the benefits and problems of online communication for their learning (Kear, 2007). The communication system used by the students was FirstClass (www.firstclass.com). It provides discussion forums, together with other communication facilities including email and chat. At the time of the research, the Open University used FirstClass to provide course-specific forums of different types – social, module-related, group-related, project-related, and so on. These were visible only to students and tutors associated with the course. In addition, FirstClass was used to provide university-wide forums on matters of general interest.

The interviews and observations with students revealed a considerable amount of information about their requirements of an online communication system. Students commented on features that they found useful, and suggested additional facilities which would help them. Analysis of the feedback from students led to the following broad areas:

- usability and flexibility;
- information overload;
- lack of social presence;
- potential benefits of synchronous facilities.

In the following I discuss each of these in turn.

All the students in the research described the FirstClass software as easy to use, and many were able to learn how to use it without referring to the instructions or help. One aspect that students liked was the ability to customize the software. For example, they liked being able to decide how messages should be listed, and what font should be used for their own messages. Students wanted to personalize the system, and to be in control of how it behaved. They disliked situations where the system seemed to be taking control away from them. For example, particular dislikes were system messages that auto-opened and mail messages that expired after a certain time.

When working in large discussion forums, many students felt overwhelmed by the number of messages. Reading through all of them took too long, and it was difficult to pick out those that could be useful. This was partly because the message title was not always a good indicator of the content of the message. Because there were so many messages arriving so quickly, students were discouraged from writing to the forum.

These problems are well known to educators using online communication on large courses (Hiltz & Turoff, 1985; Salmon, 2002). One solution is to break the student cohort into smaller groupings. However, this is sometimes not well received by students, who may want to be in touch with all the other students on the course (Weller & Robinson, 2001). Another approach is to break the forums into sub-forums on different topics, and students reported that this was helpful. Students also noted the value of connecting messages into 'discussion threads' of messages, replies and replies-to-replies, allowing them to follow conversations more easily. These findings are largely in line with those of Ahern (1993, 1994) and Warren and Rada (1998) in which structured, graphical interfaces were more likely to encourage participation than purely text-based interfaces or ones where the message relationships were not clearly structured.

Many of the issues raised by students in the interviews related to the idea of social presence (introduced in Chapter 2 of this book), although this was not a term that students used. Students wanted to feel that they were communicating with real people, even though the communication was online. This is consistent with the finding of Barab et al. that there is a 'need for familiarity with the people in the community before online communications can be substantive, or even sometimes initiated' (2003, p. 250).

Text-based asynchronous communication was seen by some students as impersonal. In particular, students felt frustrated by the delay between submitting a message and getting a response. This can be alleviated somewhat by a facility that tells students who has read their message, and when. The feeling of impersonality could partly explain the problem of poor, or even offensive, communication that can arise online. If the environment feels anonymous, there is little to inhibit students from posting ill-considered messages.

Many students said that they valued the user profile facility (or resumé), which gave them a chance to learn something about a fellow contributor, and possibly to see a photograph. Some students suggested that profiles should be compulsory, or that users should be prompted to complete their profile when they first logged on. Students need to know something about the people they are communicating with, so that they can gain a sense of a real person behind the screen.

Another prevalent theme in students' responses was the use of synchronous facilities. Some students found the FirstClass synchronous chat tool helpful and motivating, particularly when carrying out group work. However, there were problems with chat because the overlapping conversations could become confusing, and the experience could be frustrating for students who could not type quickly. Another issue was that there was not normally a record of a chat session. This might be an advantage, because it encourages spontaneity, but if chat is to be used for collaborative tasks and decision-making, an option is needed to save a transcript. When carrying out group work, some students used the normal discussion forum facilities, but tried to have all members of the group online together. This speeded up decision-making considerably.

A feature that many students wanted was an alert when certain people came online – as in an instant messaging system. Students wanted to be told when their friends or members of their tutor group logged in. This would enable them to make contact via chat, email or in a forum. Students also said that audio- or videoconferencing tools would be useful to them. However, it can be difficult for all students in a group to get together online at a particular time. A mix of synchronous and asynchronous technologies therefore provides a more flexible learning environment.

Several issues emerge from this research. One is that there are often significant feelings of being overloaded among students, as communication proliferates. Another is that students appreciate a sense of connection with other students, and this can help build good working relationships.

The case study below, 'Pedagogical Discourse', describes tools that were provided within an online discussion environment in order to help students identify relevant contributions and find other students who could support them.

CASE STUDY

PEDAGOGICAL DISCOURSE: TOOLS FOR PROMOTING LEARNING AND PARTICIPATION IN AN ONLINE DISCUSSION FORUM

Erin Shaw and Jihie Kim, University of Southern California, USA

The Viterbi School of Engineering at the University of Southern California uses discussion forums to support distance learners. These students participate in courses virtually, concurrently with their on-campus peers. Students use the discussion forums to collaborate, exchange information, and seek answers to problems from their instructors and classmates. Although studies have shown that forums can be an effective medium for collaborative problem solving and discovery-oriented activities (Scardamalia & Bereiter, 1996b), online discussions are not always effective in promoting learning. Even when participation is high, message threads may consist of only one or two messages. The goal of the Pedagogical Discourse project is to develop tools that help students and instructors use discussion forums more effectively.

The project has developed two discussion forum tools intended to promote student discussion, participation and learning. *PedaBot* was designed to connect the current discussion thread to relevant past discussions and course documents. *MentorMatch* was designed to identify students who often provide answers on a given topic (i.e. mentors). Both tools have been integrated into a live discussion forum used in an undergraduate computer science course. Details and further results are described in Kim and Shaw (2009).

The research on PedaBot and MentorMatch took place in the context of a course discussion forum for an undergraduate course in Computer Science. Students connect to the discussion forum through their Blackboard Course Management System account. The forum is an open source phpBB bulletin board (phpbb.com) that has been used as a research testbed since 2004. The corpus of past discussions includes seven semesters of discussions from the same undergraduate course, two semesters from a related graduate course, and text from related course documents. There are 6,622 messages in the current corpus.

PedaBot: Scaffolding Online Discussions with Past Discussions

PedaBot scaffolds student learning by automatically matching a current discussion question to relevant responses from previous course presentations (Kim et al., 2008). These prior discussions provide new perspectives and should be of interest to current students. The system dynamically processes student messages, mines a corpus of relevant past discussions, and displays portions of messages that best match the student's question (Figure 3.4). Results are updated as the thread grows and include the year and author (role), and a link to the discussion thread they comprise.

PedaBot was integrated into a live course discussion forum in fall 2007. Data was collected during the 2007 and 2008 fall semesters. Among 147 discussion participants, 114 students used the feature. A questionnaire was emailed to students at the end of the semester. Thirty-four students who had used the feature responded (9 in 2007, 25 in 2008). Students were asked to rate how interesting, useful, and relevant the feature was on a scale of 1–4. The average ratings were 2.46 for 2007 and 3.13 for 2008. Students reported finding the feature highly interesting, moderately relevant and somewhat useful. Comments were generally positive, for example,

> Good way to find all the relevant questions at one place. Results of past discussions were useful for my project work.

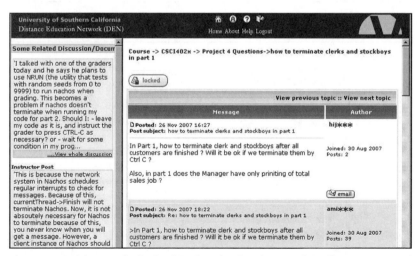

Figure 3.4 Pedabot result display interface (students' names have been anonymised using asterisks).

Source: Reproduced with permission.

I liked that the system tried to provide me with relevant posts (even though most of the results were not relevant). This new feature saved me the trouble of typing in a search keyword to explicitly fetch related topics or posts.

MentorMatch: Promoting Participation of Class Mentors

MentorMatch matches help-seekers to course mentors, i.e. course peers with relatively good understanding of a particular domain topic (Shaw et al., 2009). When a help-seeker initiates a new thread, the system identifies the message topics, and searches for potential mentors by matching topics and student discussion profiles. Email links to mentors are provided above the thread (Figure 3.5), with a note that 'These authors may be able to assist you with this question'.

Two menu links were added to promote use and awareness of the feature. One displays a course-wide topic-mentors list (Figure 3.6), which is updated

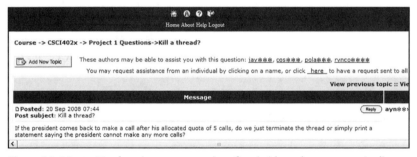

Figure 3.5 MentorMatch assistance request interface (with students anonymised).

Source: Reproduced with permission.

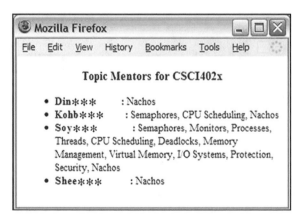

Figure 3.6 MentorMatch course mentor list (with students anonymised).

Source: Reproduced with permission.

dynamically. The other displays a personal topics list, with links to discussions for which the student has been asked to provide assistance.

MentorMatch was deployed in October 2008. To evaluate the effect of mentor participation within the limited time available, mentors were automatically sent a request for assistance instead of waiting for other students to send personal requests. To gauge this effect, we compared the number of topic-related replies to non-topic-related replies subsequent to mentor notification. As the number of notifications increased, student replies increased overall, although there was more increase in non-topic related discussions.

A questionnaire was emailed to students at the end of the semester. 52 per cent (13/25) of respondents reported opening the mentor list or noticing the menu section. Of those who noticed, 69 per cent (9/13) reported clicking through to a discussion. Students who used, or were aware of, the feature were asked to rate their interest in it, and its usefulness on a scale of 1–5. The average ratings were 4.2 for interest and 4.0 for usefulness.

Comments were mostly positive, for example,

> It helped find people who could directly assist with a topic and mail them if the discussion forum didn't get a response.

> It was easier to communicate with the mentors and moreover easier to decide whose suggestion to take into account.

Conclusions and Future Work

The questionnaire results show that students found both PedaBot and MentorMatch to be of value. They found PedaBot results useful and moderately relevant to their discussions. Comments on MentorMatch indicate that students appreciated attempts to help match them to other students who might be able to provide answers. As the number of topic notifications increased, student replies increased overall.

For future development, a deeper assessment of user activity patterns may prove useful in improving the performance of the tools. For example, identifying whether a message contains questions or answers would help in selecting the most valuable information to send to students.

Acknowledgements

The authors are indebted to Dr Michael Crowley for his continuous support. The work was funded under a NSF CCLI Phase 2 program grant (award #0618859).

Choosing and Using Tools for Online Communities

As we have seen in this chapter, there are many communication tools that can be used to support online communities of learners. Faced with such a wide choice, educators can find it difficult to decide which tools to use, and for which purposes. The key is to begin with a clear view of the educational aims. These could be very broad, such as increasing a sense of community among students. Alternatively, they could relate to specific learning outcomes, such as developing students' information literacy skills.

Once the aims and intended learning outcomes are reasonably clear, activities can be designed to fit them. At this stage, the palette of possible communication tools can be considered, in relation to aspects of the learning context. These aspects include: the students' prior experience; the teachers' current skills; the curriculum subject; and the institutional context. For example, a relevant question is whether students are 'digital natives' (Prensky, 2001) who are very comfortable using new technologies, or whether they are less confident users. Similar considerations apply to the course teachers or tutors. Are they happy to be educational technology innovators? Or would they prefer to use tried-and-tested communication tools?

In terms of the curriculum subject, what sort of activities will be most useful to students? If the subject is based on discussion, debate and the exchange of ideas, a discussion forum will be an appropriate tool, and a wiki could also be used to develop a shared perspective. In a more practice-based subject, where students need to carry out tasks together, a simulation within a virtual world, or sessions via videoconferencing may be of value.

The institutional context also needs to be taken into account. Are there already established online tools that can be used, such as those within a virtual learning environment? If tools outside the normal institutional context are being considered, what are the implications for technical support, reliability, privacy, accessibility and so on? These issues are discussed further in Chapter 9, *Supporting Online Learning Communities*.

Key Points for Practitioners

- A range of tools exists for supporting online learning communities. These tools can address the issues of separation in distance and time. They can be categorized as synchronous (real-time) and asynchronous (delayed time).
- The tools can support many different purposes, such as discussion, collaborative writing, sharing resources and building community. Tools need to be selected to match learning activities and aims.
- Students can experience problems, as well as benefits, when working online. Suitable tools, and features of these tools, can help. Examples include synchronous tools to build social presence, and threading in discussion forums to address overload.

Further Reading

Barab, S.A., MaKinster, J.G., Moore, J.A., Cunningham, D.J. and The ILF Design Team (2001) 'Designing and building an on-line community: the struggle to support sociability in the Inquiry Learning Forum', *Educational Technology Research and Development*, 49(4), pp. 71–96.

This paper discusses the development of the Inquiry Learning Forum, an online environment for teachers to share good practice. The paper explains how the environment was designed, problems that emerged in its use, and the resulting focus on social aspects of online communication.

Mason, R. and Rennie, F. (2008) *E-learning and social networking handbook: resources for higher education*, New York: Routledge.

This book discusses a wide range of social software tools, and considers how they can be used to support learning. It includes many examples from educators who are using these tools in practice, and considers the advantages and issues in each case.

Preece, J. (2000) *Online communities: designing usability, supporting sociability*, Chichester, UK: John Wiley & Sons.

This book explores online communities, and how to support them effectively using communication tools. It is not limited to educational contexts, although these are covered. The book explains how online communities can thrive when attention is paid to sociability as well as usability.

4

Benefits and Problems of Online Learning Communities

This chapter discusses the benefits of online communication for learning, and also the problems that can arise. Based on research findings and experience from practice, the chapter considers benefits such as: flexibility of communication; opportunities for peer learning; engagement and motivation; feelings of belonging. The chapter then goes on to discuss problems such as: overload; low participation; impersonality. The chapter ends by discussing steps teachers can take to increase the benefits and reduce the problems.

This chapter explores the benefits and problems of online learning communities. We will consider the findings of a range of research studies, look in more detail at the emerging themes, and consider some examples that illustrate these ideas. The aims of the chapter are:

- to discuss the potential benefits and problems of online communities;
- to consider how the benefits can be achieved and the problems minimized.

Benefits of Online Learning Communities

Online communities can offer many benefits in education. They can support different kinds of learning activities, such as debates, group projects, peer review, resource sharing and collaborative writing. Online communication tools can provide flexibility for learners in terms of place and time. Students can communicate with their teachers and their fellow students from any location where an Internet connection is available. Using asynchronous tools, they can communicate at any time of day or night.

Online communities can increase social contact and sense of belonging among students. This is valuable for encouraging trust and openness, which are needed for genuine collaborative learning. Interacting online as part of a group also provides opportunities to develop important 'employability' skills in team working, self-management and interpersonal communication, as well as the practical information technology skills needed for online communication and collaboration.

Benefits: Lessons from the Literature

We will begin with a brief overview of research studies that have identified the benefits of online learning communities. Some of these studies go back a number of years, while others are more recent. The authors of these studies have used online communication in their educational practice, and have considered the outcomes from the perspectives of learners and teachers. For example, Hiltz and Turoff claimed that online communication is:

> the ideal technology for extending the ability of students to discuss material and to work in collaborative groups as an integral part of the learning process. It is also the ideal technology for extending education or training to segments of the population who have difficulty in taking the time to attend face to face sessions.
>
> (Hiltz and Turoff, 1993, p. 471)

The above quotation illustrates two kinds of benefit that online communication can provide: improved learning through dialogue and collaborative activities; improved access to learning by overcoming distance and time limitations.

Support for dialogue and discussion has been highlighted as a key benefit of online learning communities. Rowntree (1995), who was a teacher on an early course that used online discussion, commented:

> Out of this stew of debate, learners can develop their own outlook on the subject and make their own meanings. But they will not have done so without being exposed to other people's thoughts and feelings.
>
> (Rowntree, 1995, p. 208)

Online communities are particularly beneficial in a distance learning context, where they can help to keep students in touch with their teachers and with fellow students. Wilson and Whitelock (1998) found that many students valued this means of contact. Students felt that asking fellow learners questions, answering others' questions, and simply observing the dialogue were all helpful for learning.

Research by Vonderwell (2003) found that students felt more comfortable asking the teacher questions online than they would in a face-to-face class. They asked more questions, and were less embarrassed about what others would think of them. Students also highlighted the benefit of an asynchronous medium for reflecting on ideas and for self-expression. Browne (2003) reported on experiences from an online Masters degree. Teaching staff found that the quality of discussion and work from students was extremely high. There was also a good sense of community among students and staff, and students reported enjoying the online interactions. Coppola et al. (2002), who interviewed 20 online teachers, found that staff had a closer relationship with their students online than face-to-face, and that, '[i]n spite of the lack of nonverbal expression, faculty found that their relationship with the students online was more intimate, more connected' (p. 179). In this study, staff reported that communication was improved generally. This was partly because online communication seemed less public to students than face-to-face communication, so shyer students had an opportunity to contribute.

Hemmi et al. (2009) discussed the use of blogs and wikis in several different courses. When students shared their reflective blogs with just the teacher, this led to a closer relationship between the two. When shared more widely with the class, blogs enabled students to see a range of different perspectives on aspects of the course. A major benefit of wikis was that they allowed students to structure their collaborative writing in a flexible way, which encouraged creativity. The experience of working in a wiki also encouraged students to consider issues such as individual versus shared authorship, and permanence versus ephemerality of the text.

McConnell (2006) argued that the use of online communication in a social constructivist framework can provide very positive outcomes for students. He based these conclusions on experience, over many years, of an online Masters course. The course placed a strong emphasis on collaborative learning and online community. Questionnaires to students demonstrated that they valued the approach and benefited from the online discussions. McConnell concluded (p. 89), 'The results are extremely encouraging, showing that when e-learning courses are designed with some care and attention to the meaning of learning in groups and communities, students' experiences can be very positive.'

The research studies discussed above have identified a range of benefits of online communication in education. These are discussed further below, under the following headings:

- convenience and flexibility;
- learning with others;
- engagement and belonging.

Convenience and Flexibility

The use of online communication means that problems of distance and time can, to a degree, be overcome. Discussion and interaction can extend beyond the walls of the classroom, and are not limited to timetabled sessions. This provides more flexibility in the kinds of learning activities that can be carried out. It is also more convenient for students, who are increasingly likely to have part-time jobs in addition to their studies.

Online communication allows teachers to be in closer and more regular contact with their students, and make more efficient use of time. Teachers can post notices and general advice online, rather than needing to contact each student individually. There is no need to restrict contact to scheduled teaching sessions or office hours. If a student has an urgent problem, they may be able to contact their teacher online within a few hours, or even immediately. However, care needs to be taken to manage students' expectations, otherwise the demands on the teacher could become unreasonable.

The use of online communication also means that students can keep in touch with each other when they are not in classes. This could be via a discussion forum, an instant messaging facility or a social network site. If a student has a problem, they can easily contact others in their teaching group to ask for help or advice. Other students may be online at the time, and able to help straight away. For example, many students have an instant messaging facility constantly available while they are working at their computer. Even though the main purpose might be social, the facility also enables students to post a comment or query about their work, and gain ideas, help or just moral support from fellow learners. If students are working on a project, they can discuss the work online, rather than needing to arrange a time when they can all meet.

Learning with Others

Online communication can support collaborative learning in many different ways. Informally, it allows students to keep in touch, discuss their work and help each other with difficulties. Used more formally as part of a course, online communication enables ongoing discussion of issues and ideas. By engaging in discussions, students are exposed to a wide range of perspectives, and they gain an awareness of other people's views. They also have increased opportunities to practise expressing their ideas and communicating them to others. Because most online communication is text-based, this can help improve students' written communication skills. Alternatively, by using an audio- or video-conferencing system for discussions or presentations, students can develop skills in oral communication.

In an online community, participants can ask questions and answer other people's questions. They can follow lines of enquiry, and share resources that they have found useful. For example, a teacher might notice that a topic students are learning about has been discussed in the news that day. In a forum or blog, the teacher could post a link to an online resource giving further information, and ask students to add their comments. As part of the resulting discussion, students might direct each other to further online resources, perhaps sharing these via a social bookmarking site. In this way, learners will gain a deeper understanding of the topic, and of how it relates to the world at large.

Online communication tools can also support the practical aspects of carrying out collaborative work and group projects. They facilitate the day-to-day communication and discussion that is needed, and they provide a shared space in which to develop the products of the group's work. For example, a discussion forum can be used for planning collaborative work and discussing ideas; a chat tool or videoconferencing facility can be used for making decisions and talking through problems; a wiki can act as a group workspace for developing and storing group products, and allowing members to monitor progress; a social bookmarking site can be used to share useful web resources that group members find.

Engagement and Belonging

When students are in regular online contact with each other, and with their teacher, this can result in an increased sense of belonging. This is particularly important for those who are studying part-time or at a distance, and helps to reduce feelings of isolation. With regular communication, and activities around shared interests, a course cohort can develop into a community. The development of a sense of community among students has many benefits. It helps them to engage more actively with the course, and to gain more value and enjoyment from their studies. Because students get to know and trust each other and their teachers, they are willing to be more open about their learning, take more risks and acknowledge when they have difficulties.

Online communication can be particularly beneficial to students who do not feel confident enough to contribute in a face-to-face group context. For several reasons, the online setting can encourage these students to participate. First, online communication can feel more 'anonymous' to some students, and hence less threatening. Second, with an asynchronous environment such as a discussion forum, there is no need to wait for a gap in the conversation before making a contribution. There is also time to reflect on what you want to say, and to edit your contribution before you submit it. Even students who do not actively contribute can learn by observing the online interactions and by following the discussions, helping them to develop the confidence to take a more active part.

Regular online communication can help to improve the relationship between teachers and students. This is important for students' motivation and retention, and for the teacher's satisfaction with their work. When teachers are in closer contact with their students, they can get a better sense of students' strengths and difficulties, both as a group and as individuals. By acting on this knowledge, teachers can tailor their teaching to their students' current needs. This helps to pre-empt problems, and allows teachers to deal with them more quickly if they arise.

The following case study discusses the benefits of one particular online technology – blogging – for supporting a learning community. The case study describes how novice teachers used blogs to reflect on their experiences and share their problems.

CASE STUDY

BLOGGING TO BUILD COMMUNITY AMONG PRE-SERVICE TEACHERS

Lisa Kervin and Jessica Mantei, University of Wollongong, Australia and Anthony Herrington, Curtin University, Australia

This initiative involved fourth year students studying for their Bachelor of Education in the Faculty of Education at the University of Wollongong. At the time, this fourth year of study was an additional year, which students typically undertook in a part-time mode while teaching concurrently full-time, part-time or on a casual basis.

The transition period from being a student of education to being a practising teacher is a challenging one. Students need to deal with a change of role and identity, while also studying and working. They need to learn about the norms, values and beliefs of the community of practice they are entering. They also need to develop a sense of their own professional identity as a teacher. During this period it is important that they can reflect on their new experiences and learning.

Online Support for Authentic Learning

In order to support these reflective activities, the Faculty of Education provided a community-based website for students, entitled *Beginning and Establishing Successful Teachers*: BEST (Herrington et al., 2006). This website was designed according to principles of authentic learning (Herrington & Oliver, 2000). These include:

- exploring problems;
- engaging with multiple roles;
- collaboration;
- reflecting on learning.

One of the features of the BEST website is a blogging facility where each student can write journal-style entries about their experiences, and other students can offer comments. This provides opportunities for the learning activities listed above, and therefore supports authentic learning.

Investigating Students' Blogging Experiences

One of the compulsory modules in the year of study for the Bachelor of Education is *Reflective Practice*. In 2007, students taking this module used the BEST website's blogging facility to support their reflection as they made the transition to being practising teachers. The blogging activity also provided the background to a written report by each student discussing the professional decisions, issues and challenges that they were facing.

The value of the blogging experience was investigated by analysing a combination of data sources:

- usage data for the BEST website;
- students' blog postings and comments;
- students' written reports;
- in-class discussion and interaction.

The findings from this analysis are reported in the following sections.

Blogging and Reflection

Students appreciated the opportunity to describe their experiences and share their feelings in writing, without the pressure to express themselves in formal academic language. One student commented that it was:

> great to be able to write freely without having to quote someone you agree with.

Students also valued the opportunity to revisit what they had written in their blogs, and perhaps to change it, based on further learning, discussion or experience. This is a process that blogs allow, because the blog author 'owns' what they have written, and can add to it or edit it at any time. This aspect makes blogging particularly supportive of the reflective process. Kervin et al. (2010, p. 694) comment that a blog entry need never be considered finished; 'its incomplete state allows the author to make tentative constructions of meaning in the face of complex perspectives.'

Blogging and Community

The blogs provided a valuable online space for the student teachers to provide support for each other, and build trusting relationships. For many students the blogs were a safe environment in which to share their difficulties, as well as their successes. Students wrote about problems that they were facing, and often received reassuring comments from other students who were facing similar issues:

> I have had exactly the same bad experience!

This kind of online support helped students to feel less isolated in their new professional environments, and contributed to developing confidence. Comments from other students could also provide alternative perspectives and ideas, which the blog author might be able to take into their day-to-day practice.

However, not all students were immediately comfortable with blogging about their experiences, and reading others' blogs. Some were anxious about 'going public' in this way, or felt intimidated when they read what others had written. Nevertheless, once students took the plunge, their concerns reduced and they were able to learn, and feel supported, by reading blog posts, and writing their own.

Linking Virtual and Physical Communities

Through the blogs, students were able to build on the community that they had already established face-to-face during the previous three years. They could also connect their blogging activities to what they were learning in their classes on campus. These face-to-face sessions provided new ideas and understanding, which students could then discuss in their blogs. For example a blog entry might begin:

As many people in the class today may have felt, [. . .]

Students also used the blogs to forge links with each other for further study activities. For example, if a student read a blog post to which they particularly related, they might seek out that blog author in a face-to-face class and perhaps work together in the future.

The supportive online environment also helped students to come to terms with their new physical environment – the school in which they were working. As beginning teachers, some experienced difficulties in 'fitting in' and being accepted by the more longstanding teachers. One student described in her blog how some of the teachers at her school:

pretend I am not there because I am a casual teacher.

In response to this, one of the other students, who already had some teaching experience, wrote a blog posting titled 'Casual teaching tips'. He invited others to:

have a quick glance and see if you can get anything from it.

This is just one illustration of how the online community, via the blogs and comments, supported its members in developing their new professional identities.

Acknowledgement

This case study is based on Kervin et al. (2010).

Problems of Online Learning Communities

So far we have been considering the benefits of online learning, but there can also be problems. For example, an online environment can seem daunting or overwhelming, particularly if there are large numbers of participants. Text-based communication, in particular, may feel cold or unfriendly, due to the lack of facial expression, tone of voice and other 'cues' that are present in face-to-face communication. With asynchronous tools, the delay between making a contribution and gaining a response can be frustrating, and may contribute to a sense of impersonality. For all these reasons, low participation is often a problem in online communities.

Problems: Lessons from the Literature

Earlier in the chapter we considered the benefits identified by researchers in online communication. These benefits are considerable, so it is clear that online communication can be an important tool for students and teachers. However, it is significant that all the researchers whose work was referred to earlier have identified problems as well as benefits. These problems can counteract the benefits in quite serious ways.

For example, Hiltz and Turoff (1993), who highlighted the benefits of online communication for discussion, also pointed out that '[a]t some size the benefit of increased communications becomes the problem of information overload' (p. 479). They explained that attempts to operate the 'virtual classroom' environment with over 90 students resulted in severe problems of overload, so that it was necessary to break students into smaller groupings.

Rowntree (1995) pointed out problems arising from the textual nature of much online communication: 'It lacks the visual and auditory cues on which we usually rely in interpreting other people's meanings (and their responses to what we have said)' (p. 210). He discussed how this can have a negative effect on students, particularly those new to online communication. In an evaluation of the course Rowntree was discussing, Wegerif quoted the view of one student:

> It is a cold medium. Unlike face to face communication you get no instant feedback. You don't know how people responded to your comments; they just go out into silence. This feels isolating and unnerving. It is not warm and supportive.
>
> (Wegerif, 1998, p. 38)

This comment highlights a particular problem with asynchronous communication: the time lag between sending a message and getting a reply. As well as being a frustration, this time lag means that decision-making is difficult (Sproull & Keisler, 1991, p. 69).

In their study of a distance learning course, Wilson and Whitelock (1998) found problems related to participation and interaction. Even in the most active group, half the messages were posted by the tutor. Students also tended to direct their messages to the tutor, rather than to each other. Vonderwell's (2003) study identified similar problems with students not engaging each other in dialogue. This seemed to be because they did not feel that they knew each other, and felt uncomfortable making contact. In line with Wegerif's

(1998) findings, the students felt that the online environment was impersonal. One student commented:

> It is not like a person to person interaction. It's more like computer to computer interaction.
>
> (Vonderwell, 2003, pp. 83–84)

Browne's (2003) study also highlighted problems with lack of participation. Some students found the online environment complicated and frustrating to use, and concerns were expressed by students and staff as to the amount of time demanded. The online teachers interviewed by Coppola et al. (2002) also mentioned the large amount of time needed. They said that there was additional managerial work in planning and running an online course, particularly in getting students started.

McConnell (2006) reported problems related to dealing with large, complex bodies of textual discussion. Some students found it difficult to follow the discussions, particularly when working in large communities rather than smaller groups. The author pointed out that:

> the information flow is often too much to handle, and the speed at which the discussion threads develop, with members opening new threads in order to organize their ideas and invite others to discuss them, is extremely difficult to manage and navigate.
>
> (McConnell, 2006, p. 73)

McConnell also reported problems related to the interpersonal aspects of online communication. Students sometimes felt isolated, dominated by other participants, or anxious about presenting their ideas publicly (pp. 69–70). Hemmi et al. (2009), discussing students' experiences of wikis, pointed out that some students found them to be rather formal places, and missed the conversational interaction with other students. This feeling of formality perhaps contributed to students' reluctance to edit each other's work in the wiki. One student commented that they 'feared treading on others' toes' (p. 27).

Murphy et al. (2001) drew together a valuable collection of case studies where educators who were early adopters of online communication discussed their experiences. A major concern raised in these studies was lack of participation and interactivity among students. Typical scenarios involved innovative teachers setting up discussion environments, and then finding that very few students used them. In their accounts, the teachers suggested possible reasons for students' lack of engagement. For example Gunawardena et al. commented:

> For highly motivated and self-directed learners who juggle online course work with several other competing duties and demands, the discussion group may not have been enough return for their time investment.
>
> (Gunawardena et al., 2001, p. 41)

Other issues were largely to do with social aspects of asynchronous communication, which some students perceived as 'faceless' (Tarbin and Trevitt, 2001, p. 65). Misunderstandings could arise, and individual students could dominate the discussions. The tone could become unpleasant and, in the extreme, these aspects could contribute to a 'flame war' of aggressive messages between students (Robertshaw, 2001). Problems of this kind were very off-putting to students, particularly if they were new to online communication.

Based on the case studies presented by Murphy et al. (2001), it appears that the problem of low participation in online communities may partly be because students are anxious about exposing their ideas in a public and permanent way. This seems to conflict with the findings of Vonderwell (2003) and Coppolla et al. (2002), given earlier, that students felt more comfortable contributing online than face-to-face. Possibly some students find online learning contexts more stressful than face-to-face ones, while others find the opposite.

The research studies reviewed above have highlighted different kinds of problems that can arise when using online communication for learning. These will be discussed further below under the following headings:

- information overload;
- impersonality;
- low participation.

Information Overload

When students are communicating in active online groups using asynchronous communication tools, contributions can build up very quickly. For example, if a discussion forum is set up for all the students on a course, each student may be faced with a considerable number of new postings to read every time they log in. The teacher will be in the same situation, but with even more pressure to read all the postings, and respond to specific queries. It can take a considerable amount of time for students and teachers to keep up with the contributions in a busy discussion forum, and even more time to actively contribute.

With a conversational communication tool, such as a forum, participants either need to read all new postings, or find a way of identifying which ones will be most useful. The process of 'sorting the wheat from the chaff' is not easy. In principle, the system threading should help students find their way through a forum, following messages and replies. But in practice, this can be problematic. Some students post messages in the wrong thread, or post them as stand-alone messages when they are really part of an existing conversation. For these reasons, the threading can be confusing – leading to even more wrongly located postings.

There can also be problems of overload when using other communication tools. With synchronous chat, there are problems following the rapid exchange of messages, keeping up with the typing, and mentally holding together the interspersed conversations. This is a particular difficulty if there are more than two or three participants. With wikis there are problems identifying when material has been added, which parts are new, and how the content has been changed. Notification facilities, together with the wiki's 'history', can help, but some skill is still needed to keep track of developments. Other communication tools, such as blogs with comments, social network sites and microblogging facilities, also present problems of overload when there are significant numbers of participants.

Impersonality

Some students feel that online communication is impersonal, when compared with face-to-face interactions. There is nearly always a loss of some of the important aspects of face-to-face communication, such as facial expression, tone of voice or body language. The extent to which these 'cues' are missing will depend on the communication medium in use. For example, a high-quality videoconferencing system can provide an experience that is similar to a face-to-face setting. In contrast, email and discussion forums depend largely on text, so the aspects mentioned above will be absent. The time lags inherent in asynchronous communication make matters worse. Rather than receiving an immediate response to their contributions, users might have to wait several days, or possibly not receive a response at all.

These aspects can make online interactions seem unnatural or stilted, and the lack of non-verbal cues can lead to misunderstandings. Some students may appear to dominate the interactions, or may post messages that are off-putting to others. Some participants may use the online environment as a place to air their grievances. Unless care is taken by students and teachers, these aspects can result in an unpleasant atmosphere in the online environment, and poor relationships among students. If this happens, the environment will seem unfriendly, students will be unwilling to contribute, and may simply stay away. It is therefore important for the teacher to deal appropriately and promptly with any difficulties of this kind, and for all participants to help make the online community supportive and enjoyable.

Low Participation

A contrasting problem to overload is low participation. Some learners tend to observe rather than taking an active part, possibly because they find the online environment daunting. They may be put off by the public and permanent nature of online spaces such as forums, wikis and blogs. Some, having read others' contributions, become anxious about contributing, and feel that they will never be able to reach the same standard.

In face-to-face contexts, there are often learners who prefer to leave the interaction to others, and this is largely accepted. But the problem in asynchronous online settings is that observing (sometimes described as 'lurking') is invisible to other participants. Unless a member actively participates, it looks as if they are not there at all. In contrast, in synchronous environments such as videoconferences or virtual worlds, all participants are visible, and quieter students may be encouraged to take a more active part.

Low participation can be a problem at the beginning of a course when students are preoccupied with other aspects of their work, or it can arise later when the novelty of communicating online begins to wear off. Participation is a particular issue if online communication is an 'add-on', as opposed to being a core element of the learning. Some students are not willing to take part in activities that seem peripheral, or are not part of the formal course assessment. They need to feel that the benefit gained justifies the time and effort involved.

In group project work, where students are dependent on each other's contributions, it is particularly problematic if some members do not participate. If an aspect of a group's work is assigned to a member who then 'disappears', this can be frustrating and cause difficulties for other members. There may be a genuine reason for that person to be out of contact, but if the other students do not know this, it will look to them as if the group member is not pulling their weight.

In addition to the level of participation, an important aspect of online learning communities is the degree of interaction among learners. There is little point in having online communication as part of a course if students are not truly communicating with each other. A discussion forum that is full of carefully crafted 'set pieces' by individual students will not be an inviting or effective place for learning. What is needed is the exchange of ideas and debate that characterizes good education. For these interactions to happen, students need to feel comfortable with each other and with their teacher, and they need to be engaged by the online activities they are asked to do.

The case study that follows discusses the issue of participation in online discussion forums. Based on experience from several courses over a number of years, the author considers how to encourage learners to participate actively online.

CASE STUDY

ONLINE DISCUSSION AND COMMUNITY: BARRIERS TO PARTICIPATION

Elisabeth Skinner, University of Gloucestershire, UK

The module *Management at Work* formed part of the first year of an undergraduate degree at the University of Gloucestershire, UK, for students of heritage, environment or community management. The student cohort combined full-time campus-based students with part-time distance learners who were already in employment. The module included a sequence of five online discussion activities, which served to bring the full-time students and the distance learners together, so that they could learn from each other (Skinner, 2009). Students were grouped online according to the main subject they were studying (heritage, environment or community). They used the discussion forums within the university's *WebCT* virtual learning environment for their online discussions.

The Online Activities

The discussion activities in *Management at Work* were designed using Salmon's five-stage model (Salmon, 2004). The activities, which took place over an eight-week period, were intended to extend classroom discussion, help the students get to know each other and develop cooperation. The five activities, together with their stages in the Salmon model, are shown in Table 4.1.

The teacher provided feedback after each activity, in order to build students' confidence and suggest improvements. This design is consistent with Laurillard's (2002) 'conversational framework'. To encourage students to participate, the discussions carried 50 per cent of the marks for the module. Students gained credit for thoughtful responses, ability to stimulate discussion and support of other students. Each activity was given a deadline to help students manage their time, with the fifth of these deadlines being the formal submission date.

Evaluating the Online Activities

An initial survey-based evaluation of the module suggested that students felt comfortable participating in the online learning community. The respondents valued the opportunity to give and receive feedback and to share different

Table 4.1 Applying Salmon's 5-stage Model

Stage in Salmon (2004) model	Online discussion activities in Management at Work
Stage 1: Access and Motivation	Give an account of personal experiences of management.
Stage 2: Online Socialisation	Suggest goals for the module and discuss motivation as a management tool.
Stage 3: Information Exchange	Share subject-related resources and discuss current issues in their field.
Stage 4: Knowledge Construction	Apply ideas from their reading to management roles in relevant professions.
Stage 5: Development	Reflect on their performance and evaluate the online discussion experience.

perspectives. The relatively small group sizes (typically eight students) encouraged participation without overwhelming students with messages.

These findings were encouraging, but only 25 per cent of students had responded to the evaluation survey, so the views of students who were less engaged might not be represented. The course designers were also aware of issues that had previously arisen in both *Management at Work* and other course modules: for example, overload of messages, and the failure of some individuals to participate in team work (Skinner, 2007; Skinner & Derounian, 2008). In relation to *Management at Work*, problems had been identified with students' lack of confidence (both technically and socially) for engaging in online discussions. The course team therefore provided additional support, including hands-on workshops with WebCT.

However, in spite of these initiatives, a significant number of students still failed to contribute to discussions until after the deadlines. A second study was therefore carried out, including skills audits, student interviews and a survey. This time the survey had a much higher response rate (69 per cent). The findings from this second evaluation are discussed below.

Findings on Confidence and Motivation

Anxiety about communicating online still proved a significant factor, with nearly a quarter of the respondents admitting that they lacked confidence. The students mentioned having significant fears or feelings of inadequacy initially, which discouraged them from participating. However, it is worth noting that more students lacked confidence for speaking out in the classroom (50 per cent) than for communicating online. Furthermore, most students expressing a lack of confidence overcame their fears and met required deadlines because they were motivated to do so.

The remaining three quarters of the students claimed to be confident with online networking, but many of them highlighted poor motivation. A number of students had little interest in management, and some were only taking the module because it was compulsory. This lack of interest explained their failure to participate. One student admitted:

> if it doesn't flick my switch, I'm just going to do the absolute necessity, and that's really it.

The first online activity had asked students to share their experiences of management:

Introduce your previous experience of management. Everyone has experiences of management – at school, at work, at home, in the community or in social groups. Tell your group about an experience of either good or poor management.

However, this activity failed to strike a chord with students, and proved a barrier to participation. In relation to the activity, one student commented:

> I don't like management; it's boring. You start the course off with that and then it's always going to be an uphill struggle [. . .] if you take it the other way, you get students all excited and then just guide them into the stuff they think is boring!

'The other way' could come from the students' enthusiasm for their own subject, as indicated in the following comment:

> I have a passion about heritage and all things like history, that's what I really enjoy. [. . .] If you're really interested in something and you are passionate about something you could talk all day.

On the basis of these findings, the first online activity was replaced with a subject-based discussion aimed at triggering personal feelings about their subject:

> You have chosen to study heritage, environmental or community management. Tell your group about something that *excites or angers* you connected with your subject.

Conclusion: Enjoyment and Engagement

Persuading students to participate actively in online discussions is a significant challenge. Feedback from students of *Management at Work* identified two main barriers to participation:

- lack of confidence;
- lack of motivation.

In the current era, where online social networking is widespread, educators might assume that confidence among students is not a problem. However, not all students are confident online, whether technically, academically or socially. This means that they need to be well supported, and also enticed to take part in online discussion.

This brings us to the issue of motivation. We might assume that if online activities are assessed, students will participate. But if the activities are not enjoyable, many students will do the bare minimum. It is therefore important to engage students from the start with activities that relate directly to their experience and interests.

Increasing the Benefits and Reducing the Problems

Earlier in this chapter I identified some of the educational benefits of online communication. They fell in the following three areas:

- convenience and flexibility;
- learning with others;
- engagement and belonging.

I then identified three potential problem areas with online communication in education. They were:

- information overload;
- low participation;
- impersonality.

I want now to suggest that these benefits and problem areas are related. In fact, there is a correspondence between the three benefit areas and the three problem areas listed above. To show this more clearly, in Table 4.2 I have listed down the first column the benefits I identified. Down the second column I have listed the problems.

Taking the first benefit in the table, 'convenience and flexibility', my comment for that row suggests that the very convenience of the communication methods leads to the large volumes of online messages and other material associated with the problem of overload. In rows 2 and 3, I similarly bring together benefits and problems, and suggest in my comments the relationship between them.

My aligning of benefits and problems suggests that we need to think carefully about how the technology is used in education if we want to minimize the problems and maximize the benefits. The technology by itself will not necessarily achieve the outcome we want.

In the remainder of this section I will consider what can be done to increase the benefits of online learning communities and to reduce the problems.

Table 4.2 Benefits and Problems of Online Communication

Benefits	Problems	Comments
Convenience and flexibility	Information overload	Increased flexibility and convenience of communication can result in large volumes of contributions, leading to overload.
Learning with others	Low participation	The full benefits of learning with others will only be gained if students actively participate.
Engagement and belonging	Impersonality	Students can experience a sense of belonging, but this may not happen if the online environment seems impersonal.

Teachers can explore a number of avenues for achieving this, by taking actions themselves and by guiding their students. I will discuss these ideas below, following the three broad areas presented in Table 4.1:

- flexible communication versus overload;
- learning together versus non-participation;
- engagement versus impersonality.

Flexible Communication Versus Overload

Teachers can help their students to benefit from the flexible nature of online communication by encouraging them to log on regularly, and keep up with discussions and contributions. Facilities for automatically notifying students of new contributions (e.g. via email or an RSS feed) can help. Students may also consider using synchronous or 'always-on' communication tools such as instant messaging, so that they can keep in contact with each other in real time.

To help avoid overload, teachers should structure the community's online spaces carefully. It is important that students know where to go to find particular types of resources and communications, and that they don't submit their own contributions to the wrong place. It is helpful for the teacher to name online spaces in a meaningful and memorable way, and where possible to use icons or graphics to support this. Colours, fonts or icons can also be used to highlight important items. For example, Figure 4.1 shows a set of forums for The Open University course Digital Communications (T305), which was discussed in the 'Hope This Helps' case study in Chapter 2. The forum names and icons indicate the purpose of each forum, making it easier for students to locate information.

At the beginning of a course the teacher will need to help students get used

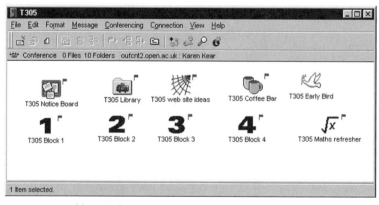

Figure 4.1 A set of forums for an Open University course.

Source: Reproduced with permission from The Open University.

to the online environment. For example, when using a discussion forum, the teacher should explain to students how the threading works, and move any messages that are obviously posted in the wrong place. When using a wiki, the teacher should explain how material is organized, how to navigate within the wiki, and how to add new pages and sections. Ways of dealing with the problem of overload are considered further in Chapter 5, *Too Much Information*.

Learning Together Versus Non-participation

To maximize the learning benefits of online communication, teachers should encourage students to communicate with each other informally, discuss aspects of the course, and share any problems they may have. Once students begin to interact online, they often comment on the value of realizing that others are 'in the same boat'. Students should be encouraged to participate actively, rather than just reading contributions. This will help to make the online community a dynamic and lively environment.

In order to encourage peer communication, the teacher should be careful not to dominate the online interactions. If a student asks a question, it is likely that another student will be able to provide a helpful response. At the beginning of the course, the teacher should make it clear that, although they will be keeping a close watch on the communications, they will not necessarily take a leading role. Setting the scene in this way will prevent students expecting the teacher to respond immediately to all their queries.

To encourage active participation it is helpful to link online activities to the course assessment. This requires teachers to design well-structured collaborative learning activities for their students, and also to consider carefully how these should be assessed. These issues are discussed in greater depth in Chapter 8, *Assessment for Learning in Online Communities*. As an example, Figure 4.2 shows a 'tutor-marked assignment' (TMA) question from the Level 1 course *Networked Living* at the UK Open University. This question was linked to an 'online tutorial' in which students took part in an asynchronous discussion in a forum and a synchronous discussion via live chat.

Engagement Versus Impersonality

There are many ways for teachers and learners to make an online community an inviting place, and to overcome the problem of impersonality. In a discussion forum or blog, a major factor is the 'tone' of the communications. Contributions should be friendly, supportive and informal. Careful phrasing is very important, and can be supplemented by emoticons (also called 'smileys') and use of colour and font. Figure 4.3 gives an example of how to convey these ideas to students. It shows an activity from the course *Networked Living*, mentioned above, together with a comment to students from one of the course authors. The purpose of the activity is to show how text-based communication can be used to communicate feelings in a positive way.

(a) For the first part of the online tutorial for Block 2 you were asked to read a newspaper article called 'Collecting friends is the new philately', find and comment on a relevant web resource, and then engage in a debate in your tutor-group forum on the question:

Do social websites enhance personal relationships?

(i) Paste into your TMA copies of the following two messages that you posted to your tutor group during this activity:

1   your message identifying and commenting on a relevant web resource

2   a second message in which you feel you contributed well to the discussion, by raising a new issue or responding to another student's contribution so as to take the discussion forward.

(5 marks)

(ii) Write a brief piece of text explaining:

- how you found your web resource for message 1 above

- why you think your message 2 above contributed well to the discussion.

(10 marks)

(b) For the second part of the online tutorial you were asked to listen to an audio extract about Second Life (or to read a transcript of this extract) and then use the First Class Live Chat facility to discuss the following question with a small group of fellow students:

To what extent are virtual worlds replacing the real one?

(i) Write a brief summary of your group's discussion of this question, and any conclusions that the group came to.

(10 marks)

(ii) Give your views on the pros and cons of synchronous Chat, as compared with asynchronous forums, for group discussion.

(5 marks)

Figure 4.2 An assignment question linked to two online discussion activities.

Source: Reproduced with permission from The Open University.

Social interactions, although not directly contributing to students' learning, help to make participants feel welcome, and make the interactions enjoyable. At the start of a course, teachers can play a major role in modeling the style of interactions that they would like to see from their students. For example, a teacher can share a little of their personal life with students (how they spent their weekend or what their hobbies are). Teachers can also encourage students to introduce themselves, to provide some personal information, and perhaps to upload a photograph. Some online communication tools have a 'member profile' facility where students can write something about themselves, and students should be encouraged to use it. Where possible, an initial face-to face session is valuable to help students get to know each other a little 'in the flesh' before they start communicating online. These and other ways of enhancing a sense of community among students are discussed further in Chapter 6, *Feeling Connected.*

Synchronous communication can also help to break down barriers between

Activity 7 (exploratory)

Look at this email exchange. What emotions are being expressed through smileys and typography? Would Jon and Sue still be on speaking terms if they hadn't used these devices?

From: Jon
To: Sue
Dear Sue,
I've messed up by overwriting a file you've just edited.
I think I've mended the damage, but could you check I did it right?
Jon

From: Sue
To: Jon
Aaaarrrgggghhhhhh. Don't do this to me. ;o)

From: Jon
To: Sue
Sorry.

From: Sue
To: Jon
:o))))
The page looks OK. No harm done.
I had a meeting at 8.15 yes 8.15 today so forgive me if I'm a bit grumpy.
Sue

⌾ **Comment - click here**

In Sue's first reply to Jon she expresses her frustration by typing 'Aaaarrrgggghhhhhh'. But she ends that message with a winking smiley. Jon's reply then says 'sorry' in a very small voice! Finally, Sue's reply starts with a happy smiley to show that everything's OK. She uses a large font when she mentions the annoyingly early meeting time.

I feel sure that Jon and Sue would still be friendly after this email exchange. But I have seen email exchanges between colleagues which had the opposite effect, when the participants have not taken care about how they express themselves in their messages.

Figure 4.3 An activity showing how emotions can be expressed in text.

Source: Reproduced with permission from The Open University.

students. Synchronous chat sessions are by their nature informal, and can be fun for participants. Audio- and videoconferencing are particularly helpful in a distance learning context, as they enable students to hear each other's voices and perhaps see each other in a live setting. The benefits of synchronous communication are considered in Chapter 7, *In Real Time.*

Summary

In this chapter we have considered the benefits and problems that can arise when using online communication for learning. Starting with reviews of the literature, we have explored benefits such as flexibility, collaborative learning and engagement. We have also considered problems such as overload, low participation and impersonality.

We then moved on to consider what teachers and students can do to increase the benefits and reduce the problems. Possibilities include: making the online spaces welcoming and well-structured; encouraging students to interact regularly and informally; linking online activities to assessment. These issues are discussed in more depth in later chapters of this book.

Key Points for Practitioners

- Online communication offers many benefits for learners and teachers. These include: convenient and flexible communication; support for collaborative learning; the development of a sense of community.
- However, there can also be problems, including: overload; low participation; and impersonality.
- Teachers can take steps to increase the benefits and reduce the problems. For example:
  - structuring online environments clearly, and helping students to navigate within them;
  - encouraging social communication, and ideally holding an early face-to-face meeting;
  - linking online activities to the course assessment, and not dominating the online interactions.

Further Reading

Murphy, D., Walker, R. and Webb, G. (2001) *Online learning and teaching with technology: case studies, experience and practice*, London: Kogan Page.

This book presents a set of case studies of teachers' experiences when using online communication as part of their courses. It takes an open, honest approach to this endeavour, sharing problems and failures with the reader, as well as successes and useful techniques.

McConnell, D. (2006) *E-learning groups and communities*, Maidenhead: Open University Press.

This book is based on many years' experience of running postgraduate courses via online communities. The learning approaches described are grounded on social constructivism, and use student-centred methods such as negotiated assessment.

Wegerif, R. (1998) 'The social dimension of asynchronous learning networks', *Journal of Asynchronous Learning Networks*, 2(1).

This journal paper is based on qualitative evaluation of an online course. It includes the findings of interviews with students where they explain how they experienced the online setting, and what encouraged or discouraged their participation.

5
Too Much Information

This chapter considers the problem of information overload in the context of online learning communities. It explores why difficulties arise in following busy online discussions, and how students can help each other to identify useful resources from the vast amount of material on the web. The chapter relates these issues to the features and user interfaces of discussion forums, and to web-based facilities such as social bookmarking.

We are all surrounded by information – from television, newspapers, the web, email . . . and so on. These communication systems provide value in keeping us informed and aware of new developments. But sometimes it can all seem too much, and we feel overloaded.

> With the information floodgates open, content rushes at us in countless formats: Text messages and Twitter tweets on our cell phones. Facebook friend alerts and voice mail on our BlackBerrys. Instant messages and direct-marketing sales pitches (no longer limited by the cost of postage) on our desktop computers. Not to mention the ultimate killer app: e-mail.
>
> (Hemp, 2009, p. 84)

With group communication systems added into the mix, the problem can be overwhelming. In a learning context, students' sense of overload can be associated with:

- busy discussion forums;
- wikis where new material is being added every day;
- activities where students are asked to find resources on the web.

Faced with large amounts of information and communication, where should students focus their attention? Which items are essential, and which (if any) can safely be ignored? Some learners find these decisions too difficult to cope with, and simply withdraw from aspects of their studies that are causing them to feel overloaded.

In this chapter we consider how to reduce the problem of information overload in online learning communities. We begin by considering overload in online discussion forums, and consider system features that might address the problem. We then move on to look at how social bookmarking facilities can help students identify and share useful resources from among the huge amount of information on the web.

Research on Information Overload

Information overload has been acknowledged as a problem for a considerable time, and over the years there has been a significant amount of research on the issue. However, much of this research does not specifically relate to educational contexts. In this section I will briefly review some of the research findings on information overload, beginning with general research in this area, and then turning to research specific to online learning communities.

Email Overload

A number of researchers have considered the problem of information overload in relation to email. For example, Denning (1982) characterized the problem as 'electronic junk' and suggested various filtering mechanisms. Adam (2002) reported that the main problem was receiving messages that were of little interest, but which stopped people dealing with the messages that were important to them. Whittaker and Sidner (1997) investigated how people deal with their email. They found that some people had serious problems keeping track of information in their email systems. Whittaker and Sidner suggested that the problems could be alleviated by system features such as conversational threading, automatic filing and the ability to mark messages as needing attention. Many modern email systems offer such facilities.

Hemp (2009) discussed more recent research, in a workplace context, which found that employees typically spent two hours a day dealing with email. About a third of the email messages received were judged to be unnecessary, and when work was interrupted by an email, it took an average of 24 minutes to resume the interrupted activity. Hemp discussed a range of improved workplace practices that could reduce overload. For example, rather than distributing non-urgent information by email, it could be posted on a website or wiki. Better subject headings would help readers to judge which messages to open, and in which order.

Overload in Group Communication

Other researchers have considered information overload in relation to group communication systems. The problem arises primarily for asynchronous communication, where all the contributions are stored so that they can be accessed later. Although the stored aspect of asynchronous communication has advantages for learners, the contributions can build up rapidly over time. This is particularly so in large or very active groups, and it can cause significant difficulties (Rennie & Mason, 2004, p. 11). Students may even feel so overloaded that they withdraw from the online environment. Palloff and Pratt found that a 'typical reaction to overload is to retreat. If a student disappears from an online class, overload may be a culprit' (Palloff & Pratt, 1999, p. 50).

One problem is the amount of time needed to keep up with the contributions. A student quoted in Salmon (2004, p. 130) said, about online communication:

> It is useful but gets clogged with messages that don't add value for me. I wasted a lot of time on it initially and felt inadequate when I couldn't keep up with all of the new messages, but I do find I get some useful info. I tend to set a time limit and stick to it.

This student's comment raises an aspect of the overload problem, which is the difficulty in picking out useful contributions. Students need to be able to differentiate contributions that will probably be of interest to them from those that will probably not be.

In an early study of online communication, Hiltz and Turoff (1985) surveyed users of six different online communication systems and found that most users reported feeling overloaded at times, although the problem reduced with time. The authors pointed out that there is a balance between avoiding overload and maintaining social cohesion. Contributions that seem 'off-topic' to some users can add important social elements for others. This means that the issue of how to deal with 'social chat' needs careful consideration. Some learners (and also some teachers) assume that messages not directly related to the topic of a course are just 'noise'. However, contributions such as these can be important for building a sense of community.

Overload in Forums: Students' and Teachers' Views

The problem of overload in discussion forums has been noted in earlier chapters of this book. Chapter 3, *Tools for Online Communities*, briefly discussed the issue, as raised by students at the UK Open University who were asked their views on using online communication. This study interviewed 10 students who used *FirstClass* discussion forums in the course they were studying. As part of the same investigation, 10 Open University tutors from a range of courses were also interviewed about their use of forums with their students. The comments of the students and tutors regarding overload are presented below.

Students' Views

Many of the students highlighted the problem of information overload in the whole-cohort forums. This was expressed in terms of 'takes too much time' or 'too many messages'. Some students spent five or more hours per week in the forums, which was a significant amount in the context of the expected study time of 16 hours per week. It is not clear whether the time spent was in addition to or a replacement for time on other study activities.

One aspect of the overload problem was deciding which messages to read. There was a view among the students that there were too many 'junk' or repetitious messages. This was characterized as 'a poor signal to noise ratio' by one student, and another said she had problems 'sorting the wheat from the chaff'. One student commented that there were useful tips in the whole-cohort forums 'so it's worth reading through'. However, students said they had difficulty judging from the message title whether to read a message, partly because the subject of a discussion thread changes over time.

Some aspects of the FirstClass forum software were helpful for dealing with the large numbers of messages. Searching was highlighted as useful by two students, though one reported that she often forgot to use it. Sorting was mentioned by two students, particularly sorting by thread. The threading of messages was highlighted as a valuable feature, particularly the 'next-in-thread' feature for reading the messages in a single thread in sequence. Two students said that sub-forums were a helpful feature for organization. One student, showing her tutor-group forum, which contained a number of sub-forums, described it as 'nicely broken down'.

Tutors' Views

The tutors pointed out that having too many messages to read was off-putting, both to students and tutors. One tutor described the problem as 'death by red flags' because FirstClass shows a red flag icon beside messages that the user has not yet read. Tutors felt that the sight of all the unread messages could be dispiriting for students, who might simply withdraw from such 'crowded' forums (as some tutors did from crowded staff forums). Tutors commented that there was a distinct variation between students who posted a large number of messages and those who did not have time to be so active. This imbalance was felt to be discouraging to both types of student. However, the tutors pointed out that the scale of the problem varied, depending on how often the student logged on.

Tutors considered that students had difficulty judging which messages to read. They pointed out that the message title should help in making this judgement, but often did not because the same title was used for all messages in a thread. A preview facility, where a user could see the first few lines of a message, was suggested – or just a very quick way to open a message. A further suggestion was that tutors should have a facility for flagging important messages.

Threading was highlighted as a valuable tool for grouping related messages and for following conversations. Tutors who had used an earlier discussion system (see Kear, 2001) put more stress on the second aspect – following conversations – and felt that the threading mechanisms in FirstClass were not as good as those in the earlier system. Not all tutors displayed their messages grouped by thread, however; some displayed them chronologically. It was noted that, although threading is of value, it is not always successful in categorizing messages. This is because threads can go off-topic, and messages on the same topic may inadvertently be created in different threads.

Following the Thread

Poor organization of contributions in an online environment can itself contribute to a sense of overload in the user. Salmon explained this in relation to discussion forums, described here using the term CMC (computer-mediated communication):

> CMC can elicit quite uncomfortable, confused reactions from participants and severe anxiety in a few. Although many people are now familiar with email, they are not used to the complexity of CMC's many-to-many conferencing, with its huge range of potential posting times and variety of response and counter response.
>
> (Salmon, 2004, p. 62)

The issue was noted by Ruberg et al. (1996, p. 266), who reported that some students found the 'multiple threads of simultaneous topics' confusing and jumbled. Harasim et al. pointed out that a feeling of confusion and overload is often associated with the early stages of online communication:

> Early in the course, as students learn to navigate around the system, the sense of being lost in cyberspace can trigger an experience of information overload. A sense of place has not yet been established, and the conference may feel like a maze. Additionally, students may send notes to the wrong conference, creating confusion for readers.
>
> (Harasim et al., 1995, p. 223)

When there are many contributions posted at different times by different people and on different topics, the contributions should be grouped and organized. Discussion systems have various mechanisms for doing this. Typically there are different discussion areas for different purposes, with potentially different memberships. For example, a student may be a member of a large forum with all the students on their course, and a small-group forum for the more structured course learning activities.

Within a forum, messages are usually grouped further into discussion threads. Users can start a new thread, or can add a message to an existing thread. Each message in a thread typically has the same subject line, possibly preceded by 'Re:' or a similar indicator that the message is a response (see Figure 5.1). Discussion forums provide tools for displaying threads and navigating through them.

The purpose of threading is to allow users to follow a 'conversation' that is spread over time, and would otherwise be interrupted by messages from other conversations. Threading organizes messages into thematic groups, and allows users to read messages in a meaningful order. As Hewitt (2001, p. 209) pointed out, threading 'makes it easier for readers of the conference to find and follow conversational chains. [. . .] It also allows the class to simultaneously pursue multiple avenues of inquiry without confusion.'

The value of threading was demonstrated experimentally in an investigation by Schwan et al. (2002), using dummy discussion forums. Groups of students were required to engage in either:

- a threaded forum (where related messages had the same subject line, preceded by 'Re:' and a number indicating the sequence in the thread); or
- an unthreaded forum (where each message had a different subject line).

The researchers found that students read nearly all the messages, rather than using the message titles to decide which to read. Students read the messages in a topic-related order, rather than chronologically. There was no significant difference in terms of learning between students who used the threaded and the unthreaded forums, but those using the threaded forum posted over twice as many messages. They also experienced fewer difficulties in finding relevant messages, mentally linking them together, and

Name	Size	Subject	Last Modified
Hazel ✶✶✶✶✶	3K	⊟ Re(3): Student review of T175	17/01/2007 16:12
John ✶✶✶✶✶	2K	Re(2): Student review of T175	15/01/2007 17:01
Ernie ✶✶✶✶	3K	Re: Student review of T175	15/01/2007 15:56
Karen ✶✶✶✶✶	3K	Student review of T175	12/01/2007 09:35
Hazel ✶✶✶✶✶	3K	⊟ Re(3): Student progress to Level2	18/01/2007 12:41
Mirabelle ✶✶✶✶✶	2K	Re(2): Student progress to Level2	17/01/2007 16:41
Hazel ✶✶✶✶✶	3K	Re: Student progress to Level2	17/01/2007 15:59
Karen ✶✶✶✶✶	2K	Re(2): Student progress to Level2	02/01/2007 14:49
Hazel ✶✶✶✶✶	3K	Re: Student progress to Level2	02/01/2007 11:54
Karen ✶✶✶✶	2K	Student progress to Level2	20/12/2006 10:26

1 Item selected.

Figure 5.1 Two discussion threads in a FirstClass forum (users' names have been anonymised).

Source: Reproduced with permission from The Open University.

generally understanding the discussion. The study therefore showed that, although students can cope with disconnected messages, good threading facilities are needed to help them to engage more fully and easily in online discussions.

The study by Schwan et al. (2002) used linear threads, which are simply a chronological sequence of messages on the same topic, as in Figure 5.2 (a). However, many discussion environments use a hierarchical approach to message threading. This assumes that the user wishes to respond to the message they are currently reading, rather than to the thread discussion as a whole. Adding a message to a thread involves 'replying' to one of the messages in it. The result is a branching structure of initial messages, replies and replies-to-replies, as in Figure 5.2 (b).

The issue of whether a reply in an online communication system should be to an individual message or to the thread was hotly debated in the early days of online communication (Rapaport, 1991). Some practitioners felt that it was important for users to be able to reply to individual messages, while others felt that a message should be a contribution to the topic as a whole. As Nicol et al. state,

> Even apparently simple acts like organising online discussions into different virtual spaces, or even threading discussions in particular ways, will have significant effects on the nature of student interaction and on the discourse structures that result.
>
> (Nicol et al., 2003, p. 279)

Students view threading, and particularly branched threading, as a helpful feature. However, they also have problems with threading, and can become confused (McConnell, 2006, p. 73). For example, although most discussion forums can group together messages belonging to the same thread, they do not all show clearly which messages are replies to which. This means that it is not obvious in what order to read the messages. See, for example, the lower thread grouping in Figure 5.1, titled 'Student progress to Level2'. In this thread it is not possible to tell unambiguously which message is a reply to which.

Hewitt (2001) claimed that branched threading was unsuitable for forum discussions, causing a lack of convergence. He argued that threads can easily drift away from the original topic of discussion because the 'reply' option encourages users to respond to a particular message, rather than to the discussion as a whole. Hewitt commented that current online environments do not help students to keep the overall context of their discussions in mind.

A further issue is the extent to which threads are visually separated from each other. In some systems, the only visual separation of threads is provided by grouping together messages that are in the same thread, within the list of all the message headers (see Figure 5.1). Other systems keep the threads more clearly separated, for example by only allowing one thread to be viewed at a

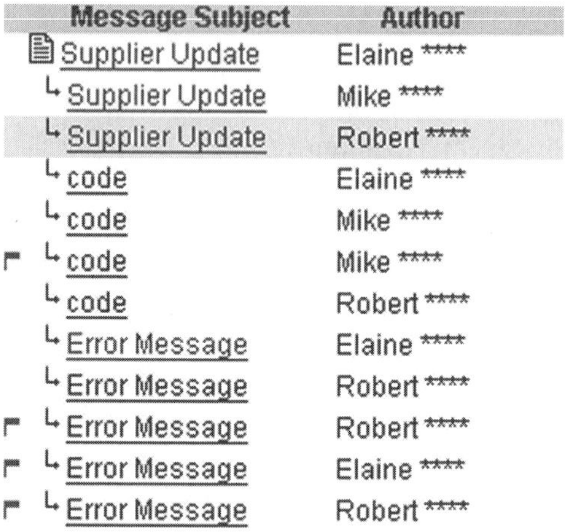

Message Subject	Author
📄 Supplier Update	Elaine ****
↳ Supplier Update	Mike ****
↳ Supplier Update	Robert ****
↳ code	Elaine ****
↳ code	Mike ****
⌐ ↳ code	Mike ****
↳ code	Robert ****
↳ Error Message	Elaine ****
↳ Error Message	Robert ****
⌐ ↳ Error Message	Robert ****
⌐ ↳ Error Message	Elaine ****
⌐ ↳ Error Message	Robert ****

(a)

Figure 5.2a Chronological threading.

Source: Reproduced with permission from The Open University.

Message Subject	Author
📄 Supplier Update	Elaine ****
↳ Supplier Update	Mike ****
↳ Supplier Update	Robert ****
↳ code	Elaine ****
↳ code	Mike ****
⌐ ↳ code	Mike ****
↳ code	Robert ****
↳ Error Message	Elaine ****
↳ Error Message	Robert ****
⌐ ↳ Error Message	Elaine ****
⌐ ↳ Error Message	Robert ****
⌐ ↳ Error Message	Robert ****

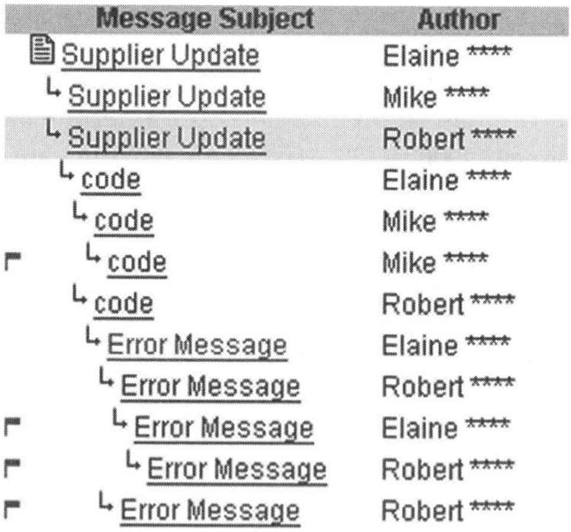

(b)

Figure 5.2b Branched threading.

Source: Reproduced with permission from The Open University.

time. The forums in the Moodle virtual learning environment operate in this way, as shown in Figure 5.3, which shows a list of discussion threads. Clicking on a thread title in the left-hand column will open that thread.

When choosing a discussion forum environment, it is worth exploring the options for threading, and the degree of control that the administrator or users will have over how threads are displayed. The best choice of threading style may depend on the purposes of the forum and the degree of experience of the learners. For discursive subjects or for intensive collaborative activities such as group projects, discussion threads are likely to be long and complex. In this case a system with branched threading, clearly displayed, will be helpful. However, less experienced students may need support in navigating through the messages, and understanding how they relate to each other. For a more technical course, where most contributions might be simply question-and-answer pairs, linear threading would probably be adequate, and students who are new to online discussion may find linear threading easier to understand.

One final aspect worth consideration is the issue of message titles. Most discussion forums use the same main title for all messages in a thread. This means that users are given only a general idea of the subject of a particular message. This is a problem in long threads, which may be subject to 'topic drift', where some or all of the discussion moves away from the original subject. One way to address this issue is to encourage learners to give their own title for a message (provided this does not destroy the connectivity of the threading). This is particularly valuable at a point where it is clear that the true topic of discussion has changed.

An alternative approach is to display the whole message text, or possibly just the beginning of the message, rather than only the header. This is the approach used in the Moodle virtual learning environment. However, it means

Start a new discussion				

Page: 1 2 (Next)

Discussion	Started by	Posts	Unread ✓	Last post ▾
The Virtual Revolution - starts BBC2 Saturday	Mike	1	1 ✓	11:03 today Mike
The Cisco material	Judith	5	5 ✓	10:48 today Thomas
Part 4 DHCP reference	Andrew	5	5 ✓	10:23 today Philip
Help-Cisco course material	Ali	5	5 ✓	08:54 today Judith

Figure 5.3 A list of discussion threads in a Moodle forum (users' family names have been removed).

Source: Reproduced with permission from The Open University.

that viewing long threads can be a rather cumbersome process, involving a lot of scrolling. The hierarchical structure of the thread, which is typically indicated using indentation, can then be difficult to discern.

Recommending and Rating

In large discussion forums it is difficult for students to decide which contributions are particularly worth reading (Kear & Heap, 2007). Many students therefore feel that they have to read every message, in case it contains valuable information. Similarly, when students are required to find and use online resources, they can struggle to identify useful material from the huge amount available on the web or in a library database.

In both these examples, students could use recommendations by others to help identify valuable resources and contributions. For example, in some community-based websites, users can rate others' contributions, and the collated ratings can then be used as a guide to which contributions to read (Dron, 2007, p. 148). However, Preece issues a caution regarding the use of rating:

> There are good reasons to be concerned about employing such schemes in online communities. What happens if people feel their contributions are not valued? Do they become disheartened and leave?
>
> (Preece, 2001, p. 351)

The idea of user ratings or recommendations is not new, and considerable research has been carried out in this area (Resnick & Varian, 1997; Konstan et al., 1997). One key aspect is how to encourage users to rate/recommend contributions, so that a critical mass of rating information is built up. A further issue is how to collate the ratings in a way that will be useful, and not misleading, even if there are not many ratings for a single item. The *slashdot* online community (slashdot.org) uses a complex system, described as 'karma', for these purposes (Preece, 2004). The Amazon online store has user-generated reviews and ratings, and even has a mechanism for customers to rate other users' reviews.

User recommendations are beginning to be explored in educational contexts. For example, at the UK Open University, Shaw and Woodthorpe (2009) investigated the use of an online environment called *fOUndIt*, where students can recommend and comment on web resources that they have found. Other students can rate these resources, and the resources that receive the highest ratings become more prominent. Students can also add further comments, or comments on comments, such that the environment takes on an aspect of community-building as well as resource-sharing. However, there can be problems gaining sufficient input from students to achieve critical mass. It is therefore necessary for teachers to 'seed' the environment with useful resources, and this can be time-consuming.

Rather than requiring learners to recommend resources or provide ratings, an alternative would be to gather information automatically. An example of this approach is provided by the Amazon store, where information on customers' purchases is used to recommend products to others. A similar approach could be used in a discussion forum, where messages could be highlighted if they attracted large numbers of readers, or if they were marked by readers as 'favourites' (see below).

Filtering

Ratings can sometimes be combined with filtering facilities, resulting in an approach described as 'collaborative' or 'collective' filtering. All the user ratings for a given contribution are combined to provide an overall rating for that item. Each user can then set a personal threshold to filter out contributions with low overall ratings. This serves to 'separate the signal from the noise', highlighting items with high ratings and effectively removing those with low ratings.

Research in collaborative filtering goes back a number of years. For example, Goldberg et al. (1992) developed the *Tapestry* system for collaborative filtering of group email communications. Resnick et al. (1994) applied the *GroupLens* system to Usenet newsgroups. More recently, some discussion-based websites (such as *slashdot*) have implemented this approach. It can be particularly valuable for dealing with objectionable or 'spam' contributions, as these will have low ratings. With an appropriate filter setting the user simply does not see them.

Contributions can also be filtered, or sorted, according to parameters other than user ratings (Palme et al., 1996). Possibilities include: the date (and time) when the contribution was made; whether the user has read it; the topic of the contribution; or the contributor. It would also be possible to implement user-controlled filtering of individual messages. A user could read a message (or just read its title), decide whether they might need to return to it later, and if not, filter it out.

One problem with filtering in a discussion forum is that, if messages are filtered out, the connectivity of a thread can be disrupted. Given that the relationship between messages is an important aspect of online communication, any implementation of filtering in a discussion forum needs to deal with this issue. Students need to see the context of a message as well as its content. One possibility would be to offer users a quick and easy way of reinstating any filtered messages, in order to provide the necessary context.

Bookmarking

Learners often want to keep a record of online resources or postings that they have found useful. Some social network sites, for example Twitter, provide an internal 'Favourites' facility for this. In relation to web resources, most people use their browser to keep a local record of their 'favourites' or 'bookmarks'. There are now opportunities to store bookmarks to web resources online, using 'social bookmarking' tools such as Delicious (delicious.com). This approach means that the stored links are all in one place, rather than scattered among different browsers and different computers. There is also the potential to share bookmarks with other people who use the same social bookmarking service. This is discussed in more detail later in this chapter.

It would be possible to apply the same approach of personal or shared bookmarks within a discussion forum. For example, when a forum user found a message that they would like to return to later, they could 'bookmark' it, and perhaps also add some tags to describe it. A reference to the message would then be stored in the user's own area in the system. When the user clicked on the bookmark, they would be taken to the original message, within its thread, ensuring that the context of the message was retained. Users' bookmarks could be kept private, or they could be shareable, forming the basis for a social bookmarking facility within the discussion forum.

The following case study discusses a number of novel features, including a bookmarking facility, that were implemented in a course discussion system. The aim was to reduce the sense of overload for students.

CASE STUDY

SORTING THE WHEAT FROM THE CHAFF: NEW FEATURES FOR DISCUSSION FORUMS

Nick Heap and Karen Kear, The Open University, UK

The UK Open University makes considerable use of discussion forums to support its students. Many of the university's courses have large cohorts, and the forums can be very active. This level of activity in forums raises the issue of overload for students. In order to address this problem, a novel discussion environment was designed, which included features aimed at reducing overload. This was evaluated with students on several presentations of a 12-week, distance learning technology course (Kear and Heap, 2007).

Students used two versions of the discussion system: the 'enhanced' version, which included a number of features aimed at reducing overload; and the 'basic' version, which did not. The features in the enhanced version were:

- branched threading of messages (as opposed to linear threading);
- a facility for recommending messages;
- filtering of messages using different criteria;
- a 'clipping' facility for bookmarking useful messages.

For the first half of the course, students used the basic version of the system, and for the second half of the course, they used the enhanced version. Students were asked to complete survey questions at the half-way point and at the end of the course, so that their use and perceptions of the two versions could be compared.

Feelings of Overload

Many students reported that they had felt overloaded when using discussion forums in previous courses. They felt similarly overloaded during the first half of the present course, when they were using the basic version of the discussion system. Feelings of overload were mainly caused by seeing large numbers of unread messages. In the second half of the course, when students were using the enhanced version, they felt less overloaded (see Figure 5.4). This could mean that the new features were effective in reducing overload. However, there could also be other explanations, such as students becoming more confident as the course progressed.

Between the first and second halves of the course, there was little difference in the percentages of messages the students read; and some students read all the messages in both halves. As Hiltz and Turoff (1985, p. 683) pointed out, some students 'feel compelled to observe all the communications they can access in order to maintain confidence that nothing relevant is being overlooked'.

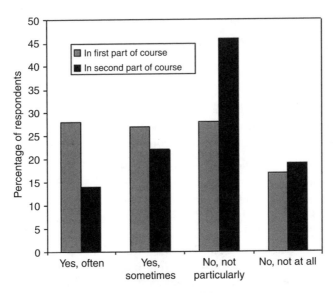

Figure 5.4 Students' responses when asked whether they felt overloaded.

Features for Message Threading

When asked their views on branched and linear threading, students expressed a clear preference for branched threading. They thought of a thread as a conversation among a group of people, with each contributor responding to another contributor's comment. Branched threading allowed students to see which comment responded to which, and to follow the progression of different 'strands' of the conversation.

Most students were also in favour of isolating the threads visually from each other, so that only one thread was visible at a time. This was seen as helpful in organising the messages, so that those on a specific topic were kept together, and separate from messages on other topics.

Recommending Messages

The issue of motivating students to recommend messages was given particular consideration. Hence the process for recommending a message was made as simple as possible. Students only needed to click a single link at the end of the message text to recommend it. Differing degrees of recommendation (that is, rating) were not catered for.

In practice the recommendation facility was used very little. This was partly an issue of 'critical mass'. Until there are significant numbers of recommendations it is difficult to make use of them (Konstan et al., 1997). However, there were other reasons for students' unwillingness to use this feature. Students commented that the value of a message was a personal matter, so a message that one person found useful would not necessarily be useful for someone else. Without knowing each other better, students felt that they could not provide helpful recommendations.

Filtering Messages

A number of filtering options were provided in the discussion system. Students could filter messages according to:

- whether the message was very recent;
- whether the student had already read the message;
- whether the message had been recommended by other students.

The last of these, filtering by recommendation, had seemed during the design of the project a useful way for students to 'sort the wheat from the chaff'. However, as recommendations were rarely given, this type of filtering was barely used.

The most useful filtering facility, according to students, was filtering out messages they had already read. This was surprising, given that unread messages were already indicated with an icon. It appeared that hiding messages that had already been read was more effective in some circumstances than simply highlighting unread messages.

'Clipping' Useful Messages

The discussion system enabled students to 'clip' (bookmark) useful messages for future reference. Although many students said that they considered this feature helpful in principle, most students did not use it. Clipping (or its equivalent) is rarely a feature in discussion forums, so students may not have registered that the facility was available.

When asked about the clipping facility, students said they would have preferred the clipped messages to be stored on their own computer, rather than on the system server. One issue was convenience: to access a clipped message it was necessary to connect to the Internet and log into the forum. This was not always possible, and not very convenient. Another issue was permanency: students realized that they might not have access to the clipped messages once the course was finished. This was important because some messages contained information or advice that students wanted to be able to refer to in the future.

Conclusions

Of the range of facilities designed to reduce overload, some were received favourably by students, whereas others were used very little. One clear finding was in relation to threading. A large majority of students found branched threading more helpful than linear threading.

The facility for recommending messages was not successful in the context of this short course, where students did not know each other very well. Perhaps students were uncomfortable making a judgement on a fellow student's contribution, as this could be viewed as counter to the supportive ethos of an online learning community.

Students' answers to the survey questions showed that they felt less overloaded in the second part of the course, which is when they were using the 'enhanced' version of the system. This suggests that the new features were helpful. As the course progressed, students would have become more experienced and confident with the online environment, which would also help to reduce feelings of overload.

Using Information on the Web

So far in this chapter, we have considered the problem of overload mainly in relation to online discussion forums. However, as mentioned earlier, another potential cause of information overload is the web. Learners are increasingly expected to seek out information via the web, perhaps as part of a resource-based or problem-based learning strategy. For example, a group of students might be asked to investigate a topic or issue, and present an up-to-date account of it to their fellow students. They would need to search for relevant material, evaluate what they find, select the material that is most appropriate, and then use it to prepare their presentation. These activities all require considerable information literacy skills.

Teachers need to support learners in developing the skills needed to find, evaluate and use web-based information. There are many ways to approach this, and many sources of advice and guidance are available to students. Academic librarians will have resources that can be used, and suggestions for how to develop these skills in students. For example The Open University Library offers a wealth of resources to students, including the 'Safari' information literacy guide (see Figure 5.5). This contains general discussion of finding and using information, as well as specific advice on searching the web, using library databases, referencing sources and so on.

If students are to become skilled web researchers, they need to be introduced to web-based techniques for finding, evaluating and storing information. For example, RSS aggregators could be useful to students for following specific topics without constantly visiting the same websites (see the brief overview of RSS given in Chapter 3). Another possibility is to use social bookmarking sites, where resources identified as useful by other web users are available for viewing, and where students can store and share their own bookmarks. Social bookmarking, which was introduced briefly in Chapter 3, is discussed in more detail below.

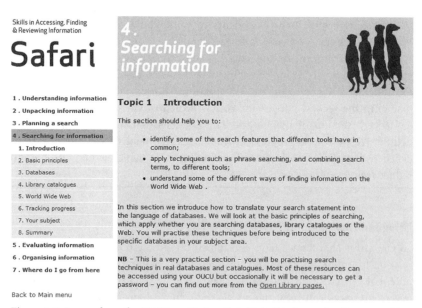

Figure 5.5 A page from the UK Open University's 'Safari' information literacy guide.

Source: Reproduced with permission from The Open University.

Social Bookmarking and Tagging

In the 'Sorting the wheat from the chaff' case study above, students were able to bookmark forum contributions that they found useful, but these bookmarks were private to each user. In contrast, 'social bookmarking' makes users' bookmarks available for sharing, so that each person can see resources that others have found useful. This approach is applied to web resources via sites such as Delicious (delicious.com) or Digg (digg.com). It is an effective way of 'sorting the wheat from the chaff' when learners are using the web as an information source.

Social bookmarking sites allow users to bookmark web resources of their choice, with the links to bookmarked sites stored in the user's area online. This means that a user's bookmarks are accessible whenever and wherever they have web access. Social bookmarking facilities often provide tools that can be added to a browser, so that creating a bookmark to a site you are browsing is quick and easy. Some websites and blogs also provide buttons to enable the user to create a bookmark in one or more of the main social bookmarking sites.

The 'social' element of social bookmarking is added by the facility to make bookmarks public and shared rather than private. If a user allows some or all of their bookmarks to be shared, these are added to the pool of shared bookmarks from other users. The popularity of each shared web resource can then be judged from how many times it has been bookmarked. There may also be information about who has bookmarked the resource, and a link to other bookmarks from that person. Users can therefore gain an indication of web resources that might be of use to them, and other users with whom they may share an interest.

With a popular social bookmarking facility such as Delicious, a large number of web resources will have been bookmarked, so the problem of overload is still present. However, this is addressed to some extent by the use of tagging. When a user bookmarks a web resource, they can also label it with 'tags' indicating something about the resource – perhaps its content, or its purpose. For example, suppose students on a course called 'English 101' were researching a project on the writing of Charles Dickens. They might label resources that they found with the tags 'Dickens' and 'English101', and perhaps also use tags for particular books by Dickens (e.g. 'Copperfield' for the book *David Copperfield*). Students could use these tags to find relevant resources bookmarked by their fellow students or by other web users. Figure 5.6 shows some of the results from Delicious for the tags 'Dickens' and 'Copperfield'.

Tagging is a more flexible process than assigning resources to pre-defined categories. Tags are defined by users, and new ones can be easily created. A resource can have many different tags, rather than needing to fit into just one category. Because of the user-centred nature of this approach to taxonomy, the

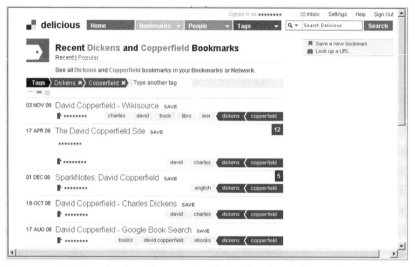

Figure 5.6 Delicious bookmarks tagged with 'Dickens' and 'Copperfield'. All user names and user-generated content have been replaced by asterisks.

Source: Reproduced with permission from Yahoo! Inc. © 2010 Yahoo! Inc. DELICIOUS and DELICIOUS logo are registered trademarks of Yahoo! Inc.

term 'folksonomy' is often used to describe it. However, there are disadvantages with the open nature of folksonomies (Guy & Tonkin, 2006). Users may create different tags for the same purpose or may use the same tags for different purposes. Variations or mistakes in spelling are one specific problem. For example, in the Charles Dickens example above, some relevant resources in Delicious are labelled with the tag 'Dickens'.

Educators and academic librarians have started to explore the value of social bookmarking tools for communities of learners (Hammond et al., 2005; Godwin, 2007). Boulos and Wheeler comment:

> Social bookmarking is an excellent resource discovery tool. It allows users to see the collective list of resources from all users who share a common research interest, and facilitates the development of communities of interest and expertise.
>
> (Boulos & Wheeler, 2007, p. 9)

Alexander (2006) comments that social bookmarking helps researchers – whether students or staff – to learn from each other and develop new collaborations. Observing how others are using bookmarks and tags can help to reveal patterns and connections, leading to new perspectives. Two examples are given of bespoke educational applications for social bookmarking within educational communities:

- The *Penntags* project at the University of Pennsylvania allows users to bookmark and tag resources, and also organize them into projects. (http://tags.library.upenn.edu/).

- Harvard's *H2O Playlist* offers a facility for grouping and sequencing resources into shareable 'playlists'. (http://h2obeta.law.harvard.edu/home.do).

Minocha (2009) and Redecker (2009) provide further examples of social bookmarking in education.

The case study below, 'Sharing with the shabab', describes an initiative to use the social bookmarking facility Diigo (www.diigo.com) with students. The aim was to build a learning community and to help students to develop learning practices that were less dependent on the teacher.

CASE STUDY

SHARING WITH THE SHABAB

Mark Curcher, Dubai Men's College, United Arab Emirates

Dubai Men's College is one of sixteen colleges that form the Higher Colleges of Technology (HCT) of the United Arab Emirates (UAE). The HCT's mission is to provide world-class vocational higher education to the citizens of the UAE. The campuses are spread across the cities and regions, with a men's and women's campus in each city. This study in Dubai Men's College involved all male students studying for the Bachelor of Applied Science in Business, and taking the final-year course *Monetary Theory*.

Most students have taken between four and five years to reach this course, one of the last they take before completing the BAS programme. The majority of students have been educated in public state schools where the language of instruction is Arabic. However, the HCT operates a western-based curriculum and all classes take place in English, so students are studying in a second language. The major experience of most students has been learning by memorization; rote learning is a highly prized skill in the local Islamic culture and is supported by both religious and secular tradition.

The Monetary Theory course had been taught for a number of years using a formal and traditional 'knowledge transfer' model, which was comfortable for the students and the former instructors. However, there is a considerable body of literature to support the idea that learning is a social activity (for example, Brown et al., 1989; Lave and Wenger, 1991; Wenger, 1998). The author was keen to make greater use of educational technology to create a community of learning among the students, with a particular focus on the sharing of resources using new social bookmarking technologies. The 'shabab' of the title refers to this community. 'Shabab' is an Arabic term for 'young people' or 'the guys', and is often used in class to refer to class members as a group.

Using Diigo for Social Bookmarking

In a social bookmarking system, users store lists of Internet resources that they believe they will find useful. The social aspect is that these can then be shared with the public at large or with a specific group. For this pilot Diigo (www.diigo.com) was chosen, after a review of the many alternatives available. It offers the ability to set up unlimited groups, useful for teaching multiple sections or sharing resources with different groups of people. It also allows the text on websites to be highlighted, and annotated using 'sticky notes'. Diigo can also host a discussion based on a particular comment or resource. The key point is that Diigo creates an environment where there is collaborative ownership of the learning resources. All participants are respected as members of a learning community, of which the teacher is just a part.

Student Participation

In the initial pilot there were 19 students taking the Monetary Theory course. Although 16 registered with Diigo, only about 10 students were active and participated enthusiastically in sharing resources and discussion. The remainder never really 'bought into' the idea, despite the fact that marks

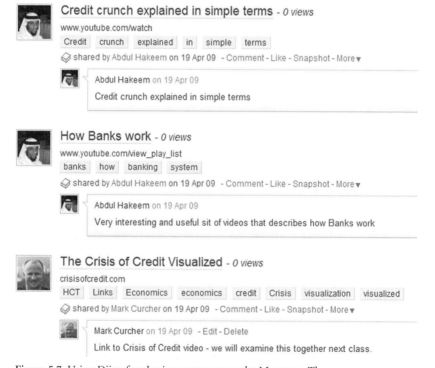

Figure 5.7 Using Diigo for sharing resources on the Monetary Theory course.

contributing towards students' course grades were attached to this activity (10 per cent of the final grade).

When questioned about lack of participation, one student responded that this was because the percentage weighting was too small. It is also important to recognize that this style of learning may not suit everyone, and was particularly difficult for these students to adopt, given their prior learning experiences. As Brown (2001) states, communities only form when the participants want this to happen. Perhaps some of the learners did not want to be a part of a community.

Based on the statistics from the Diigo group, most of the students who were active shared between three and four bookmarks during the course. The outliers were two students who shared more than 10 different resources each, and another who shared only one site during the course.

An examination of the resources shared, and the discussions among students, gave some encouraging results. There were many examples of students supporting each other, clarifying ideas and knowledge, and checking their own understanding in a spirit of trust and support. There were also many examples of students encouraging peers to read a particular article or watch a video, to gain an insight that the recommender had already gained from the resource. A typical post might be:

> Try watching this Ahmed, it helped me understand Money Supply and the difference between M1, M2 and M3.

All posts were respectful and there were no cases of flaming or abuse during the course.

Student Feedback

All students on the course were asked to complete an online survey, and 10 of the 19 students did so. Of the respondents, only eight actually participated using Diigo. The reason given for not signing up was that it was 'too complicated'. For all students it was their first experience of using a social bookmarking system and some struggled with the complexity of using the site.

All the participating respondents felt that Diigo had helped their learning; 63 per cent said that it helped their learning a bit, and 37 per cent said that it helped a lot. Two students said that they found the site difficult to understand and use at first. This is a fair comment, and more could have been done in class to scaffold the students' skills in using the website. Overall the feedback from the students who used Diigo was that it was enjoyable and had a beneficial effect on their learning.

Conclusion

The use of social bookmarking technologies contributed to the development of a small learning community in the Monetary Theory class. Those students who actively participated took to the new approach with remarkable enthusiasm, particularly given their prior learning experiences. They seemed to value the opportunity to have a voice and share their knowledge and opinions. The use of Diigo also moved learning beyond the classroom's formal setting. Students were now engaged with learning at the times that suited them and their family and work commitments.

A minority of students were very active, really engaging with the subject, the materials and other learners. However, a small group of students were very resistant to the changes in the course, and vocally expressed the view that it should be the teacher who provides all the resources and provides the students with answers.

Using social networking technology for learning requires proper planning and implementation, and a re-evaluation of learning activities and assessments. Adequate scaffolding is also needed to help students develop the skills required for participation. With these provisions, the technology can improve the learning experiences of students and make learning much more enjoyable.

The Collective

We have seen above how social bookmarking facilities can support members of learning communities. Resources can be shared within a small project group, a course cohort, an educational institution, or potentially among all web users. Social bookmarking works most effectively when there are many contributors. Dron (2007) and Wiley (2007) both use the term *stygmergy* to describe the phenomenon where contributions from many individuals combine to create something of value. A similar concept is 'the wisdom of crowds' (Surowiecki, 2005). In this context, Dron and Anderson (2007) use the term *collective* for the 'crowd'.

In relation to social software, Dron and Anderson (2007) characterize three different kinds of grouping: the *group*; the *network*; and the *collective*. They define these as follows:

> Groups are more or less tightly knit teams of individuals who are committed to each other and usually to a task or tasks.
>
> Networks connect distributed individuals. People may be connected to other people either directly or indirectly, but may not be immediately aware of all those who form part of the wider network.
>
> Collectives are aggregations, sets formed of the actions of individuals who primarily see themselves as neither a part of a group nor connected through a network. Like the Network, the shape of the collective is emergent, not designed.
>
> (Dron & Anderson, 2007, pp. 2461–2462, quoted in Ryberg et al., 2010)

In this categorization, a student class or project team would be a group. A network is more fluid, in that membership can evolve (for example, a set of friends and friends-of-friends on Facebook). A collective is even more loosely connected, but results in an emergent structure (for example, members of *Delicious* who tag and share their bookmarks). Social software for sharing, tagging, recommending and filtering gains its power from the collective. It provides a way of benefiting from large quantities of online information, rather than being overwhelmed by it.

Shirky (2008a) discussed the implications of the huge increase in user-generated material on the web. He characterized traditional publishing and editorial processes as 'filter-then-publish', and contrasted these with newer web-based approaches, which he described as 'publish-then-filter'. He went on to claim:

> Filter-then-publish, whatever its advantages, rested on a scarcity of media that is a thing of the past. The expansion of social media means that the only working system is publish-then-filter.
>
> (Shirky, 2008a, p. 98)

In a presentation later that year, Shirky explicitly made the connection between filtering and the problem of information overload – 'Thinking about information overload isn't accurately describing the problem; thinking about filter failure is' (Shirky, 2008b, quoted in Asay, 2009).

Shirky's argument is that dealing with information overload is a question of finding adequate methods, both technical and social, for filtering. This includes structuring information (for example, threads in forums or tags on social bookmarking sites), using recommendations, and applying information literacy skills. But it also requires us to think about how we interact with each other and how we share information so that it does not become overwhelming.

As communication software improves, more effective methods for filtering and managing information will become available. However, filtering as traditionally performed has tended to be a compromise, in which capturing everything relevant has been at the price of letting in some irrelevance; and excluding irrelevant material has been at the price of excluding some relevant material. Whether this dilemma can be resolved by purely technological means remains to be seen. For the time being, though, there is no doubt that overload is a major problem with the use of online resources. Teachers therefore need to support students in developing strategies, both collaborative and individual, to overcome this.

Key Points for Practitioners

- Overload can be a significant problem for members of online learning communities. In particular, it can be caused by:

- ○ large numbers of postings in discussion forums;
- ○ the challenge of identifying useful web resources.
- In relation to forums, the problem can be alleviated by clear structuring of forums and by consistent use of system threading.
- For identifying useful learning resources from the large amount of material on the web, students need information literacy skills.
- Students will also benefit from the sharing, recommending and tagging facilities provided by social bookmarking tools.

Further Reading

Dron, J. (2007) *Control and constraint in e-learning: choosing when to choose*, London & Hershey, PA: Idea Group Publishing.

This substantial book covers many aspects of using social software for learning. The theme is learner control in online settings. The book discusses students' and teachers' use of a number of tools, including forums and social bookmarking.

Hilt, S.R. and Turoff, M. (1985) 'Structuring computer-mediated communication systems to avoid information overload', *Communications of the ACM*, 28(7), pp. 680–689.

This paper gives a valuable insight into the issue of overload in online discussion systems. It shows how early researchers in this area gave careful thought to the design and use of online communication systems. The authors advocate facilities for users to control and structure their online environments.

Wiley, D. (2007) 'Online self-organising social systems: four years later' in Luppicini, R. (ed.) *Online learning communities*, Charlotte, NC: Information Age Publishing, pp. 289–298.

This book chapter considers online settings where contributions from a large number of people combine to create something of value. It discusses a number of 'web 2.0' applications where this principle applies, in particular social bookmarking. Other chapters in the book will also be of interest.

6
Feeling Connected

This chapter focuses on ideas of community among online learners, and also discusses the concept of social presence – whether online communication feels 'real' to participants. The chapter considers the extent to which online learners feel a sense of community, and how this varies between individuals. It considers the steps educators can take in order to build online community among learners. The chapter ends by looking at the potential of social network sites for supporting online learning communities.

Online communication can help to develop a sense of community and belonging among students. By enabling regular communication and contact, it helps students to feel in touch with each other and with their teachers. Attending to these social aspects can make a significant difference to how students feel about their learning environment, their fellow learners and their studies. For learners who are experiencing difficulties, or feeling isolated, these affective aspects could make the difference between successfully completing a course and dropping out.

In this chapter we will be looking at the role of online community in an educational setting. We will also be exploring the related concept of social presence, to see whether learners feel that online communication is sufficiently 'real' to fulfil their needs. I begin the chapter with a brief review of the literature, and then go on to consider learners' views about online community. We will then look at how teachers can help to build community among learners. In this chapter we will be focusing primarily on asynchronous communication tools, such as forums, blogs and social network sites. Then in Chapter 7 we will move on to discuss the role of real-time communication tools.

Research on Social Aspects of Online Learning

A number of research studies have investigated students' feelings and experiences when learning together online. The studies consider whether students:

- feel a sense of belonging;
- feel that the communication is real and meaningful.

These two aspects are closely related, but tend to be addressed in different areas of the academic literature. The first aspect is typically discussed as 'online community', while the second is characterized as 'social presence'. In this section I will look at research findings under these two headings. All the studies investigate whether learners feel a sense of connection when working in an online context, and how this affects their learning and motivation.

Online Community

Brown (2001) found that a sense of community in an online course helped overcome isolation, increase student satisfaction and retention, and support learning. Brown found that the sense of community a student experienced was related to their level of participation in the course. Some students felt no sense of community, because they had no need for it, or could not commit the necessary time to online interaction, or believed that community could only be experienced face-to-face. Those who did feel a sense of community reported that it took longer to develop online than it would have face-to-face. Opportunities for students to learn more about each other (e.g. through self introductions, or from the content, timing and tone of messages) helped the process.

The development of online community in a part-time Masters degree was investigated by Haythornthwaite et al. (2000). The degree programme began with a face-to-face 'boot camp', followed by study via asynchronous and synchronous communication. Interviews revealed that students felt a sense of belonging, and that the initial face-to-face period helped, by giving a clear sense of others who were part of the community. One student commented:

> Even though they would be just a name on a screen in the chat room or on the webboard, you still had the memory of knowing them from boot camp, which was such an intense experience. That gave you a connection. It was almost like they were there. You could imagine them.

The learners in this study also said that synchronous communication was helpful in alleviating feelings of isolation, and some students used email in a near-synchronous way when online at the same time as others. Haythornthwaite and her colleagues concluded that students need 'multiple means of communication: public and private, synchronous and asynchronous, multi-party and one-on-one, distanced and face-to-face for sustaining group interaction.'

The importance of an initial face-to-face meeting for fostering a sense of community was underlined by Conrad (2002). Investigating mainly online courses, Conrad found that the initial meeting helped students to visualize each other when communicating online. Subsequently, when online, many students made efforts to build community through their messages, although this took time and effort. Conrad concluded that participation in online intellectual exchanges was made more comfortable for students by their increased sense of community.

Social Presence

Gunawardena and Zittle (1997) investigated whether social presence affected the degree of satisfaction of learners who were communicating online. Social presence was defined as 'the degree to which a person is perceived as "real" in mediated communication' (p. 8). Their research found that students' sense of social presence was a strong predictor of satisfaction with the online learning experience. The researchers concluded that, even when using a text-based communication medium, participants could create social presence through the ways in which they interacted with each other:

> In spite of the characteristics of the medium, student perceptions of the social and human qualities of CMC will depend on the social presence created by the instructors/moderators and the online community.
>
> (Gunawardena and Zittle, 1997, p. 23)

Whereas Gunawardena and Zittle, above, used questionnaires to assess social presence, Rourke et al. (1999) analysed students' messages in online forums for two courses which used different communication systems. They observed that, when social presence is high, participants:

> feel a sense of affiliation with each other and a sense of solidarity with the group. This environment of approachability and closeness encourages the students to regard the conference and their interactions as valuable and educationally profitable.
>
> (Rourke et al., 1999)

Using the same research approach, Swan (2002) investigated social presence in an online postgraduate course. Her findings supported an equilibrium model of social presence. She argued that, because text-based communication does not easily convey feelings, participants in online communities explicitly add affective aspects into their communications. For example, they might include some personal or social content in their messages, or they might use emoticons or punctuation to convey their meaning.

This brings us back to the findings of Conrad (2002), that students make efforts to build community in an online setting. When using a communication medium that does not itself provide many 'cues' (Sproull & Kiesler, 1991) to support communication, some students use the content, timing and style of their messages to add this 'social glue'. However, this takes considerable effort, time, sensitivity and skill, so not all students will be willing or able to do this.

Students' Views on Online Community

In this section I will present the findings of a study that investigated students' views about online community (Kear, 2007). The students were distance learners at the UK Open University, registered on a 12-week part-time undergraduate course on a technical subject. The students had no face-to-face contact with each other, or with the course facilitators, but instead communicated via discussion forums. During the course, students were asked a number of survey questions about online communication and online community. For example:

- Is online contact with other students in the course important to you?
- Is it important to you to feel part of a community of students on the course you are studying?
- Can you gain a sense of community purely though online communication?
- Do you think synchronous communication facilities in an online course environment can help to create a sense of community?

The research took place over two presentations of the course, both with more than 90 students. The response rates for the survey questions were over 69 per cent.

Although many students were uncertain about online community, most felt it was important to have online contact with other students. Considerably more students thought online contact important than thought feelings of community important. Students reported that they liked reading others' contributions, but they were not all convinced that this involved a sense of community.

Students made some thoughtful comments about community, explaining why it was, or was not, important to them. Those who felt that feelings of community were important related this to a sense of identity as a member of the course, and of the university. They commented that this could last for several years, as they used online communication to keep in contact with students they had met on earlier courses. Several students commented that a sense of community could help them to keep going when they were struggling with motivation.

Synchronous communication, according to most students, could help create a sense of community. However, they seemed to place more value on asynchronous communication. It fulfilled their needs and they felt more comfortable with it. Initiating real-time contact with people they did not already know made students feel uncomfortable. However, an awareness that others were online and working on the course was seen as helpful. One student commented that there is a place for both approaches, with synchronous chat for light-hearted conversations, and discussion forums for more reflective and inclusive course discussions.

Students were divided as to whether a sense of community could arise in a purely online setting. Some students thought it could, others thought it was difficult, and others said that it might depend on the individual. Nevertheless, students found value and interest in reading online contributions from other students. Some students thought a sense of community could only be developed through face-to-face meetings. They felt that just reading messages and viewing member profiles was not enough to enable them to get to know each other well. Trust was also seen as an issue in online environments. Some students felt that without meeting people face-to-face they could not be sure that others were truly as they presented themselves. One student said that, after some time, he felt that he was interacting with real people, rather than just reading text on a screen. He added that asking for help, or giving it, helped to establish this rapport.

The case study below, 'Sharing images, creating communities', from the UK Open University, discusses an online environment where students helped each other develop skills in photography. The case study highlights the connection between practical learning and the development of a community (Wenger, 1998).

CASE STUDY

SHARING IMAGES, CREATING COMMUNITIES

Georgy Holden, The Open University, UK

This case study discusses OpenStudio, a photo-sharing interface that is based on the web 2.0 photo-sharing interface, Flickr. OpenStudio is used as an integral part of student learning for a Level 1 course in digital photography (T189) offered by the UK Open University (see Minocha, 2009, pp. 54–58). The challenge faced by the course authors was how to teach a subject as visual as photography, at a distance with no tutorial support.

The course attracts around 2,500 students per year, in two presentations. Students are drawn from a diversity of educational backgrounds and experience, and more than 50 per cent are new to the university. The course materials are delivered entirely online and, as well as OpenStudio, students can communicate in a number of support forums.

Using OpenStudio

OpenStudio is an unmoderated, peer support environment, although the moderators of the course forums have access to it, and some choose to engage with it out of interest. The main affordance of the interface is that students can post an image and others can comment upon it. The interface has a 'report' facility to enable students to report any problems, whether social or technical. The system administrator can, if necessary, remove or restrict images and comments.

The interface has five main areas:

- *My Photos*, an area where each individual posts up to 10 photos per study week;
- *My Group*, an area that displays the images from everyone in the student's allocated group week by week;
- *My Community*, an area that displays all of the images from the entire course community week by week;
- *My Favourites*, a virtual album that contains any images that the student has chosen to 'fave' from others' photo-collections. The images are linked so this can be used as a way of keeping track of comments on images, or keeping in touch with fellow students;
- *Search*, an area where students can search for images by photographer or by self-allocated tags.

The allocation of students to random groups is designed to make commenting more practical in a large community. Students are advised to give priority to their own group when critiquing images, though many comment on images from the community pool as well. Students can add descriptions and comments on their own images, and this is encouraged as a means of reflecting on the photography.

The interface allows the student to reveal as much or as little information about themselves as they wish, including their name (the default name is their initialized computer i.d.). Many choose to reveal some personal details but others prefer to remain anonymous.

Students' Views on OpenStudio

An evaluation carried out with a sample of students revealed that a large majority found the interface helpful or very helpful. The most cited reason for this was the value of comments received on photos. A significant proportion of students also cited the camaraderie, motivation and inspiration OpenStudio engendered. This student comment sums it up:

> Extremely helpful. T189 was my introduction to serious photography and so I really appreciated the comments I got. I also found that evaluating other people's work made me think about the various aspects that make a good photo, again helping me to improve.

For the students who found the interface less helpful, reasons cited were: lack of meaningful comment; technical limitations; and social issues.

For a small but vociferous minority, the lack of expert guidance in Open-Studio and the unsupervised nature of the interface were problematic. The issue of expert help is an interesting one. One of T189's sister courses teaches web design without any personal tuition and this has never been raised as an issue. It would seem that the intensely personal nature of photography leads students to require affirmation and approval from experts that they do not expect on other courses. This may stem from perceived differences between knowledge and skills acquisition, photography being seen as predominantly skills based.

Interaction Among Students

The vast majority of students comment in a constructive way on one another's images. To facilitate this, advice is provided in the course materials about critiquing and commenting. In the first presentation of the course, early guidance was by example, with explicit guidelines coming later. However, student feedback led to the explicit guidelines being moved to the beginning of the course.

The success of the interface as a social medium is evidenced by the post-course creation, by students, of a number of Flickr groups based on the course. Students write about their experience of both OpenStudio and the Flickr interface on which it is based, as a social experience as well as a learning community:

> Firstly I think of it as a social medium where I have contact with people with a common interest. Hopefully it is helping me to improve my photography and I still get a buzz when I receive comments on my images so I suppose it is also to showcase my images.

> I miss the Open Studio community and feedback and Flickr has filled that void for me.

Conclusion

Evaluation of OpenStudio shows that it is achieving its intended outcome of enabling students to learn digital photography through peer support. The scope for use of image-sharing interfaces in other disciplines is also significant. Engagement via the visual image is undoubtedly rich and fruitful. Possibilities might include: the use of photo-sharing in art and media courses for discussing images and the issues surrounding them; in science to collect and share samples virtually and seek opinion or comment upon them; in languages as a stimulus for discussion or as a basis for language games.

The study showed two specific areas that are critical to the success of such an interface. First, guidance and encouragement are needed to enable students to engage in meaningful dialogue within the online environment. Where student skills and abilities vary enormously, the timing and pitching of this guidance is crucial. Second, integration of the interface into the learning strategy for the course is important if the students are to have an incentive to contribute.

In this case OpenStudio was a key element of the learning strategy and almost all students on the course used it, though the extent of engagement varied.

The study also showed that offering opportunities for social interaction could strengthen the student cohort, aid retention and encourage future studies. However, findings indicate that there is a need to allow and facilitate social interaction at different levels to suit individual preferences.

Encouraging Community Online

As we have seen earlier in this chapter, not all students need to feel part of a community, but for those who do, it can make all the difference to their experience of studying online. In this section I will consider the steps that teachers can take to encourage a sense of community among learners. To illustrate my points, I will use examples of online environments, activities and resources from the UK Open University. The discussion is mainly focused on online forums, but the principles of how to build community among learners also apply to other online environments.

Creating a Welcoming Online Environment

An initial responsibility for the teacher is to create a welcoming and friendly online environment for students. There are different ways of doing this, depending on the communication tools being used and the degree of control that individual teachers are given. Taking discussion forums as an example, the teacher may be able to influence:

- how many forums there are;
- what they are called;
- what they look like;
- what students find when they first arrive in a forum.

It can be helpful to differentiate forums by purpose (for example, one for course discussions and one for social chat). However, having too many could mean that students are not sure where to make their contributions. It could also mean that interactions are spread too thinly, so all the forums look rather empty. There is a balance to be struck, so that the forums are lively, but not crowded and confusing. This balance will depend on how many students are involved, and how active they are online.

Naming the forums appropriately helps students to understand the purpose of each, and to make their contributions in the right place. Names can also be used as a way of setting the tone of the interactions. For example, a forum for general conversations could have various names, such as 'Coffee Bar' or 'Common Room'. The name chosen will influence how students feel about the online space.

The visual appearance of forums can also be used to give online spaces a sense of identity. For example, in the FirstClass system, each forum has an icon to represent it. A suitable icon reminds students of the purpose of the forum and the kinds of interactions that take place there. Figure 6.1 shows a set of forums for the photography course described in the 'Sharing images, creating communities' case study. In this course, whose code is T189, the students are divided into several groups, named after colours. Figure 6.1, which shows the forums for the 'Green' group in the '2009J' course presentation, demonstrates how names and icons can be chosen to represent the purpose of each forum.

When students first arrive in an online forum it is important that they find a welcoming message from the teacher or moderator. This is analogous to arriving at a social event and being welcomed by the host. A good example is given in Figure 6.2, which shows part of the welcome message for the first module of the course *Information and Communication Technologies* (T209). The message conveys a sense of personal contact from the moderator of the forum, as well as explaining the forum's purpose. The moderator, Pat Crawford, has chosen a friendly font style, and in the original the text was in colour. In her message Pat mentions the use of icons for other forums, and for personalizing her own messages. Pat is from Scotland, and she has added a nice final touch by signing off with the word 'Sláinte', which is 'good health' in Scottish Gaelic.

Encouraging Supportive Interactions

I have discussed some of the steps that teachers can take to create welcoming online spaces. Another important consideration is encouraging students to interact with each other in ways that support online community. Early chapters have shown that many students use their messages to good effect in building community and enhancing social presence. To some, this comes naturally, and they may not even realize they are doing it. But other students, particularly those who are new to online communication, may find it difficult to judge how their contributions will come across, or may not even think about this.

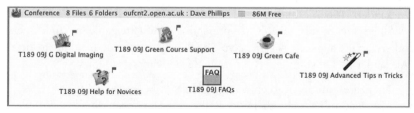

Figure 6.1 A set of forums for the course T189 Digital Photography.

Source: Reproduced with permission from The Open University.

Hi everyone!
Welcome to T209 and, in particular, to this Module 1 conference. This conference exists to give you all an opportunity to offer each other support and encouragement.

My name is Pat and I'll be moderating this conference, with the support of the T209 Course Team, until the 13th March, by which time the Module 2 conference will be well underway. As moderator, I will 'drop-in' most days to see that everything is running smoothly and I will archive old messages in the folder with the treasure chest icon. I will usually use the red butterfly icon for my messages so that you can easily identify my moderator comments.

I am sure that it will not be necessary but it would also fall within my remit to remove any unsuitable messages (e.g. illegal or offensive material or anti-social communications) from the conference.

This is your conference and you can use it to discuss the contents of the module, to share ideas about how you might approach assignments and generally offer support to each other as you work through the course.

[. . .]

I hope you enjoy this Module and that you can find time to contribute to what I am sure will be worthwhile discussions. I'm looking forward to getting to know you all.
Enjoy the module and the course.

Sláinte!

Pat

Figure 6.2 Part of a welcome message from a course moderator.

Source: Reproduced with permission from The Open University.

To some extent, teachers can address this issue by modelling an appropriate style in their own messages. If the teacher sets the tone of the interactions at an early stage, students can pick this up, either consciously or unconsciously, and follow the example. However, it is wise to augment this with discussion and guidance on good practice for interacting with others online. This is often described as 'netiquette'. Figure 6.3 shows material on netiquette from the Level 1 course *Networked Living* (T175). This material is included near the beginning of the course to set the scene for students' activities in the course forums. It is based on work by Gary Alexander and Bob Zimmer (Zimmer & Alexander, 1996; Alexander, 2000).

Some care must be taken when presenting netiquette guidelines to learners, otherwise the advice may come across as condescending, or as rather artificial. Alexander (2000) comments on netiquette guidelines as follows:

These are not meant to encourage groups to be overly polite and agree with everything each other says. Rather, they are meant to allow groups to really engage with issues, to disagree and learn by resolving their disagreements without upsets and hurt feelings.

Netiquette

Introduction

Netiquette is the unwritten rules of good behaviour online. Although the principles are similar to face-to-face conversation, the limitations of a text-based medium mean you have to learn new techniques. Other people can't see the expression on your face or hear your voice, so it is what you write that sets the tone of the conversation.

Thank, acknowledge and support people

People can't see you nod, smile or frown as you read their messages. If they get no acknowledgement, they may feel ignored and be discouraged from contributing further. Why not send a short reply to keep the conversation going? This can make a big difference in a small group setting like a tutor-group conference. (But bear in mind that in a large, busy conference, too many messages like this could be a nuisance.)

Acknowledge before differing

Before you disagree with someone, try to summarise the other person's point in your own words. Then they know you are trying to understand them and will be more likely to take your view seriously. Otherwise, you risk talking at each other rather than to each other.

Make clear your perspective

Try to avoid speaking impersonally: 'This is the way it is . . .', 'It is a fact that . . .'. That will sound dogmatic and leaves no room for anyone else's perspective. Why not start, 'I think . . .'? A common abbreviation is IMHO (in my humble opinion) – or even IMNSHO (in my not so humble opinion). If you are presenting someone else's views, say so, perhaps by a quote and acknowledgement.

Emotions

Emotions can be easily misunderstood when you can't see faces or body language. People may not realise you are joking; irony and satire are easily missed. Smileys or emoticons such as :-) and :-(can be used to express your feelings (look at these sideways). Other possibilities are punctuation (?! #@*!), <grin> or <g>, <joke>, or even using mock HTML tags such as <rant>smileys are stupid</rant>.

Remember that many discussion systems only support plain text so you can't rely on fonts and colours to add meaning.

Be aware of your audience: people from widely differing cultures and backgrounds may read what you write online. What you find funny may be offensive to them.

AND DON'T WRITE IN CAPITAL LETTERS – IT WILL COME OVER AS SHOUTING!

Flaming

If you read something that offends or upsets you, it is very tempting to dash off a reply and hit Send – but don't! Online discussion seems to be particularly prone to such **flames**; often an unwitting breach of netiquette will escalate in a flaming spiral of angry messages. So if you feel your temperature rising as you write, save your message, take a break or sleep on it – don't hit Send.

Figure 6.3 Netiquette guidelines for students.

Source: Reproduced with permission from The Open University.

Helping Learners Get to Know Each Other

At the beginning of an online course, it is helpful to have an 'icebreaker' activity to encourage students to interact and to get to know each other. Icebreakers are often used at the beginning of face-to-face tutorials or workshops to help participants feel comfortable with each other.

Figure 6.4 shows an extract from an online icebreaker activity in the *Networked Living* course mentioned above. The activity is followed by a comment from one of the course authors, showing students the type of message they might contribute to the forum for this activity.

Activity

Using a search engine such as Google, find three websites that somehow describe an aspect of yourself that you wish to share with fellow tutor group members. The sites could refer to a hobby, something that you are interested in, or perhaps the place where you live.

Make a note of the web addresses of the sites that you have selected [. . .].

Once you have completed your search, compose a message to the rest of your tutor group including the three website addresses. Add a few sentences about the sites in your message indicating why you have chosen them. The subject of the message should be something like 'Chris's website choices'.

Now post your message into your FirstClass tutor group conference and have a look at the messages that others in the group have posted. Try responding to one or two people's messages in order to get to know them a little better.

Comment

This is the sort of thing I might post to the conference:

Hi everyone – here are my three websites by way of introduction – look forward to finding out a bit about all of you over the next few days . . .

1. I live quite near to the Grand Union canal, and often go for walks along the towpath. Here is some information about the part of the canal which goes through Milton Keynes.

http://www.mkweb.co.uk/canal/home.asp

2. I enjoy running as well as walking, and I sometimes enter charity running races. One example is the Race For Life, which raises money for cancer research. http://www.raceforlife.org/default.aspx

3. I've been a member of the Open University choir for many years. For the 40th anniversary of the university, in 2009, we performed with other singers and musicians in the Milton Keynes Theatre.

http://www.open.ac.uk/wikis/ouchoir/OU Choir

Figure 6.4 An online icebreaker activity.

Source: Reproduced with permission from The Open University.

The icebreaker activity above invites students to introduce themselves, so that they can learn something about each other. Another way of helping learners to get to know each other is to encourage them to complete a member profile. This is discussed in more detail in the next section.

Member Profiles

Most online communication systems have a facility that allows users to add some text about themselves, and perhaps to include a photograph. This feature has different names in different systems (for example, in the FirstClass system it is called a résumé), but I will refer to it as a member profile. In some systems the member profile is structured into topics (such as location, hobbies, education, favourite music or films) whereas in others it may be completely open, so that users can add any information that they wish to share with others. Figure 6.5 shows my member profile in the Open University's virtual learning environment.

In the remainder of this section I will consider some of the research literature related to member profiles, and consider more detailed findings from a research study of member profiles in a learning context.

Literature on Member Profiles

Member profiles have been advocated by online learning practitioners for many years. For example, Zimmer et al. (2000), in their discussion of building online learning communities, advised that:

Socialisation can be enabled by setting up the community in a way that allows individuals to gain an understanding of who is addressing them

Location: United Kingdom

View Karen Kear's blog

I am a senior lecturer at the UK Open University. I teach information and communication technologies, specialising in online communication. I work on the following OU courses:

- T175 *Networked Living*
- T215 *Communication and Information Technologies*
- TU100 *My Digital Life*

I also carry out research in online communication and collaboration, particularly in the context of learning.

Outside work, I enjoy running, walking and music. I sing in the OU choir and I play the piano (not particularly well!)

Figure 6.5 The author's VLE member profile.

Source: Reproduced with permission from The Open University.

in what can be an impersonal textual environment. This could include: photos, résumés and biographies and general introductions to the online group.

(Zimmer et al., 2000, pp. 3–5)

Barab et al. (2003) used member profiles within their Inquiry Learning Forum for peer support among teachers. They encouraged members to create member profiles so that they could learn more about each other. Bonk et al. (2001), discussing the 'Smartweb' system, reported that students were asked to include in their member profiles such things as their hobbies, where they lived and their computer experience. Photographs have also often been recommended. Kim suggested that photos should be included because they would 'help your members express their identity in a more immediate way' (2000, p. 100).

Nicol et al. (2003) describe a system used by the Open University of Catalonia, where each contribution is accompanied by a thumbnail picture of the contributor. In this way a mental picture of the contributor is reinforced. The Moodle virtual learning environment also adopts this approach (see Figure 6.6).

Song et al. (2004) reported that the use of photographs helped build community in an online course that had an initial face-to-face meeting. However, other researchers have found drawbacks as well as benefits from member

Figure 6.6 Messages in a Moodle forum, with images representing the senders.

Source: Reproduced with permission from The Open University.

photos. Cress (2005) found that member photos had a positive effect on group interaction for some members of online groups, but a negative effect for others. Tanis and Postmes (2007) also found that member photos had mixed results. In both these studies, the authors suggest that member photos can reduce some participants' sense of solidarity.

Investigating Students' Views on Member Profiles

It is clear from the literature presented above that many online learning practitioners advocate the use of member profiles and photos for enhancing social presence. However, little of this literature is based on the views of learners themselves. The remainder of this section therefore presents a brief account of a study investigating learners' perspectives on member profiles.

The context of this research was the short distance-learning course mentioned earlier in this chapter, which used online discussion forums to support the study of the course (Kear, 2007). The discussion environment provided a facility for students to create a member profile, to add any text they wished, and to upload a photograph. Once a student had created their member profile, a small icon representing a face appeared beside their name wherever it was displayed (for example, when they were shown as the author of a message). Other students could click on this icon in order to read the person's profile and view their photo, if they had uploaded one.

In two course presentations, data was gathered on students' use of the member profile, and their views on its value. Students were asked several survey questions about their use of member profiles. These included:

- Had they created a profile?
- If they had not, what was the reason?
- Had they looked at other students' profiles?
- If they had, was this helpful, and in what ways?
- Was it helpful to have photos or images in member profiles?

In both course presentations, students were encouraged to write something in their member profile. In one of the presentations about two-thirds of the students did so, and in the other about half the students did. In some cases students chose not to post any information, for reasons of privacy. In other cases students were uncertain about what to write; perhaps a more structured format for the profile, or some guidance, would have been helpful.

About half the students looked at others' profiles. Mainly, students read profiles of other students who had posted messages. About a third of the students reported that they found profiles helpful for getting to know other students. However, some students felt that reading messages was a better way to find out about others. When asked their views on the value of photos in profiles, about a third of the students reported finding them useful.

The research described above found that member profiles and photos were important to some students, but not to the majority. Some students said they preferred to learn about others from reading their postings, and that this seemed a more genuine and natural way of getting to know them. This underlines the importance of encouraging students to interact and engage with each other through their messages.

Since this research study was carried out, social network sites such as Facebook and MySpace have become widespread. Most current students will be familiar with these sites and many will be using them regularly. In social network sites the member profile is a central focus, and within this profile the user's photo is a key element. It will be interesting to see whether familiarity with these sites encourages students to make more use of the member profile facility in other online environments.

Social Network Sites for Learning Communities

Social network sites are designed to connect people together. They therefore have significant potential for supporting learning communities. Although social network sites first began to appear in the late 1990s, the best known sites – MySpace, Facebook and Twitter – are more recent (boyd & Ellison, 2007). MySpace started in 2003 and Facebook became available to any web user in 2006, as did Twitter. There are also more specialized social network sites for media sharing, for example Flickr and YouTube.

Social network sites continually evolve, influenced by their users as well as by developers. Having started as a way of building networks of friends, and 'friends of friends', they now facilitate many kinds of communication:

- synchronous or asynchronous;
- private or public;
- one-to-one or one-to-many.

They also provide facilities for sharing media, providing short status updates, playing games, and many other activities (Donelan et al., 2010). Some researchers suggest that these sites have considerable potential for learning and identity development among young people (Greenhow & Robelia, 2009). It is also suggested that use of social network sites may improve the relationships between students and teachers (Mazer et al., 2007). At the time of writing, educators are beginning to explore the use of social network sites to support online learning communities. In this section we will consider the findings from a few of these exploratory studies. Further examples are reported, in the form of case studies, by Minocha (2009).

Using Facebook for Learning Communities

Schroeder and Greenbowe (2009) investigated the use of a Facebook group in a course on chemistry. The course already used WebCT, but there was very little participation by students in the WebCT discussion forum. In contrast, although the Facebook group was entirely optional, 41 per cent of students joined it. There were about four times as many postings in the Facebook group as in the WebCT forum, and the Facebook discussions were more involved and interactive. The discussions continued in Facebook throughout the course, while the WebCT discussions faded away and then stopped altogether. The instructors felt that a key factor in the success of Facebook was that students were already using it for other purposes, so they could easily check the course group while they were logged in.

In another study, this time with students of architecture and visual arts, Durkee at al. (2009) identified several advantages of using Facebook, as compared with using an institutional virtual learning environment. These included: opening up participation to alumni, potential employers and other practitioners; and allowing students to 'publish' their work for critical review, using a range of media. Durkee et al. pointed out that, because most students are already familiar with Facebook, there are few technical barriers to overcome. Facebook is constantly available, even via mobile devices, and enables students and teachers to freely mix synchronous and asynchronous communication. Because Facebook is a 'student-owned' environment, the teacher can be viewed more as a peer than as a remote expert.

Tools for Implementing Social Network Sites

An alternative to using an existing social network site is to develop a tailored site, using tools such as Elgg (elgg.org) or Ning (www.ning.com). Use of Elgg for learning was discussed in the case study on *Ekademia* presented in Chapter 2 of this book. Elgg has also been used at the University of Brighton, UK, in order to develop an institutional online community (Minocha, 2009).

Dron and Anderson (2007) reported on the use of Elgg for an individual course at Brighton. An Elgg 'Community' was set up for the course, and students communicated with each other via the blogs and other social software tools offered within Elgg. Students also had access to the wider Elgg community, and although this was potentially beneficial, the blurred boundary between course environment and the wider social network caused problems. Dron and Anderson (2007) characterized this as being 'lost in social space'. Students were unsure whether they were in their own personal space, the course, the university or the wider public space.

Ning is widely used as a tool for setting up and running a social network site. It is well structured and easy to use, both for the administrator and the student. Ning includes advertisements, but these can be removed in a paid-for service. Ning is a hosted service, which means that it runs on Ning's own servers. Many examples of Ning networks for communities of educators can be found on the web (see for example www.classroom20.com and edupln.ning.com).

To date, there appears to be little published research on the use of Ning in a course context. However, one example is the course 'Women in popular culture' at the University of Nebraska-Lincoln, USA (Schueth, 2008). Students on this course have access to a Ning social network site for interacting with their fellow students and the course instructor. Joining the site is a simple process of going to the generic Ning site and adding the instructor as a 'friend'. Students are then given access to the private course Ning site, where they can write and read blogs entries, upload photos and videos, take part in forum discussions and so on.

Twitter for Learning

To complete this section we will look at the use of the microblogging facility Twitter. This is a blend between a blogging tool and a social network site. It allows users to post short updates ('tweets'), which can then be read by other users who are 'following' that person. Each user's network can be extended by observing who is following whom, and adding new people to be followed. In general, there is no requirement to ask a user's permission to follow them, though users can set up their accounts to make this necessary if they wish.

Twitter has protocols that allow tweets to be directed to individual users (via the @ symbol), tagged (using the # symbol with a keyword) or re-distributed ('re-tweeted', labelled using the code 'RT'). Tweets can include links to other websites, so users can easily direct each other to resources, blog posts and so on. Users can also send private messages to each other. The combination of these facilities, which can be used equally well on mobile devices or desktop computers, makes Twitter a valuable facility for building communities.

There is an increasing amount of material appearing on the web, and in the academic literature, related to how Twitter can be used in a learning context (see, for example, Skiba, 2008; Educause, 2009). The case study below provides a good example with which to end this chapter.

CASE STUDY

USING TWITTER TO BUILD PEER COMMUNITIES

Jo Badge, Stuart Johnson, Alex Moseley and Alan Cann, University of Leicester, UK

In 2008 Leicester University carried out a study of the Twitter microblogging service (twitter.com) to investigate its potential in an academic context. The study participants were ten campus-based first year undergraduate students in the School of Biological Sciences at the University of Leicester, all 18 to 19 years old, and in their first semester of higher education. Five members of staff were involved in the project: one academic staff member, two e-learning technologists and one member of the central Student Support and Development Service.

Participating students were each provided with an iPod Touch mobile device, and required to post status messages ('tweets' in Twitter terminology) at least four times per day (for example, 'I am in the library writing an essay for module x'). To encourage recruitment, several students, selected at random, were allowed to keep their iPod Touches at the end of the project. Students were asked to label their tweets with a specific, unique hashtag (a community-driven convention for adding metadata to tweets), which they all did rigorously. This provided a powerful means of gathering a stream of information for later analysis, as the hashtags were easily tracked using the RSS syndication technology. The evidence collected online was supported with a short online survey that asked the participants about their previous experience of Twitter and their impressions of using it on this project.

Findings

All but one of the study participants had not used Twitter, or any similar microblogging service, previously. The participants had access to online training materials via a project wiki, but Twitter proved to be very intuitive, and little instruction was needed beyond the initial set up, which was done in a short face-to-face meeting. All the participants used multiple interfaces to access Twitter, including mobile devices.

In a relatively short time, these students formed quite sophisticated peer networks, following up to 60 Twitter accounts, with the ratio of following to followers at 1.5. Although many messages posted consisted of simple status updates carrying the designated hashtag, students were also highly conversational in their use of Twitter, with over a third of their messages being @ replies to other people. Messages were sent from across the University of Leicester campus, student halls, cafes, bars, on buses and any other locations where students were working or networking. Some typical examples of messages posted during the project were:

> Doing metabolism questions over msn, testing each other is a fab way to learn! If only I knew any answers.

> Has the words 'russian bride' written on his hand, and can't remember much of last night. . . . Now for chemistry revision.

> Is rather worried about the assessment tomorrow and is preparing herself for failure.

These first year undergraduate students were very open in their Twitter postings and a strong community soon grew between those using the devices. Nevertheless, the students were conscious that their messages were public, and they exercised restraint in their online behaviour, with no incidences of inappropriate content being posted during the project. Although students knew that their messages were being monitored by academic staff, in survey responses they said they did not regard this as an intrusion. Indeed they frequently used Twitter in preference to alternative channels, such as email, to contact tutors to ask questions or arrange meetings. Approximately half of the students continued to use Twitter after the end of the project.

Emergence of Peer Support

Peer support became a key feature of this student network, with activity rising just before assessment deadlines or during revision for exams. Content analysis of the messages shows clear evidence of personal learning networks emerging. Students used these networks when they were preparing assessed work or revising for tests, often in situations when they were physically isolated from their peers. They also frequently used the service to arrange social meetings in cafes, lunch between classes, or evening social events. There were no incidences of students using Twitter to collude on answers for assessments, in part because assessments had been designed to preclude the possibility of cheating by simple answer sharing.

In addition to directly academic-related content, students also posted a considerable amount of social chat:

> After eating almost my own body weight in Pistachio's life doesn't seem so bad anymore :)

> The Presentation Queen has churned out another awesome one.

> I have a conundrum are cornflakes better with milk or without?

> Wonder if Asda 30p Foamy Fruits sweets count as one of my five a day?

Far from being spurious, this type of message formed the social glue that facilitated and enhanced the emergence of peer-support networks.

Summary

The benefits of using Twitter for data collection have previously been described (Aspden & Thorpe 2009). The use of Twitter in this study enabled data about the student experience to be collected and analysed using a wide range of free, and increasingly sophisticated, online analysis tools.

From the student perspective, using Twitter helped to:

- develop peer support, with activity rising just prior to deadlines or during revision;

- develop personal learning networks, often used when students were isolated from their peers;
- arrange social and academic meetings.

The staff involved in the study were so impressed with the value of Twitter that they have continued to use it in their teaching. They also plan to promote its use across the university as a lightweight communication tool for a range of academic and social purposes.

Acknowledgements

This case study is adapted from an article 'Twittering the Student Experience' which appeared in *ALT-N*, vol. 17, October 2009.

The authors are grateful to JISC TechDis (www.techdis.ac.uk) for their support under the HEAT3 scheme.

Key Points for Practitioners

- Online contact is important to learners, helping to avoid isolation and increase motivation. For many learners, over time, this develops into a sense of community.
- Community can develop if the communication feels real to participants. This is described as experiencing social presence.
- Social presence and feelings of community can be enhanced by:
  - a face-to-face meeting early in the course;
  - attention to the tone and content of postings;
  - activities to help learners get to know each other;
  - use of member profiles and photos;
  - a mix of methods for communication.
- Social network sites have significant potential for learning communities. Students already use them for social purposes, encouraging regular participation.

Further Reading

Brown, R.E. (2001) 'The process of community building in distance learning classes', *Journal of Asynchronous Learning Networks* 5(2), available at http://www.sloan-c.org/publications/jaln/v5n2/v5n2_brown.asp.

Based on interviews with students, this paper provides a detailed exploration of how a sense of community can develop online. It identifies three stages in this process: making online contacts; taking part in discussions; and long-term camaraderie. The paper also points out that some learners do not experience community online.

Haythornthwaite, C., Kazmer, M.M., Robins, J. and Shoemaker, S. (2000) 'Community development among distance learners: temporal and technological dimensions', *Journal of Computer Mediated Communication*, 6(1).

This paper discusses the development of community in an online course. It considers how feelings of belonging are affected by the use of different communication channels (asynchronous and synchronous, public and private, online and face-to-face).

Gunawardena, C. and Zittle, F. (1997) 'Social presence as a predictor of satisfaction within a computer-mediated conferencing environment', *American Journal of Distance education*, 11(3), pp. 8–26.

This paper provides a foundation for discussions of social presence in online learning settings. It offers a clear definition of social presence, and uses empirical data to demonstrate the link between the degree of social presence and the degree of course satisfaction.

7

In Real Time

This chapter looks at the role of synchronous (real-time) communication in supporting online learning communities. It relates real-time communication to the concept of social presence, encountered in earlier chapters of this book. The chapter discusses different kinds of synchronous communication: real-time chat; instant messaging; audio- and videoconferencing; and virtual worlds. It considers the benefits of these technologies, and the issues that need to be considered when using real-time communication for learning and teaching.

In the earlier chapters of this book we have focused mainly on asynchronous communication, but synchronous (real-time) communication can have distinct benefits in educational contexts. Facilities such as instant messaging, videoconferencing and virtual worlds can add vitality to an online learning community, help students get to know each other better, and enable them to keep in closer contact. When using synchronous communication, 'a sense of social presence develops that often leads to a greater sense of community' (McInnerney & Roberts, 2004, p. 75).

The enhanced social presence arises because of the real-time nature of the interactions. Synchronous communication does not suffer from the delays and uncertainties of response that frustrate students when using asynchronous tools. This means that even a simple text-based communication facility, such as a chat tool, can offer a strong sense of connection and interaction.

More advanced real-time communication tools offer the further benefits of a mix of different media. For example, synchronous conferencing systems can provide voice communication and live video, as well as different kinds of shared workspaces. When using a videoconferencing system, students and teachers can hear each others' tone of voice, and see each other's expressions and body language. Developments in synchronous communication also include virtual worlds, where learners can communicate and work together in an online environment that is a representation of a physical space.

In this chapter I will consider the potential of synchronous communication tools for supporting learning, and discuss the issues that need to be borne in mind. I will begin by looking at synchronous chat and instant messaging, and then move on to consider the benefits and problems of audio- and videoconferencing. Finally I will discuss the possibilities of virtual worlds for learning and building community.

Synchronous Chat

In a synchronous chat system (often called a chat tool or chat room) participants are online at the same time. Chat discussions can be one-to-one, but in educational contexts they are often group discussions facilitated by the teacher. Users interact by typing messages, and these appear on-screen preceded by the writer's name (or the name they have chosen to use). The interactions are normally shown in a simple chronological list, which means that different participants' messages, and possibly different topics of conversation, may be interspersed. This can make chat interaction confusing, particularly if there are several participants. A certain degree of competence in typing is also needed in order to take part in the quick-fire of the interactions. In spite of these disadvantages, chat can be a lively and engaging medium, which is perhaps why some educators have been keen to explore its possibilities. The findings of a number of these explorative studies are discussed below.

A study by Honeycutt (2001) compared email and synchronous chat for peer-review tasks in courses on writing. When using synchronous chat, student reviewers showed greater personal involvement with the student writer. There was also more off-topic and social behaviour which, although enjoyable, was distracting to students. Students felt that email was more helpful for this task, because it allowed time for reflection and more detailed feedback.

In research by Kirkpatrick (2005) a session using a chat tool appeared initially to be anarchic, and dominated by social interactions. However, analysis of the chat transcript revealed that many of the interactions were discussion of the class content. Students felt that the experience was enjoyable, though not very useful for learning. Kirkpatrick's findings were partly supported in a study by Cox et al. (2004), who used chat in two courses. In one of the courses students used chat for several lab-based discussion sessions. The first session contained a significant proportion of social interactions, but as students gained experience the discussions became more focused. In the second course, the chat tool was used as part of a role-play exercise, and this was more successful. Students engaged with the task and found the chat tool empowering and motivating, though also frustrating at times.

Pilkington et al. (2000) investigated the use of chat in a course with full-time students and part-time distance learners. The researchers found that nearly half the chat interactions were content-related and of good quality. However, participation by the part-time students was low, largely because of the timing of the sessions. The discussions also tended to be dominated by the tutor and two or three students. A subsequent presentation of the course used a discussion forum as well as chat. Neither of these tools adequately fulfilled the distance learners' needs for a sense of presence, but students felt that chat was better for this purpose, because of the speed of response.

These studies suggest that chat tools can be useful for learning, provided they are integrated into the course activities. Otherwise there is a risk that discussions via chat will be unfocused, and dominated by social interactions. Chat can be an enjoyable way for students to interact, helping them to feel more in touch with each other, which is particularly important for those students who can rarely meet face-to-face. However, it relies on finding a suitable time when students can be online together.

Instant Messaging

Instant messaging (IM) is, like synchronous chat, a text-based tool for real-time communication. A key difference is that an IM tool lets users know who else is online (that is, who else is currently using the same IM service). Typically an IM system allows users to create lists of 'contacts' or 'buddies'. Then when one of these contacts comes online, the user is notified. IM systems may also indicate further status information for each contact, for example 'busy' or 'away'.

An early study on workplace use of IM (Nardi et al., 2000) suggested that it is used to 'maintain a sense of connection to others' (p. 79) and for quick questions and clarifications. However a disadvantage was that IM could be distracting. To overcome this, recipients of IM requests did not always respond straight away, and this was considered acceptable behaviour. Compared with communication via email, participants found that IM messages gave a greater sense of a shared context. Users found value in knowing who else was 'around', even if they had no need to make contact at that time. One user commented:

> You feel like you know where other people are, so you feel like you're not the only one working on a weekend. To me it's just fascinating to know that someone else is somewhere else doing something while you're doing something. You feel like you're in this world together, so you create a little universe.
>
> (Nardi et al., 2000, p. 85)

A study by Baron (2004) reported on the use of IM by college students. The research confirmed the findings of Nardi et al. (2000) that some users leave long intervals before responding. IM was effectively being used as an asynchronous technology by some of the students in Baron's research. This contrasts with the findings of a study by Matthews and Scrum (2003) that student IM users found it difficult to resist responding immediately to messages (which were typically of a social nature). This appeared to impair their concentration and academic work.

A more recent study (Quan-Haase & Collins, 2008) found that IM was important for helping students to feel in touch with each other when they were studying on their own – even if they did not actually communicate. However, the students found that IM could potentially disrupt their work, so they used a number of control strategies. Most of the students dealt with the problem through the IM status settings. If they were working, they would set their status to 'away', and ignore some messages and answer others.

Hrastinski (2006) investigated the effect of introducing an instant messaging system into a distance-learning course. The course already used asynchronous communication, but students found the time lags frustrating. Most of the IM communication was within small work-groups, and was focused on the work, rather than being used for social support. The lack of social interaction seemed to be partly because students on the course did not know each other well, and partly because there was not a critical mass of students online.

Use of IM in a distance-learning course was also investigated by Nicholson (2002). The course was mainly taught asynchronously using the *WebCT* virtual learning environment, but at the request of students, an IM service was provided. Just under half the students used the IM facility, mainly the younger ones. Some students were concerned that IM would be distracting or time-consuming, and some were ambivalent about contacting other students whom they did not know. The students who used IM reported feeling a stronger sense of community than those who did not. One student commented, 'Nothing else I used to communicate was as funny and friendly and warm as the conversations I had via IM' (p. 369).

Contreras-Castillo et al. (2004) reported that use of IM increased the level of interaction among students and helped reduce feelings of isolation. Awareness of others who were online, and notifications of arrivals, were particularly important for helping students feel part of a learning group.

Rutter (2009) found that students used IM both for social support and for mutual help. However, students found it distracting, and most students turned it off when they needed to concentrate. This study investigated the relationship between students' grades and their use of IM, and found that students who did not use IM scored the highest grades. However, students who used IM heavily also performed well, and gained higher scores than intermittent IM users. There are several possible explanations for these findings, but one interpretation is that IM is supportive of learning for expert users, who can manage the issue of distraction.

As the above discussion shows, findings on the potential of instant messaging for education seem to be mixed. Although there are problems related to distraction, there is evidence that IM can be beneficial for enhancing social presence. When using an IM system, students may feel reassured to know that their peers are online and that they can easily communicate with them in real-time for help or just for personal contact. As Nicholson suggests, instant messaging 'can serve to provide a stronger sense of community in the solitude of asynchronous online course work' (2002, p. 363).

Students' Views on Instant Messaging

In this section I will look at the findings of a study carried out at the UK Open University to investigate distance learners' use and perceptions of an instant messaging facility (Kear, 2007). Prior interviews with Open University students had indicated that they saw synchronous communication as potentially beneficial, and a number of students had positive experiences of using synchronous chat in courses they had studied. Some students also said that they would like a 'buddies' facility, so that they could easily see which members of their tutor group were online.

An instant messaging tool was therefore implemented as part of the online communication environment for a new, part-time course in technology. The instant messaging facility was incorporated within the online discussion environment for the course. The main window of the discussion environment indicated the number of users who were logged in. Clicking a link opened a small pop-up window that listed these users (see Figure 7.1). If any of the users were logged in but inactive (for example, they were away from their computer), the system detected this and displayed a cross against their name.

If a user wished to initiate an instant messaging session with one of the online users, they simply clicked on the speech bubble icon next to that person's name. This alerted the recipient, and offered three possible response options:

- accept the instant message request;
- decline that particular instant message request;
- decline all instant message requests during this online session.

Figure 7.1 List of users logged in (with a cross if logged in but inactive).

Source: Reproduced with permission from The Open University.

These options allowed users some control over possible interruptions.

The new IM facility was evaluated with students via two surveys – one part way through the course and one at the end of the course. Students were also invited to provide feedback via the course forums. The findings from the surveys and forum contributions are discussed below.

Although most of the students had prior experience of synchronous communication, the course IM facility was not used by many students. A survey about half way through the 12-week course found that only a quarter of the students had used the facility. When asked why they had not used it, some students said that they did not feel the need for this form of communication. Others commented that there were typically only one or two other students logged in at any given time. For some students, instant messaging was seen as a potential distraction or interruption in a busy study schedule, and some were stridently against it.

Several students commented that they did not know each other well enough to make contact via instant messaging. Those who did try to make contact felt even more uncomfortable and embarrassed if they received no response. This raises the issue discussed earlier of whether instant messaging is perceived as a purely synchronous communication tool. If it is, then the sender will expect an immediate response and the recipient will feel obliged to provide one. One student suggested that an option to set your status to 'busy' would help alleviate this problem. As in other types of online communication, it is important that students have shared norms for communication via IM (Quan-Haase et al., 2008) and that the tools support these.

As time went on, some students began to benefit from the instant messaging facility, finding that it gave a more personal experience, and complemented the discussion forum. Students used the facility to make contact with the course facilitator, with students whose forum messages they had read, or with others who happened to be online at the time. They used IM primarily to discuss the course content, rather than for social purposes. When asked whether scheduled chat sessions with the course facilitator would be of value, a large majority of respondents said that they would.

Students found it reassuring that they could see who else was online, even if they had no desire to contact them. In a feedback message via the course forum, one student used the metaphor of looking around a university library and seeing that others were studying at the same time. This seemed to strike a chord with other students. As noted earlier in this chapter, awareness of the other students who are logged in can generate a feeling of solidarity which students find helpful, even when they have no need for actual communication (Contreras-Castillo et al., 2004). Judging from the students' use of the library metaphor, a feeling of co-presence was created. So the concept of 'social presence' seems to apply here in the sense of making learners feel closer together.

This section has discussed the potential of instant messaging for informal peer support among students. The following case study considers its use in a more formal context, for online tutorials led by a teacher.

CASE STUDY

REAL-TIME COMMUNICATION IN A MATHEMATICS ONLINE LEARNING COMMUNITY

Birgit Loch, Swinburne University of Technology, Australia and Christine McDonald, University of Southern Queensland, Australia

Mathematics is recognized as posing a particular challenge for synchronous online communication (Smith & Ferguson, 2004). All parties need to be able to contribute mathematical symbols and visualisations to the discussion. Although instructors are often trained in mathematical typesetting software such as LaTeX or Microsoft's Equation Editor, typing mathematics in real time can take considerably longer than writing out a mathematical expression on paper. In addition, students, particularly those with weak mathematical skills, are often unwilling to learn how to use these tools. Students who are already struggling with the mathematical content may despair if they also have to deal with typesetting issues. This leads to a slow, one-way transfer of visual information from the instructor to the students, making it difficult for the instructor to tell whether a student can really produce the solution to a mathematical problem.

Instant Messaging (IM) Chats with Handwriting

This dilemma prompted the use of MSN Messenger, now Windows Live Messenger, with a handwriting component, in order to post inked contributions as well as typed messages. MSN Messenger was used in the context of two first-year mathematical sciences courses at the University of Southern Queensland, in course presentations offered via distance learning during the Australian summer semester.

In order to create a community of learners, it was decided to offer weekly online tutorials through MSN Messenger. All students who were enrolled in the two courses were invited to participate. The tutorials fostered discussion of the previous week's material and encouraged students to ask any questions they might have. Tutorials generally started and concluded with a few minutes of social chat, and at the end of a session students often arranged to meet online at times other than the designated tutorial.

During the sessions, the inked messages were mainly posted by the instructor, using a tablet PC or graphics tablet. However students used their mouse to make contributions when prompted, or to show that they had understood a concept, and present their solution. Student contribution was actively encouraged, with the instructor acting as facilitator rather than dominating the tutorial.

Findings on the Use of IM with Handwriting

Initial results from analysis of chat logs (McDonald & Loch, 2008) suggest that the online interactions are in line with the Community of Inquiry model (Garrison et al., 2000). Evidence was found for social presence, cognitive presence and teaching presence, as specified by Garrison et al., even though their model was proposed for asynchronous, rather than synchronous, contexts.

Instructors and students responded positively to the tutorials. The instructors were able to monitor how students were progressing in the course, and could provide timely support where needed. The students said that they were no longer feeling isolated and that they appreciated the opportunity to participate in the tutorials. Students commented that the synchronous sessions would not have been as effective without the presence of the instructor. The tutorials provided the opportunity for students to ask questions about the course material, and work through solutions together, with guidance from the instructor. The instructor could help immediately if students were going in the wrong direction, or were simply stuck (Loch & McDonald, 2007).

Some of the students on the course would have liked to join the tutorials but could not fit them into their calendars. This is an issue for all types of real-time online communication. Distance students often enrol because they are working full time, and need the flexibility to study at any time suitable to them.

Skype and IM Chats with Handwriting

To improve efficiency of the online tutorials, and because some explanations are more easily given orally, it was felt that an audio component was needed. Windows Live Messenger supports audio and video chats, but these are currently limited to two participants. Therefore a combination of Skype and Windows Live Messenger was trialled the following summer. In this case, the IM component provided the visual support for the oral explanations via Skype.

An interesting observation was that, even with the audio component, participants had to wait just as long to see the mathematical visualization of a concept that was being described. This is because an IM message is not seen by recipients until it is 'sent' by its author. This delay became very distracting and resulted in incomplete IM messages being posted continually while the handwriting happened.

Comparing IM with and without Audio

The dynamics of IM with and without an audio component are entirely different. With an audio component, typed comments may not be used very often, because information can be conveyed more quickly via audio. Typed messages would distract from listening/speaking, so the IM postings are mainly for visual aspects. Using audio allows the discussions to proceed at a much faster pace, with little time for reflection.

Conversely during a text/ink-only IM session, it is possible to complete other tasks on the side, like writing an email, or even leaving the room for a short while. Participants will probably not even notice, and will assume that others are focusing on the discussion without actively typing or writing a response. IM chats are slower than audio conversations because of these delays, and sometimes require patience from instructors and students.

During audio-supported chats, when the instructor asks a question and there is no immediate answer from students, an awkward silence can occur. An inexperienced instructor may try to cover this by providing the answer. This delay is similar to the delay described for typed/inked chat, but the audio component appears to produce a need for an immediate response.

Future Plans

Both Skype and Windows Live Messenger are free tools and are accessible to most students and staff. However, this combination was not considered successful for online mathematics learning, and is therefore no longer used.

The next step in exploring combined audio and visual communication is a move to a web conferencing tool such as Elluminate Live (Loch and Reushle, 2008). This will allow immediate access to the visual component through a shared whiteboard, which can be used in parallel and synchronously with the audio interactions.

Audio- and Videoconferencing

The increasing availability of broadband connections means that voice communication, video and other modes of multimedia interaction are now possible from the desktop. These technologies offer many possibilities for learning activities and social support among students. The benefits of communicating via voice rather than just text are clear (de Freitas & Neumann, 2009) and the addition of video allows body language and facial expression to be conveyed. Videoconferencing is considered a 'rich' communication medium (Daft & Lengel, 1986) because it can convey these more subtle aspects of communication. It therefore has potential for significantly increasing social presence.

In addition to audio and video, synchronous conferencing environments include a range of other facilities for interaction among participants, such as shared whiteboards and chat tools (see Figure 7.2). This combination of communication facilities makes them well suited to subjects like mathematics and design, where visual interactions and explanations are needed. Synchronous

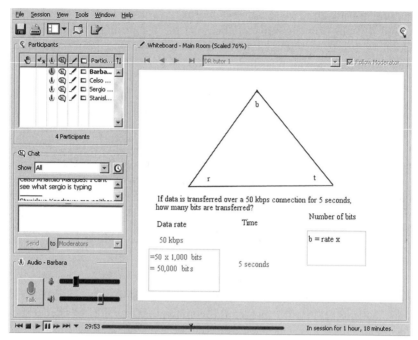

Figure 7.2 The Elluminate synchronous conferencing environment.

Source: Reproduced with permission from The Open University.

conferencing is also valuable for supporting language learning, and there is a growing research literature in this area (Lamy & Hampel, 2007).

The real-time nature of audio- and videoconferencing systems can increase social presence for learners. However, a disadvantage is that it can be difficult to arrange a time when the teacher and all the students are available. If some students cannot attend a session, one solution is to record the session, using facilities provided within the system, and to make the recording available for future viewing.

I will now look at audio-conferencing environments in a little more detail, before moving on to consider videoconferencing.

Audio-conferencing

Audio-conferencing has its origins in the telephone system, where several speakers can communicate with each other in a form of an audio meeting. This technology has been used in distance education for many years (Laurillard, 2002). The benefit of computer-based environments over telephone conferencing is that visual forms of interaction, for example via a shared whiteboard, are possible in parallel with the voice communication. This is why such systems are sometimes described as 'audiographics'.

A shared whiteboard is a particularly important visual tool in an audio-conferencing system (Wang & Chen, 2009). The whiteboard is an area of the computer screen where participants can create, edit and share diagrams, text, and so on. The whiteboard will have a number of tools for adding text and symbols, moving and changing items, pointing and highlighting. Teachers can load pre-prepared materials, or create them during the session, and students can interact with these materials. For example, a teacher might show a diagram explaining a mathematical concept or method, and then invite students to try an example by adding to the whiteboard. Alternatively, students might use the whiteboard to build up a mind-map of ideas related to a particular topic.

Audio-conferencing systems also include other facilities for creating a shared visual environment (see Macdonald, 2006, p. 84 for a summary). For example, in the Elluminate synchronous conferencing system (www.elluminate.com), it is possible for the teacher to take students on a 'web tour'. Here the shared area is used to display a sequence of websites that all the students can see at the same time. Elluminate also offers application sharing, which means that a software application can be run within the shared area. For example, a language teacher might open a wordprocessor file for collaborative writing, or an economics teacher might use a shared spreadsheet to explore numerical modelling techniques.

A particular issue that needs to be addressed is how to manage turn-taking when there are several people online together (Mason & Rennie, 2008, p. 128). When we are communicating in a face-to-face context, it is reasonably easy to manage a conversation with several people. We use subtle cues such as pauses, nods, facial expressions and tone of voice to help us to carry on a conversation fluently, without interrupting each other or leaving awkward gaps. In a larger meeting this is more difficult, and may need to be handled more formally. For example the chair of the meeting might invite people to speak in a particular order – or people might raise their hands to indicate that they have something to say.

When working in an audio-conferencing environment, turn-taking generally needs to be handled explicitly, particularly if there are more than two or three participants. Audio-conferencing environments have different ways of dealing with this (Hampel, 2003). For example, the Elluminate system mentioned above can operate in an 'open mic' mode, so that anyone can speak and be heard at any time. However, more commonly the system is set up so that only one or two people can have the microphone open. An explicit handover is therefore needed (by clicking on a button to claim, and subsequently to release, the microphone).

It might seem that the first of these two modes, 'open mic', would be preferable. However, when there are several participants it is difficult to avoid interrupting each other, partly because the visual cues mentioned above are missing. There can also be technical problems such as time lags, background noise and echo, which make communication in this mode difficult. As technical aspects are improved and experience with these systems increases, this open form of communication may become easier, particularly if video is used to supplement the audio communication, so that body language can be conveyed.

Audio-conferencing systems often include a text chat tool, and this can be surprisingly useful, particularly as a 'back-channel' to the spoken communication. Wang & Chen describe how students used the text chat area to convey actions – 'For example, "papapa" was used to represent applause, e.g., to congratulate a student's performance – the longer the "papapa" ', the warmer the applause' (2009, p. 11).

Text chat allows participants to make contributions and give short responses without interrupting the person who is speaking, and without the need for a handover of the audio channel. Some systems also have response icons available for similar purposes. For example, there might be 'Yes' and 'No' response buttons for users to click on, when asked, to indicate agreement or understanding. A further benefit of the text chat and response tools is that if participants have technical problems with the audio, they can still communicate. Even if students do not have a microphone, they can still take part in a limited way, provided they have speakers or headphones.

I will end this section with some brief comments on the more technical aspects of audio-conferencing. Although the technology and connection speeds will continue to improve, at the time of writing there can still be problems with poor audio quality (noise, time lags, gaps in the audio). A broadband connection, though not essential, is advisable, particularly if video is to be used. Users need a microphone and speakers or headphones. In order to minimize problems from echo and background noise, it is best to use a headset (integrated headphones and microphone). Finally, if a teacher plans to do significant amounts of drawing on the whiteboard, a tablet PC or graphics pen is useful.

Videoconferencing

Synchronous conferencing environments are increasingly likely to offer video, in addition to audio and graphics. Depending on the system, the video may be seen as an additional facility, or it may be the main communication medium. Videoconferencing technologies have been used within organizations for a considerable time, and there has been much research on their value for communication.

One school of thought is that video images of participants do not add much value, and may even be detrimental (Rosell-Aguilar, 2005). From this perspective the video is seen as a distraction, which takes people's attention away from more important aspects of the communication (Maturazzo & Sellen, 2000). There is also the possibility that some students and teachers might feel uncomfortable being watched by others online. The counter argument is that good quality video can play a role in enhancing social presence, and therefore easing communication. This is because it offers visual cues such as facial expression and body language, which help to convey meaning and support affective aspects of the communication.

This raises the question of what is meant by 'good quality video'. There are several aspects here, and I will discuss them only briefly. One issue is the size of the video image of each participant. This needs to be large enough that the person can be recognized, and their expression and body language interpreted. A larger size image will also allow for a wider view of the participant, rather than just a close-up of their face. A related issue is the screen resolution of the image, which affects the clarity and detail available. Finally, the refresh rate of the video will influence how realistic the video image seems; a slow or jerky image will detract from feelings of presence and live communication. These characteristics (image size, resolution and refresh rate) are dependent on the data rate of the connection. If the available data rate is low, it may be necessary to turn off the video, in order to improve the quality of the audio (Wang & Chen, 2009).

The quality of the video also depends on the hardware, including the video camera. In the case of desktop videoconferencing, the camera will be a webcam – either a separate device or an integrated part of the user's computer. The quality and cost of webcams is variable, but low-cost models are easily obtainable. When first setting up a webcam it is worth experimenting with the position, angle and zoom level in order to get a satisfactory image, and avoid glare from windows or lights.

Teaching via Synchronous Conferencing

Having covered the basics of audio- and videoconferencing technologies, I will now discuss what it is like to teach using these systems. The first point is that even desktop conferencing systems are complex applications. At first they may seem daunting to students, who will therefore need support and guidance. The teacher needs to take on the role of the moderator, which means that there are even more facilities to manage and control. Training and practice are important when first using synchronous conferencing systems. The teacher needs to feel confident in using the system facilities, coping with any technical problems and also managing the social and learning aspects of the session. These responsibilities all need to be carried out 'live', dealing with any unexpected events as they occur. One teacher described this as:

> like trying to read a newspaper, hold a conversation and watch TV at the same time.

When using synchronous conferencing with learners, the teacher has similar responsibilities to a host (Finkelstein, 2006). They need to be online early in order to welcome learners, check that they are comfortable, and make sure they can use the equipment and the system facilities. Then, as the session proceeds, the teacher will need to encourage interaction from students. It is important to keep students engaged, and provide opportunities for them to contribute. When using synchronous conferencing tools, there is a danger that sessions will be too teacher-centred (Laurillard, 2002, p. 155). For example, the whiteboard could just be used for showing slides, and the audio for 'lecturing'. But synchronous conferencing can be used very effectively for more collaborative, student-centred learning. Systems typically provide 'breakout rooms' for small group work and once students gain confidence they can even run their own sessions, for self-help or informal, serendipitous communication.

In a synchronous conferencing environment there are many parallel channels of communication – audio, video, whiteboard, text chat – and the teacher must use, and keep a watch, on several at once. This is challenging, and can also be quite tiring, so it may be worth pairing up with another teacher to run joint sessions, if possible. Contexts where there are several different media of communication are described as multi-modal (Kress & Van Leeuwen, 2001). Hampel notes that these contexts allow for:

> greater choice as users can select modes to suit the task in hand as well as catering for different learning styles. However, a multimodal system also makes greater demands on the user because of its more dynamic and unstable nature.
>
> (Hampel, 2003, p. 25)

The use of multiple media within one environment can place a high 'cognitive load' on the learner, so this needs to be carefully managed. For example, using voice to explain a diagram is helpful to learners, because they can easily take in the spoken explanation while looking at the diagram. But using a textual explanation would be unhelpful, because learners would then need to divide their visual attention between the text and the diagram (Sweller & Chandler, 1994).

In synchronous conferencing, as in face-to-face teaching, planning and preparation are essential. Teachers need to create resources, and design learning activities for students to carry out. They also need to plan and schedule these activities so that they fit into the duration of the session. It typically takes longer to teach a topic online than it would face-to-face, because of the need to manage the various tools and keep checking that students are following. When using an audio-conferencing system, interpreting the feelings of the group is a particular challenge because of the lack of facial expressions and body language, and the lack of direct feedback. For this reason, it is helpful to pause from time to time to ask students whether they are still 'on board'. Students can respond quickly and easily using response icons or text chat.

The above discussion has focused on taught sessions using audio- or video-conferencing, but students can also use these systems without a teacher present. Synchronous conferencing can be used for informal, self-help meetings or to carry out collaborative activities that form part of a course. The case study 'Synchronous conferencing for language learning' discusses the latter scenario.

CASE STUDY

SYNCHRONOUS CONFERENCING FOR LANGUAGE LEARNING

Joseph Hopkins, Universitat Oberta de Catalunya, Spain

The Open University of Catalunya (UOC) offers distance-learning courses in a range of subjects, including English as a second language. To support the development of students' skills in speaking English, the university has begun to use synchronous conferencing. The software used is the *Flashmeeting* audio- and videoconferencing system, developed by the Knowledge Media Institute of the UK Open University (flashmeeting.open.ac.uk/about.html).

The Flashmeeting software includes voice communication, video, text chat, emoticons and other facilities for collaborative working. Turn-taking is managed via a button that all participants can access, and which allows an individual to 'broadcast' or 'stop broadcasting'. Participants can virtually 'raise their hands' if they wish to speak, and the software then gives each of them the floor in the order in which they raised their hands. When using video via webcams, the person speaking is shown in a fairly large video window with a reasonable refresh rate, while other participants are shown in smaller windows with low refresh rates (for example, once every 30 seconds).

Online Speaking Activities

At UOC, online speaking activities were developed for students to carry out in groups, using the Flashmeeting software. These activities were an assessed part of the course, so they were undertaken without the support of a tutor. The first trial of these activities involved 146 students (93 females and 53 males). The age range was typical of the Open University of Catalunya, with an average of 37 years old.

The students self-formed into 40 groups of approximately four students (using the university's virtual learning environment to arrange the groups). They were offered induction into the Flashmeeting software with a tutor, and 128 of the 146 students (87 per cent) attended one of these sessions. Students were then provided with optional speaking tasks, in order to prepare for the assessed activities, but only 8 of the 40 groups (20 per cent) opted to do these.

The activities were linked to the topics students were studying at that time. For example, in one activity students were asked to produce a list of items that would be important for survival on a remote island, in order of importance. Student groups were given a script to guide them through the activity, and were asked to appoint a moderator (to facilitate the online session) and a spokesperson (to be responsible for providing an account of the session afterwards). The sessions were all recorded using a facility in Flashmeeting. Course tutors reviewed the recordings afterwards, and gave marks and feedback to students.

Evaluating the Online Activities

The online speaking activities, and the software, were evaluated afterwards to investigate how well they supported students' learning. The evaluation aimed to answer the following questions:

- What were students' perceptions? Were they satisfied with the experience? Was it useful?
- Was there evidence of learning taking place? Could this be deduced from the recordings of the sessions?

The following sources of data were used to address these questions:

- an online survey of students;
- interviews with students and tutors;
- quantitative data provided by the Flashmeeting software;
- recordings of the Flashmeeting sessions.

The recordings were analysed by a group of four observers who were experienced in foreign language teaching and in linguistics. The observers looked for interactions that were conducive to language learning, and coded them into predetermined categories. Each group's recording was coded independently by two observers, and this coding stage was followed by a discussion and negotiation stage. After three such rounds, the coding agreement between the two observers was approximately 85 per cent.

Table 7.1 shows a selection of the coding categories, together with illustrative examples from the students' online sessions.

Table 7.1 Categorising Examples of Students' Learning Interactions

Category	Example
Comprehension checks	*Do you understand me?*
Explicit statements of non-understanding	*Could you repeat please?*
Requests for assistance	Student A: *How do you say the thing you use to cut trees?*
	Student B: *An axe?*
Clarification requests	Student A: *I think that we should meet again in a fortnight.*
	Student B: *What means 'fortnight'?*

Results of the Evaluation

The survey of students revealed that 93 per cent of the respondents found the sessions useful, and 76 per cent had learned new aspects of English from the sessions. Figure 7.3 shows an example of the interactions from one student group, who were discussing items for survival on a remote island. The figure illustrates students sharing ideas via audio, raising hands to take turns, using text chat for help with words, and using emoticons to convey feelings.

Analysis of data from the interviews and Flashmeeting sessions is ongoing, but some initial findings are summarized below.

Students benefited from the opportunity to practise speaking and listening with others. There were a number of examples of negotiation of meaning, although this did not happen often. Students used text chat to a limited extent for confirmation of spelling, and so on. When students had difficulty understanding each other, it was often because of problems with audio quality.

There were particular issues related to the software's arrangements for turn-taking, where one speaker at a time has control over audio transmission. This meant that other participants could not easily intervene to give help, or to briefly comment. Students could not speak until the current speaker had finished and their turn in the sequence of raised hands arrived. This had several unfortunate consequences, for example questions or requests being ignored, or discussions getting 'out of synch'. These phenomena are similar to those

Audio		Hand raising	Text chat / emoticons	
Maria:	I'm thinking in seed... well I dunno if I'm pronouncing it well... but it's umm... s-... well I'm going to write it, OK, because I don't know if I'm pronouncing this fine... seeds... because you can... you can make grow plants and vegetables so you can eat something.		Maria:	seed
Pepa:	I think that's a great idea. I hadn't thought of that. I was thinking about an axe.... a handaxe... so you can make a... you can cut down trees and build a shelter... a good shelter.	← ANNA RAISES HAND		
Anna:	Yes... an axe to cut down trees. Are you thinking about that?			
Pepa:	Yes, yes... to cut trees and... wood...			
Anna:	Yes.. I had this one in my head because it's very difficult to cut a tree and I think we would need it to... to make shelters or beds or trying to do a... (laughs)... a tree house. I think it would be necessary.	← MARIA RAISES HAND		
Maria:	For me that's fine. I understand the general sense of the word but I don't know which word you are talking about, so you can write it down because I think that it's... OK... that's fine. Thank you very much.		Pepa: Anna: Maria:	axe axe 😊

Figure 7.3 Example of student interactions via Flashmeeting.

Source: Reproduced with permission.

that can occur with text chat, and also in discussion forums. They arise because the turn-taking conventions are unlike those in face-to-face speech. This is an example of how the design features of the software had effects on the interactions between students.

Future Work

The study reported here forms part of an ongoing research project into the use of synchronous conferencing for language learning. Future work will investigate other aspects of online language learning through synchronous audio and video. For example:

- Are there changes over time, as students gain experience?
- Is the video interaction important to students?
- What is the influence of the task students are asked to carry out?

Virtual Worlds

So far in this chapter we have moved from considering text-based communication to looking at audio and video. Now we will take a brief step back to follow a separate path, from text-based multi-user environments to graphical virtual worlds. The original virtual worlds, called MUDs (multi-user dungeons), created a descriptive 'world' in which players could interact and communicate, entirely via text (Curtis, 1997). Later developments added elementary graphics, to create a visual representation of a world. Drawing on research in virtual reality, current virtual worlds aim to create a three-dimensional environment that users can inhabit together.

There are many different kinds of virtual worlds (also called multi-user virtual environments), serving a range of purposes. These include simulation, business communication, training, commerce, social interaction and education (de Freitas, 2008). Virtual worlds vary in the type of online spaces they provide, the degree to which these spaces can be built and changed, and the facilities available to users (Virtual Worlds Review, n.d.). Key features of virtual worlds are (Dickey, 2005):

- a visual representation of a physical space which users can explore;
- a visual representation of each user, which is under the user's control;
- a way for users to communicate with each other.

The space represented in a virtual world can be as simple as a bare desert island or as complex as a virtual city. When virtual worlds were first used in education, there was a tendency to reproduce a university campus or lecture room. Although this approach has the benefit of creating a familiar context for learners, it does not make best use of the facilities virtual worlds can provide. Instead of staying with real-world metaphors, there are opportunities to create environments that are more stimulating and more conducive to collaboration. Many educators who use virtual worlds are now adopting this approach.

In particular, virtual worlds offer possibilities for simulations and role-play, allowing learners to experience contexts which they could not access, or which do not exist, in real life. For example, Edirisingha et al. (2009) report how simulations of traditional dwellings were used with students of archaeology. Another example was given as a case study in Chapter 1 of this book, where students took part in a role-play simulation of a border crossing. Setting up and developing learning spaces within virtual worlds can be a time-consuming, and hence costly, activity. It is therefore important to be clear about the purpose for the learning space, so that this effort is used to good effect.

As well as visually representing a space, virtual worlds have visual representations of their users. These are described as 'avatars'. Users normally have some control over the appearance of their avatar, and some users pay considerable attention to this. The choice of avatar name is a further important aspect. Nicosia, discussing her experiences with students in the Second Life virtual world, commented:

> Over time, students develop an attachment to their avatars and invest much of their real-life personalities into the graphical representations they have created for themselves.

> (Nicosia, 2009, p. 629)

Some users prefer their avatar's appearance to be quite unlike their own (possibly even non-human). A young learner in Second Life explained his views on this issue:

> My avatar looks completely different to me in real life, and I enjoy that. The ability to change my persona every day if I wanted, is really good, you can reflect your mood like sometimes I might change my hair colour for different reasons.

> (Twining, 2009, p. 511)

There is much debate over the extent to which users identify with their avatars. When users experience this identification, and when they feel that they are really *in* the virtual world, this is described as 'immersion' (Bartle, 2003; Castronova, 2005). There are clear connections with the concept of social presence, where users experience themselves and others as 'really there' together in a shared online environment. This sense of presence, and the visibility of other learners, can help to build feelings of community (Mason & Rennie, 2008, p. 88).

Virtual worlds offer possibilities for collaborative learning (Dickey, 2005; Jarmon et al., 2009). But this is dependent on communication between learners – or between their avatars. Until recently, the forms of communication available have been restricted to implementations of synchronous chat (looking back to the roots of virtual worlds as MUDs). For example, in Second Life users engage in text-based chat with others who are nearby, or they may choose to send an instant message to someone who is elsewhere in Second Life. However, text chat is a rather limited mode of communication, and may not be adequate for collaborative learning and socialization. A learner in the study by Edirisinga et al. commented, 'My thoughts are not short sentences. It is a chain of thoughts. . . . It is difficult to translate these long sentences into *Second Life* sentences' (2009, p. 472).

Some virtual worlds, including Second Life, now have facilities for voice communication. However, there is much debate about the use of voice in virtual worlds, and some users prefer the text-based mode of communication. This is partly because it maintains a degree of anonymity, allowing users to adopt their preferred identity within the virtual world. Use of text chat also enables participation by people who have difficulties with hearing or speech.

This brings us to the general issue of accessibility. Although progress is being made, virtual worlds such as Second Life are not yet accessible to a wide range of learners. Those with visual impairments will have particular problems because of the graphical nature of these environments, which means that technologies such as screen readers are not effective. There are also more general access issues in relation to the technology needed to run a virtual world application. Depending on the specific application, users may need to have powerful computers and graphics cards, as well as broadband connections. There are also issues of usability – virtual worlds are complex applications, and the user interfaces can be very challenging to begin with. It can take learners – and teachers – quite some time to become competent in moving around, communicating with others and so on, and some users find this frustrating (Berge, 2008).

Although current virtual worlds have a 'steep learning curve' (Nicosia, 2009, p. 634), they have considerable potential for experiential and authentic learning. An impressive example is given by Jarmon et al. (2009), who report how a group of graduate students worked together in Second Life to create a model of sustainable housing, based on actual architectural designs. The students interacted with architects, expert Second Life 'builders' and many other people outside their project team.

Another example of authentic learning is given by Twining (2009), who describes how young learners in Teen Second Life organized a virtual sailing regatta:

> a student would take on the role of race officer and would coordinate all aspects of the regatta, including: publicizing the events (which sometimes spanned 2 or 3 days); setting out the course with marker buoys;

posting a map of the course (with different courses for different events/ categories of boat); checking that the boats complied with the rules for each race; managing the races, including arbitrating over any disputes; recording the results

(Twining, 2009, p. 509)

The discussion in this section has shown the potential for learning in virtual worlds, and has also identified some of the issues that need to be considered. Some students love the freedom to engage in a highly visual, imaginative environment, meeting new people, exploring their surroundings and creating things together. Others may think that the environment is artificial and strange, and may feel uncomfortable trying to interact as an avatar. Educators therefore need to be aware of different students' reactions to these new environments. In the future, when learners have grown up with online environments such as Club Penguin and Habbo, and when virtual worlds have been developed further, they may play a key role in supporting online learning communities.

Key Points for Practitioners

- Real-time communication can enhance social presence and add enjoyable social elements to learning. Awareness of other learners provides a sense of togetherness and increased motivation.
- Real-time communication gives little time for reflection. When using instant messaging, learners also need to manage the risk of distraction from study activities.
- Audio- and videoconferencing add beneficial 'cues' to communication through tone of voice and body language. Tools such as shared whiteboards allow for a range of learning activities.
- Teaching via synchronous conferencing needs considerable preparation beforehand and management of the live session, to make sure each student can participate actively.
- Virtual worlds can add creativity and imagination to learning. They are of particular value for simulations and role-play. However, current virtual world software can be difficult to use.

Further Reading

Finkelstein, J. (2006) *Learning in real time: synchronous teaching and learning online*, San Francisco: Jossey Bass.

This book provides a practical and thoughtful guide to teaching via synchronous communication tools. It discusses a range of tools, and considers issues that the teacher needs to bear in mind.

de Freitas, S. and Neumann, T. (2009) 'Pedagogic strategies supporting the use of synchronous audio conferencing: a review of the literature', *British Journal of Educational Technology* 40(6), pp. 980–998.

This paper is a wide-ranging review of research and practice using audio-conferencing for learning. It also includes some discussion of the use of video.

Jarmon, L., Traphagan, T., Mayrath, M. and Trivedi, A. (2009) 'Virtual world teaching, experiential learning and assessment: an interdisciplinary communication course in Second Life', *Computers and Education* 53, pp. 169–182.

This paper discusses a group project carried out by students using the virtual world Second Life. It describes how the students' activities, and communication with others, went well beyond the bounds of the normal course context.

8
Assessment for Learning in Online Communities

This chapter discusses how assessment can be used to support online learning. The role of feedback is considered, whether provided by the teacher, by computer, or by learners themselves. The chapter considers how tools such as forums, wikis and e-portfolios can be used for assessment purposes. It also discusses the issues raised when assessing collaborative activities. In particular, the chapter considers how online group projects can be assessed fairly, taking into account the process of the collaboration as well as the product.

Well-designed assessment plays a key role in encouraging and supporting students' learning. It focuses attention on the important aspects of a course, provides opportunities for feedback and helps students to pace themselves and judge their progress. Assessment is not just a way of measuring what students can achieve. It also significantly influences what they do achieve (Hartley, 1998; Gibbs & Simpson, 2004–5).

In this chapter we will be looking at how to design assessments that support learning in online communities, and which give fair and valid measures of students' achievements, both as individuals and as a part of a group. In order to consider how to develop good assessment practices for online communities, we first need to consider some ideas about assessment in general. I will therefore begin by introducing a number of concepts that apply to any kind of assessment of learning. I will then move on to consider how these apply in an online context.

Assessment for Learning

Students want to do well in their assessments, and most students put considerable effort into them. Quite reasonably, students assume that the topics and skills that are assessed are those that are the most important in the course – 'From our students' point of view, assessment always defines the actual curriculum' (Ramsden, 1992, p. 187).

If the assessment aligns well with the intended learning outcomes of the course, then students will be directing their time and attention to the key aspects, and their learning will benefit as a result. This idea is encapsulated by the term 'constructive alignment' (Biggs & Tang, 2007). Constructive alignment means that the aims, learning activities and assessment of a course all work together to lead students in the right direction. If the aims, activities and assessment are not aligned, students will be confused as to how to progress in their studies. They may find that little of the material they have studied is assessed, or that the assessment activities do not relate to the stated learning outcomes of the course. This will be frustrating to students, and may affect their motivation and confidence in the course.

In order to achieve constructive alignment, it is best to start by thinking about what the course is setting out to do. Many different terms are used in education to represent the purpose of the course – for example, 'aims', 'objectives', 'learning outcomes', 'intended learning outcomes'. Regardless of the terminology used, it is important to be clear about what students will learn from the course. What will they be able to do better after they have studied it? What will they understand that they did not know or understand before? I will use the term 'intended learning outcomes' to encapsulate these ideas.

The intended learning outcomes, activities and assessment for a course are so interdependent that an iterative process is needed, in which each aspect is revisited in turn. Considering the assessment at an early stage helps to focus on whether the intended learning outcomes are appropriate, and how the learning resources and activities will help students to achieve them.

As an example, consider a course for which the main aim is to help students develop knowledge and skills related to team working. The intended learning outcomes for this course might include:

- students should have increased their awareness of the skills, attitudes and approaches needed for successful teamwork;
- students should have improved their skills in working with others to plan and carry out a team project.

The course would provide students with resources on effective team working, and would also provide opportunities for students to put these ideas into practice. The course assessment would encompass the ideas covered in the course material and the practical team working skills that students were developing.

Assessment is not just a way for the teacher to focus students' attention and to measure their progress. It is also a key process in learning. If assessment is to fulfil this purpose, it should include useful feedback to students. I will discuss the use of feedback in the next section.

Assessment and Feedback

Feedback on assessments can take many forms, from a single grade to an extensive commentary on students' work. Feedback that is little more than a grade will be of limited value. On the other hand, feedback that is too detailed can be overwhelming and difficult for students to absorb. Ideally, the feedback will focus on the most important areas of development for that particular student and will give a clear indication of what the student can do to improve their work in the future (Nicol & Macfarlane-Dick, 2006; Walker, 2009). This type of feedback is sometimes described as 'feedforward', because it looks forward in time instead of back.

The timing of feedback affects its usefulness to students (Gibbs & Simpson, 2004–5). If feedback is timely, students will be able to relate it more easily to the work that was assessed, which will still be fresh in their minds. Virtual learning environments typically have facilities for students to submit their work, and receive their marks and feedback online, minimizing delays. However, one problem when using online systems for submission and feedback is how to deal with non-text material. Subjects such as music and mathematics are dependent on diagrams, notation and other non-textual material, so the use of online assessment in these subjects is difficult. There can be problems for students in creating these types of non-text material in digital form, and for teachers in giving feedback digitally. Research is in progress to address these problems, for example via markup languages for mathematics and tablet PCs for diagrams and hand-written feedback.

For the teacher, delivering feedback online can be an efficient use of time, because some of the feedback can be provided in a generic form. For example, if there are aspects of an assessment that many students find difficult, the teacher can easily distribute relevant resources and comments to all students who need them. However, there are pitfalls when using templates, or copy-and-paste approaches for giving feedback. The result can be feedback that is too generic, and not focused on the particular needs of individual students. Also, if students receive very similar feedback, they might lose faith in the process. In such cases the teacher would do better to state explicitly that the feedback is generic.

Computer-assisted Assessment

In the previous section I focused on feedback provided by the teacher, but assessment and feedback can also be carried out automatically by computer. Systems for computer-assisted assessments (also described as online quizzes or e-assessments) have been available for a considerable time, and are typically included within virtual learning environments. Using these facilities, teachers can create online tests with different kinds of questions and feedback options (Heap et al., 2004).

However, creating good questions and feedback for e-assessments is not easy, and it can take considerable time (Schwartz, 2002). Finding stimulating ways to test students' understanding, rather than their factual knowledge, is difficult. It is important that questions and answer options are not ambiguous, and that the feedback provided makes sense to students.

The simplest e-assessments consist of a set of questions with multiple-choice answer options. More advanced systems offer question types where students might be asked to type an answer, drag items onto a diagram, put a list of items in order, and so on. Feedback can be as simple as telling the student whether their answer is right or wrong, or it can include hints, opportunities for further attempts, and guidance on which resources to consult. The software keeps a record of students' input, and a score for each question, so teachers can see how each student is progressing, and which aspects of the course they are finding easy or difficult. Recent advances in computer-assisted assessment allow short pieces of free text input from students to be marked automatically. Testing of these systems has demonstrated that they compare well with human markers (Jordan & Mitchell, 2009).

E-assessments, like other kinds of assessments, can be either summative or formative. In summative assessment, students' work is given a mark that contributes to their overall grade for the course. In formative assessment, students' work is marked and they are given feedback, but the assessment does not contribute to their grade. The process of completing a formative assessment and receiving feedback helps students' learning, and enables them to see how they are progressing. Many students appreciate the challenge and immediate feedback that formative e-assessments can offer, and are therefore willing to take the time to complete them (Ross et al., 2006; Nicol & Milligan, 2006).

An example of the use of computer-based assessment is Cisco's CCNA (Cisco Certified Network Associate) academy programme. This includes an extensive set of teaching and assessment materials on the topic of computer networking, which are delivered via a virtual learning environment. A feature of the academy VLE is a sequence of online multiple-choice exams for students to take as they progress through the course. In addition to determining grades, these exams are designed to support students' progress through the CCNA curriculum, and enable them to judge how well they are learning the material. The system provides each student with a summary of their progress towards the intended learning outcomes, and directs them to the relevant curriculum for each question where they gave a wrong answer. Class tutors can review the performance of all their students, making it easy for them to pick out areas where many students had difficulty. This information can be the basis for further tuition and discussion via the class email facility, an online forum or a face-to-face class.

Peer Assessment and Review

We have seen that assessment and feedback can be provided by the teacher or delivered automatically by computer. Learners can also provide feedback for each other, through peer assessment. Because the feedback comes from fellow students who are facing similar challenges, it can be particularly relevant. The process of peer assessing also helps students to review their own work in the future.

In relation to peer assessment, I first need to clarify some of the terminology used. Sometimes an activity described as peer assessment is more in the nature of peer review, where students give qualitative feedback on each other's work, rather than assigning marks. Even in cases where students are asked to provide marks, these may not contribute to the final grades students receive for their work, or they may be combined with marks provided by the teacher. Part of the reason for the variation in practice, and the resulting confusion of terminology, is that teachers and students can feel uncomfortable with the prospect of summative peer assessment. Formative peer review provides a useful alternative.

Peer review has many benefits, both for the students who are being reviewed and for those who are reviewing (Robinson, 1999). Learners rarely see work done by their peers, and doing so can be a valuable experience for them. It helps them to gain confidence that their own work is of a suitable standard, and it allows them to see that there are different, but equally valid, approaches to their own. The feedback received from fellow students is a useful addition to that provided by teachers.

Many educators have experimented with peer review in face-to-face contexts, but the practicalities of organizing and managing it can be difficult. The teacher needs to provide copies of submitted work to other students, perhaps anonymised, and keep track of who is providing feedback to whom. When learners are studying in online communities, dealing with these practicalities is considerably easier. There are a number of possible routes for students to make their work available to each other, and provide feedback. For example, it might be done via an online forum, blog or wiki. Alternatively an e-portfolio could be used (see below).

When peer review is used as part of a course, it is important to prepare students in advance, both for giving feedback and for receiving it. It is helpful to discuss, and even negotiate, the criteria that will be used, and to write these down so that all students are clear about them. Giving students some practice is also helpful, perhaps using an actual answer from an earlier course presentation, suitably anonymised. Students need to be advised on how to give feedback in a way that is supportive but also sufficiently critical.

When carrying out peer reviews, students can be over-generous to each other (Falchikov, 2002). This may be because they do not feel confident enough to judge others' work, or because they do not wish to give offence. For these reasons, there may also be a tendency to focus on relatively minor issues (such as spelling or wording) at the expense of higher level aspects of the work.

Self-assessment

Self-assessment encourages students to be reflective about their learning, and helps to develop their skills in judging, and therefore improving, their work. O'Reilly & Morgan describe self-assessment as 'a process of reflection that encourages learners along the path towards independent and autonomous learning' (1999, p. 152).

As in the case of peer assessment, students may be asked to review their own work, and perhaps decide on what mark they think it deserves, but this need not contribute to their final grade. The value for students of self-assessment is in the reflective process of considering their work and progress.

Self-assessment can be unnerving for learners who have had many years of education in which their work was judged by others. Some students, when asked to assess their own work, resist, saying that this is the teacher's job (Falchikov, 2002) and that they cannot make judgements about their own work. The underlying message is that, if they could see how to improve their work further, they would have done so before submitting it. To some extent, this is a sound argument. However, students can assess and improve their work, provided they allow themselves the space and time needed. Students typically do not do this; even if they have finished an assignment well before the deadline, they are unlikely to review it. This is quite understandable – we have all put off looking at a nearly completed piece of work, for fear that it will not be good enough, and will need significant re-working.

To address these issues it is helpful to provide a framework within which students can undertake self-assessment. The first aspect of this is to have clear criteria for students to use. Discussing and negotiating these criteria within the class is helpful, and gives students a sense of ownership and responsibility for the criteria. A further possibility is to establish a two-stage process for self-assessed assignments. In the first stage, students complete a draft, and then set this aside for several days. The second stage requires them to review this draft, using the agreed criteria. Based on this self-assessment, students can make changes and then submit an improved version. This will help them to see that putting their assignment answer aside, and revisiting it with fresh eyes, will help to improve it. A self-assessed assignment could ask students to submit: their draft work; their assessment of it; comments on how they have improved on the work; and their final version. In an assignment of this kind, students are assessed on how they reflect on their work, as well as being assessed on the work itself. I will discuss the process of reflection further in the next section, in the context of e-portfolios.

E-portfolios for Reflection and Feedback

An e-portfolio is a personal online repository where students can:

- gather examples and evidence of their work;
- reflect on this work and on their own progress;
- receive feedback on their work and on their reflections.

E-portfolios allow different types of evidence to be gathered and stored. This might include: textual documents; diagrams, photos or other images; links to web resources; audio and video files. Students can also create a reflective narrative to link these items of evidence together. The process of reviewing their work in order to select what to include in the e-portfolio can be of considerable value to students (Bowie et al., 2002). Access to an e-portfolio is usually restricted in various ways, but in the main the teacher has access to at least part of it. E-portfolios can also be opened to fellow learners, employers and so on, in order to seek feedback.

E-portfolios can be used for employability purposes. Students can build up evidence of specific skills they have developed, and present this skills audit to prospective employers. They can also use the e-portfolio to create and maintain a curriculum vitae. Via the e-portfolio they can even receive feedback from current or potential employers. E-portfolios can also be used by students to review their learning needs and plan their development activities – a process described as 'personal development planning'.

E-portfolios are often used for formative assessment, with teachers providing feedback at different stages. Using them for summative assessment is more of a challenge. Judgements need to be made about which aspects of the e-portfolio are to be assessed, and how marks will be assigned. There is also a risk that, if e-portfolios are to be assessed summatively, students will not use them in an authentic way for reflective learning. One approach is to require students to maintain and submit an e-portfolio in order to pass the course, but not to assign a grade (Cotterill et al., 2006). The requirement to submit the e-portfolio will encourage participation, and hopefully once students begin to use the e-portfolio, they will experience benefits and continue the practice.

This brings us to one of the main purposes of e-portfolios, which is to encourage and support the process of reflection. Reflection requires learners to take a step back and consider:

- how they are approaching their work;
- how effective their approaches are;
- whether they need to make any changes.

Reflection is a very challenging process for students (and indeed for anyone), so guidance and support is needed. It can be difficult for students to understand the process of reflection, or to see its value. Often, when students are asked to reflect on their learning, they produce a description of their activities, rather than an analysis of whether those activities were effective. Interacting with other students may be helpful in this respect. If students' e-portfolios are opened up to each other for feedback, the process of reflection can seem more natural and purposeful.

The following case study discusses a course in which students provided feedback for each other via e-portfolios. A specific issue was whether it is better for feedback to be provided anonymously, and how this might depend on the educational and cultural context.

CASE STUDY

PEER ASSESSMENT VIA E-PORTFOLIOS: THE ISSUE OF ANONYMITY

Youmei Wang, Wenzhou University, China

Wenzhou University in China has developed a web-based e-portfolio system for students to use as part of their courses (Wang, 2004). The system, called *WePS online*, offers each student an online learning space in which they can record:

- learning objectives;
- activities and outcomes;
- performance, progress and results;
- reflection about learning processes.

Using WePS, students can collect learning artifacts that they have created, assess their own work and that of others, and reflect on their learning and development. With the teacher's permission, each student can access other students' e-portfolios.

Peer Assessment and Anonymity

E-portfolios provide opportunities for self-assessment and peer assessment (Barrett, 2004). These approaches, which are typically formative rather than summative, can be valuable for developing higher order thinking and improving motivation. They are particularly appropriate assessment models for adult learners.

However, one issue that has been debated is whether peer assessment should be anonymised. In an online context, it is reasonably straightforward to anonymise peer feedback and assessment, and this can have both advantages and disadvantages. Zhao (1998), investigating peer assessment via email, found that anonymity can encourage peer assessors to take a more critical approach, but it can also lower the quality of the feedback.

This finding was in a Western cultural context, but there may be differences in other educational cultures. In particular, attitudes to learning and conceptions of self and others may be different in Eastern cultures. The study described here was carried out at Wenzhou University to investigate the effects of anonymity in peer-assessment via the WePS e-portfolio system.

The Investigation

The study was carried out with students in the Department of Educational Technology at Wenzhou University, who used e-portfolio-based peer assessment in their courses. The course chosen for the investigation was about instructional design and project management. The investigation took place part way through the course, with 40 students. The students were not told the purposes of the investigation beforehand, but were given an assessment scale, and asked to complete their mid-term assessment activity as normal. This activity was to analyze and design case studies of constructivist learning.

After finishing the task, students posted their work to their e-portfolio, and carried out self-assessment and peer assessment, including both qualitative and quantitative elements. For these activities, the students were divided randomly into two groups of 20. One group submitted their work, and carried out the peer assessment, anonymously. The other group submitted their work and their peer assessments using their own names. Each student was required to assess at least one student from the anonymous group and one from the named group (see Table 8.1).

Students were then asked to complete a questionnaire about their views on the peer review activity. Of the 40 students, 38 handed in completed questionnaires, and the findings from these are discussed below. The investigation also took into account data from the e-portfolio self-assessments and peer assessments, and from the teachers' own assessments (i.e. the extent to which they agreed with the peer feedback).

Questionnaire Results

In the questionnaire, students were asked the extent to which they agreed with a number of statements related to carrying out the peer assessment. The response

Table 8.1 Process for the Investigation of Anonymity in Peer Assessment

Group	Selection	Requirements	Assessment
Anonymous group	20 students, chosen randomly in terms of seats in the class.	Submit work and assessment without real name; all information is anonymous.	Assess at least one anonymous and one named peer.
Named group	As above.	Submit work and assessment using real name.	As above.

Source: Adapted from Wang, 2008.

options were on a five-point scale, where 1 was 'strongly disagree' and 5 was 'strongly agree'. The questionnaire data was analysed to see whether the responses of students who carried out the peer assessment anonymously were different from those who carried out the assessment using their own names.

The results (shown in Table 8.2) demonstrate that there were relatively small differences between the two groups. Students in the named group were slightly more likely to consider how their peer would respond to their assessment; but this difference was not statistically significant (see Wang, 2008 for details of the statistical analysis). Both groups claimed equally that they paid more attention to the material they were assessing than to who had written the material. The named group had more confidence that their assessment would help their peer's learning, and this difference was found to be statistically significant. Finally, the named group made a stronger claim that they carried out the peer assessment seriously, but this difference was not statistically significant.

Conclusion

The findings of this study suggest that, in the context of this Chinese university, anonymity in peer assessment has no advantage over named peer assessment, and may be detrimental. It was found that students reviewing anonymously were slightly less confident that their feedback would support their peer's learning.

These results are in contrast to those of an earlier study (Zhao, 1998), which was carried out in a Western context. In Zhao's study, anonymity was found to be beneficial in focusing students' attention on the content that was to be assessed, and encouraging them to take a more critical approach.

Table 8.2 Comparison of Average Responses from the Anonymous Group and the Named Group (where 1 = strongly disagree; 5 = strongly agree)

Statement	Average response score for anonymous group	Average response score for named group
'I have thought of how the author will respond to my assessment when I assess others' e-portfolios'	3.42	3.47
'When assessing others I pay more attention to the quality of the peer's task and content, rather than [to the] author themselves or other aspects'	4.16	4.16
'My assessment can promote the peer's learning'	3.26	3.84
'I fulfil the responsibility of peer assessment seriously'	3.89	3.95

The contrasting results from these two studies could be accounted for by differences in attitudes and approaches of Eastern and Western students. However, there are also other differences in the two contexts, which need to be taken into account (for example, using e-portfolios rather than email for the peer assessment).

The study reported here has contributed to debates on e-portfolios and peer assessment, and in particular has considered whether the effect of anonymity in peer assessment may be dependent on culture. Further research is needed, in different cultures and contexts, to investigate whether anonymity in peer assessment is helpful or unhelpful to learners.

Collaboration and Participation

So far I have largely focused on assessment of students' individual work. I will now move on to consider the assessment of work that students carry out collaboratively. Assessment is one way of addressing the problem of low participation in online group activities. Linking collaborative activities to the course assessment encourages students to take an active part.

The most familiar example of online collaboration is where a group of students discuss an issue or topic in a forum. The discussion might be based on resources provided by the teacher, or resources that students find themselves. Students are asked to make contributions to the forum during a set period of time, in order to develop their shared understanding of the issues and resources under discussion.

Figure 8.1 gives an example of a collaborative activity of this type, from a distance learning course at the UK Open University. This activity was near the beginning of the Level 1 course *Networked Living*, mentioned in Chapter 6.

Activity 8 (exploratory)

Your task is to discuss the following question in your tutor group:

What is the most important ICT invention of all time?

- Start by posting a message to your tutor-group forum with your own suggestion, and your reasons for choosing it. If your choice of ICT invention has already been suggested by another student, post a reply to their message (using the FirstClass Reply option) explaining why you would also choose that invention.

- Then comment on at least one of your fellow student's suggestions, by posting a reply to their message in the forum (use the Reply option). Say whether or not you agree that the invention is important, giving your reasons.

As you are writing your messages, bear in mind the netiquette guidelines that you have just been reading about

Figure 8.1 An online discussion activity.

Source: Reproduced with permission from The Open University.

The main purpose of the activity was to help students get used to discussing ideas from the course in an online forum (using the *FirstClass* system) and to put into practice 'netiquette' guidelines (see Chapter 6).

There are benefits and problems in assessing online work of this kind. Assessment encourages students to participate, but can result in rather stilted discussions, where students are writing for the assessment rather than for each other. There is a danger that students' postings will be more a performance than a genuine contribution to the debate (Henri, 1995).

In order to minimize such problems, careful consideration needs to be given to how an online discussion should be assessed. Should this be on the basis of:

- how many contributions students make?
- the quality of their contributions?
- how their contributions relate to those of others?

These are questions that online educators have struggled with, and which I will discuss further below.

If a collaborative activity is to be useful and interesting, there needs to be active participation for the duration of the activity. In order to achieve this level of participation, some teachers require students to post a specific number of contributions (Fox, 2001). However, as mentioned above, this can act against the authenticity of the activity.

The value of a discussion also depends on the quality of students' contributions. Ideally students will think carefully about the issues under debate, and will read relevant learning resources. They will then be in a position to make contributions that are informed and well-argued. In order to encourage such contributions, some teachers allocate marks for the 'quality' of individual postings. However, care needs to be taken that teachers and students have a shared understanding of what is meant by 'good quality' in this context (Goodfellow, 2001; Sadler, 2002).

This brings us to the issue of how students' contributions relate to each other. A discussion is by its nature interactive. When the discussion is online, and carried out asynchronously over an extended period, it can lose the sense of dynamism and interaction. If students are posting carefully crafted contributions, they may be paying more attention to what they want to say themselves than to what others have already said. Tarbin and Trevitt reported this problem when using an email list for an assessed student discussion:

> while we had secured student participation, we felt that the quality of interaction between students had not been that high. For example, most students e-mailed their thoughts on a topic to the list without relating them to the ideas expressed by others, so that the 'debate' became little more than a series of utterances lacking explicit connection.
>
> (Tarbin & Trevitt, 2001, p. 68)

This problem is not unique to the online context, but it can be more apparent online. To help avoid this situation, some teachers allocate marks for the way students' postings build on those of others. This encourages students to take note of each other's perspectives, and to see how these relate to their own point of view.

As discussed above, assessment methods for online discussions should encourage students to submit messages that are thoughtful and which relate to the contributions of others. Figure 8.2 illustrates one approach. It shows a question in the first assignment for the course *Networked Living*, mentioned earlier. The question assessed students' reflections on their messages, rather than the actual message contents.

This activity and assessment was reasonably successful in engaging students. However, in relation to part (b) of the question, there were some occasions when students intentionally posted a less than perfect message, so that they could be sure of having something to say in the assignment about how the message could be improved.

The issues discussed above were considered in relation to discussions in an online forum. But similar issues apply in other collaborative learning contexts, for example making contributions to a wiki or sharing resources via a social bookmarking site. With all collaborative activities, low participation is a potential problem, and assessment can be used as a tool to address this. However, this use of assessment needs to be managed carefully. When a learning activity is part of the course assessment, there is an element of performance involved, and the activity can become less natural.

As a starting point for this question, look back over the netiquette principles outlined in Part 3, Study Session 4.

(a) Choose a message that you have sent to your T175 tutor-group forum that you feel was successful. Include the text of your chosen message by copying it from the forum and pasting it into your answer.

With reference to the netiquette principles, explain why you consider the message was successful. You should specifically refer to the netiquette principles that you have followed.

(10 marks)

(b) Choose a message that you sent to your T175 tutor-group forum that you feel could be improved. Include the text of your chosen message by copying it from the forum and pasting it into your answer.

Explain how you could apply one or more of the netiquette principles to improve your message.

(10 marks)

(c) Marks are awarded for including a copy of both your chosen messages.

(5 marks)

Figure 8.2 An assignment question linked to the activity in Figure 8.1.

Source: Reproduced with permission from The Open University

Online Group Projects

In the previous section we considered individual assessment of work carried out in a collaborative context. We will now move on to consider assessment of group or team work. Group projects play an important role in education and training, partly because team working skills are valued by employers, but mainly because a group can be an effective learning environment. Members of the group can learn from each other, as well as learning how to work with each other (Kaye, 1992).

When working as part of a group, students engage in a range of activities, including:

- exchanging ideas and resources;
- negotiating strategies and tasks;
- commenting on each other's work;
- creating shared documents and other group products.

Group work has long been a feature of face-to-face learning, and thanks to the availability of communication technologies, online group work is now a practical option. In the remainder of this section I will discuss what is involved in designing, running and assessing online group projects.

Setting the Scene for a Group Project

If students are to undertake a group project using online tools, it is important to set up the online groups early. This helps members to get to know each other, and enables the group to 'form' (Tuckman, 1965). It is also useful for the group to have an early face-to-face meeting, if possible (Thorpe, 1998). A further advantage of setting up the project groups early is that students can get used to the online environment in which they will be working. This might include a discussion forum, a chat tool, a wiki, or any combination of online tools that are suited to the project work.

One question to address at this stage is how large the groups should be. An appropriate size will depend on the task that is to be carried out, but in general each group should be small enough that students feel comfortable with each other, and large enough that it can still function if one of the members fails to participate. Between five and eight students per group seems to work well. A second question is how to form the groups. Should students choose the groups they wish to work in, or should the teacher decide? Again, this is a matter for judgement, but experience suggests that it is preferable, and easier, for the teacher to set up the groups. This reduces the possibility of some students feeling left out, and it also means that students develop skills in working with other people whom they may not already know.

The choice of task for an online group project will depend on the subject matter and aims of the course. It must be chosen carefully, and should catch students' imagination. It should provide scope for different kinds of interaction, but should not be too dependent on complex decision-making, which is difficult to carry out online (Kaye, 1992). A typical task for a group project might involve students creating some kind of group product. This could simply be a joint document, or it could be something more involved, such as an audio or video production.

It is a good idea to give the group a chance to try out collaborative work before starting on the main project. This helps the process of getting to know each other and developing a sense of belonging. An early, small, assessed collaborative task is a good approach, as it can:

- 'build' the group;
- give students confidence with the online environment;
- provide experience of what collaborative work involves;
- encourage group members to participate;
- give the group an early objective to achieve.

A number of online tools are useful for supporting group work. If students are working entirely online they will need an asynchronous discussion facility such as an online forum. A synchronous tool such as a chat room or video-conferencing environment is also beneficial, particularly for planning and decision-making.

If the task set for students is to develop a shared document, a wiki is a particularly useful tool, allowing any member of the group to add, edit or delete material (West & West, 2009). The wiki's 'history' facility alleviates the problem of version control, and allows changes to be reversed if necessary. In addition, participants can see the current state of the joint document at any time. This visibility and sense of creativity and progress can be highly motivating (Wheeler et al., 2008). However, students can feel uncomfortable with the openness of a wiki, where any of the material can be edited by any group member. Students may be reluctant to modify other members' contributions, and to have their own modified, particularly if the work is to be assessed. A student quoted in Hemmi et al. (2009, p. 28) commented, 'In thinking about editing the text produced by someone else – I felt a considerable reluctance. It somehow seemed unacceptable to mess around with someone's work.'

To alleviate this problem, it is helpful for students to discuss how they will approach their collaborative work in a wiki, and the protocols that they will adopt for editing. If the wiki has an embedded commenting facility, students can use this to provide feedback on each other's work, and to explain the reasons for any changes made (Trentin, 2009).

Carrying out a group project using online tools can be enjoyable for students, particularly if it involves some element of hands-on, creative work, but it is demanding. The complexity of the process can be reduced by breaking the task into smaller parts, some of which can be carried out individually by students, and then joined together. This type of group working is described as 'cooperative' rather than 'collaborative'. If an approach based largely on cooperative working is adopted, some aspects of the project can be designated as the responsibility of the group as a whole, to ensure that students experience the challenges of truly collaborative work.

Assessing an Online Group Project

With any assessed group project, deciding how to mark the work fairly is an issue (Miller et al., 1998). Should there be a single mark for the whole group? Should individuals be given separate marks, and if so, how should these marks be determined? Group members will have different levels of availability and commitment, and so will contribute differently to the work of the group. For these reasons an approach is needed which gives credit for the contribution of each individual student and also for the collaboration within the group as a whole (Bryan, 2006).

Dividing the task into a group component and an individual component can work well for online group work. In this approach, some of the available marks are allocated for a student's individual contribution, and the remaining marks are for the work of the group as a whole. Each student is potentially given a different mark for the individual component, but all students are awarded the same mark for the group component. Any student who makes only a trivial contribution to the group's work does not receive the group mark, and is awarded a low mark for the individual component.

When using this approach, the balance between the individual component and the group component needs careful thought. Students who are used to individually based assessment can have difficulty adjusting to the idea of relying on other students for a part of their grade. Students are very conscious of the issue of fairness, and they need to feel that their mark is not pulled down by poor work from others. Because of this, some students express a preference for a highly weighted individual component. However, this must be balanced against the need for the project to be a group effort, and to be perceived as such by students. Experience from online group projects at the UK Open University suggests that 20–30 per cent for the group component is viewed as fair by teachers and students (Kear & Heap, 1999; Kear, 2004).

For group work to be marked fairly, a method is needed for judging the quality of the group's collaborative process and of each individual student's contribution to this process. Online group work can have an advantage over face-to-face group work in this respect, as the teacher will have access to a record of students' online interactions. For example, when students are using a forum or wiki, the teacher can see how each student has contributed, and when. Other communication tools also have facilities that could be used by teachers to monitor and assess the process of a group's collaboration (see Table 8.3).

To enable the teacher to assess the process of the collaboration, students

Table 8.3 Possibilities for Assessing the Process of Online Collaboration

Communication tools	Record of collaborative process
Forums and blogs	Contributions and comments are stored for later viewing. Some forums also show who has read contributions, and when.
Wikis	Additions and edits are recorded in the wiki history, with a record of who did what, and when.
Social network sites	There is typically a record of 'events' such as posting messages, adding comments, and uploading files. There is often a facility for users to enter status updates.
Instant messaging and chat	A transcript can be kept of a chat/IM session. However, it may be necessary to switch on this option.
Audio- and videoconferencing	A recording can be made of a session. Again this option may need to be switched on.

need to use online tools to carry out, or at least to record, their joint activities. For example, students can be asked to develop their documents within a wiki, and undertake their project discussions in a forum, or use a chat tool and make a transcript available. If students meet face-to-face or have a telephone conference, they should write notes of these meetings and post them to a forum or wiki. Students need to understand that the teacher will be assessing their collaboration only through these records, and will be unable to take into account any activities that are not visible in this way.

Using this approach, the teacher can monitor and assess the process, both during the project period and when marking the students' final work. However, monitoring and assessing collaboration in this way is very time-consuming (Mason & Bacsich, 1998). When a teacher needs to do this for several project groups, the burden of time can be too great. For this reason it is worth considering other ways of assessing the group process. One possibility is to ask students to write a reflective account of the collaboration, either as a group or individually. Another possibility is to ask students to assess each other's contributions to the work. For example, a certain number of marks might be allocated for the group process, and students asked to divide the marks among themselves according to each member's contribution. Peer assessment approaches such as this are helpful in developing students' aware-ness of group processes, but they place a burden on students, which is some-times not well-received.

Perspectives on Group Projects

Many students find group projects stimulating and enjoyable. They learn from each other's experiences and viewpoints, and gain confidence from the feedback given by fellow students. However, there are also difficulties and frustrations when carrying out group work online. The main problem is in coping with the different levels of participation by group members (Thorpe, 1998). Learners have different priorities and commitments in relation to their studies and to other aspects of their lives. As a result some group members may contribute a great deal to the work, while others may do very little. If a group is to work well together, it is crucial that all members are active during the period of the project. But in an online learning context, it is easy to 'disappear' (Kear, 2010) or 'fade back' (Haythornthwaite et al., 2000).

A related problem is the variation in pacing of contributions (Mason & Bacsich, 1998). Some members make their contributions early or on time, while others contribute at the last minute, or even after deadlines have passed (Skinner, 2009). Flexibility in when to study is one of the major benefits of online learning, but some of this flexibility must be sacrificed when undertaking group work. Even though most of the communication may be carried out using asynchronous technologies, a degree of synchronization is still needed among group members.

Despite the challenging nature of group work, it can be successful, and students can learn a great deal as a result. At the UK Open University, the lessons learned over many years of running online group projects have been put to good use in a number of different courses. As a result, students have developed skills in teamwork and online communication, as well as learning from each other about the subjects they are studying. The following case study discusses an assessed group project in an Open University course. It considers a move from using forums for communication to using forums and wikis together.

CASE STUDY

USING FORUMS AND WIKIS FOR A GROUP PROJECT

Judith Williams and Helen Donelan, The Open University, UK

The UK Open University course *Information and communication technologies* was presented from 2002 to 2009, and attracted between 500 and 2,000 students per year. Learners studied the course part-time at a distance, over a period of nine months, supported by a local tutor. The course made considerable use of information and communication technologies to support students (Kear et al., 2004).

One of the modules in the course was based on the concept of the 'cyborg' – a merging of people and technology – and in this module, students worked remotely on a group project. In groups of up to eight, they collaborated to produce a set of linked web pages relating to the cyborg concept. This was a substantial project, running over a period of seven weeks.

Assessment

Each member of the group was responsible for contributing an article, in the form of a web page, on one of eight specified cyborg topics. The group was jointly responsible for writing an overview web page to introduce these articles. In addition, each member of the group was required to provide peer reviews on the draft articles of two other group members. Students used the peer reviews they received to help improve their own articles. Finally, the assessment asked students to give a reflective account of the collaborative process, making reference to group work theory introduced in the module. The work of the group was assessed on both product and process.

Eighty per cent of the project marks were for individual achievements, and 20 per cent for group achievements. This was designed to limit the effect of under-performing team members, while still offering appropriate reward for group collaboration. In judging each individual's contribution to the group collaboration, tutors looked for high quality contributions that were sustained throughout the period of the project. This was to encourage students not to leave all their efforts to the final week or two.

Collaborative Tools

In all but the two final years of the course, online collaboration was conducted via dedicated group forums, together with use of instant messaging. Students prepared their final web pages using an html template, which was provided as part of the module materials. One member of the group collated the group's html pages and submitted the linked pages for assessment. All students were required to submit a word-processed document to their tutor for marking. This included copies of: the group's overview page; the student's own topic page; and their reviews of other members' pages. Tutors also assessed each group member's contribution to the collaborative process, and the group's collaboration as a whole. The tutors made these judgements solely from what they read in the group's forum.

In the penultimate year of the course, tutors were given the option of providing their student groups with wikis. Almost two-thirds of the course tutors took up the opportunity, despite the small extra workload required. Each of these tutors' groups could choose whether to use the wiki or the html template for developing their web pages. The wikis were set up with template pages for the group's overview and for the individual topics. Students still had access to a group forum, where they were expected to conduct their discussions. Before the start of the group project, students had many opportunities to become familiar with forums, and most students could use forums effectively. But for many students, their first experience of a wiki was in a short familiarization activity prior to the main project period.

The Students' Wiki Experiences

Following the trial, feedback was obtained from a subset of students via an online survey. A total of 167 students were invited to complete the survey, and 74 (44 per cent) did so. The survey investigated what proportion of the respondents used the wiki, why they chose to use it, and what their experiences were. Despite being new to wikis, most of the students who were given the option chose to use the wiki. Many chose the wiki because they felt that it would make the collaborative process easier. The wiki provided each group with a central resource area where documents could be stored and developed, and all members could keep an eye on the progress of pages. As expected, most groups used the wiki for contributing material and the forum for discussion.

Overall, the feedback received was positive, with 93 per cent of students reporting that the wiki was easy, or fairly easy, to use, and 70 per cent saying that members contributed equally, or fairly equally, to group tasks. Groups developed strategies for working with the wiki. For example, some groups came to an agreement on how contributions should be managed, and some assigned a moderator or leader. These strategies tended to be negotiated in the forum. Ninety-seven per cent of students who used the wiki said that it was useful to have both the wiki and forum available for undertaking the collaborative work.

The Tutors' Wiki Experiences

Tutors were generally positive about the use of wikis, and identified several benefits arising from their use. Tutors commented that:

- wikis encouraged more students to have direct involvement;
- the group could see their collaborative document develop;
- students and tutors could easily identify who had done what, and when.

Tutors initially thought that they would be able to mark solely from the wiki, but this proved not to be the case. Most tutors found they needed to copy and paste text from the wiki into each student's assignment document, in order to provide coherent feedback. This added to the time needed to mark an assignment.

Another disadvantage was that the tutors had to consult two sources in order to assess students' contributions to the group process. Tutors needed to study the forum, where the discussion took place, and the wiki, where the group's documents were developed. Tutors said that this increased their work-load, but agreed that the wiki alone did not provide the collaborative tools necessary for students.

Tutors reported that students generally found the wiki easy to use, even if they had no previous experience. One said that his students 'took to it like ducks to water'. Problems reported tended to be limitations of the particular wiki tool, such as difficulties in inserting images and tables.

Conclusions

Following the success of the wiki trial, use of the wiki was made compulsory in the final year of the course. Very few problems arose from its use, other than specific software issues, as mentioned above. Tutors again expressed some concern about their increased workload and felt that copies of wiki documents should be included in the assignment sent to them for marking. However, overall, students and tutors remained enthusiastic about the use of the wiki for this collaborative activity.

Collusion and Plagiarism

Collaboration is a key feature of learning within an online community. However, when assessment is involved, a line needs to be drawn between collaboration and collusion. Similarly, there needs to be a clear line between appropriate use of third-party resources and plagiarism. The two main purposes of assessment are to provide a measure of a student's work, and to support their learning. Neither of these will be achieved if the work being submitted is not really the student's own. The assessment process will not be a valid one if students are copying from each other (collusion) or using third-party material without attributing it (plagiarism). These problems have always been a part of education, but they are becoming more prevalent as students work together online, and have access to resources on the web (Gibbs, 2006).

Detecting plagiarism or collusion is a first step towards helping students avoid it in the future. If plagiarism is suspected, copying a phrase into a search engine is an effective way of checking whether material has been copied from the web. Specialist software can also be used to compare a student's assignment with those of other students or with documents such as web pages. *CopyCatch* (cflsoftware.com) and *Turnitin* (turnitin.com) are two possibilities.

Educators have been discussing the problems of collusion and plagiarism for many years, but there are no easy solutions. Although some students know they are 'cheating', others do not fully understand what is acceptable and what is unacceptable in an educational context. They may be uncertain at what point collaborative working turns into collusion, and when the use of online resources becomes plagiarism (Morgan & O'Reilly, 1999).

These problems are not easy to solve, but teachers can take steps to reduce them by:

- Explaining and discussing the issues with students, and giving clear guidelines on when collaboration is encouraged and when it is not allowed;

- Helping students to understand how to use references, quotations and paraphrasing appropriately, and giving them plenty of examples and practice;
- Encouraging students to make notes when working with sources, and to write their assignment from the notes, not directly from the source;
- Giving students examples of work that demonstrates plagiarism, and work that avoids it;
- Designing assignments that cannot easily be plagiarized, by requiring something more than the reproduction of standard material.

Key Points for Practitioners

- Assessment supports students' learning, as well as measuring their progress. It focuses students' attention on the important aspects of a course.
- Assessment can be formative or summative. In either case, feedback plays a key role.
- Peer assessment and self-assessment are valuable for learning and reflection, but are challenging for students.
- Assessing online discussion encourages participation, but can make the discussion less authentic.
- To assess group work fairly there is a need to consider:
  - the process of the collaboration as well as the product;
  - group members' individuals contributions as well as the work of the group as a whole.
- Tools such as forums and wikis facilitate group work online. They make the process of collaboration visible, which can help in assessing the process.
- Collusion and plagiarism are potential problems in online work. Students should be taught how to avoid them, and assessments should be designed to minimize them as far as possible.

Further Reading

Bryan, C. and Clegg, K. (2006) *Innovative Assessment in Higher Education*, Abingdon: Routledge.

This edited collection contains a number of interesting chapters by experts in assessment for learning. Some of the chapters specifically focus on the role of technology in assessment.

Schwartz, P. and Webb, G. (2002) *Assessment: Case Studies, Experience and Practice from Higher Education*, London: Kogan Page.

This is another edited collection, this time of reflective case studies from experienced practitioners. Again there are many interesting chapters, including material on e-portfolios and peer assessment.

West, J.A. and West, M.L. (2009) *Using Wikis for Online Collaboration*, San Francisco: Jossey-Bass.

This book is a guide to using wikis for collaborative learning. It is valuable for its in-depth coverage of the educational use of wikis, and also for discussing the role wikis can play in assessment.

9
Supporting Online Learning Communities

This chapter brings the book to a close by focusing on the role of the teacher in supporting online learning communities. It discusses a number of aspects that teachers need to bear in mind when designing online settings and activities: the learners; the course topic; the tools; and the teachers themselves. The chapter considers what is involved in moving from face-to-face teaching to an online or blended learning context. It also presents the perspectives of teachers who have made this move.

In this final chapter I focus on the teacher's role in supporting online learning communities. This brings together many of the topics discussed in earlier chapters of the book. I will discuss issues that need to be considered when designing and facilitating online learning activities, and how online teaching relates to face-to-face teaching. To illustrate these ideas we will explore the views and experiences of teachers who have made the move from face-to-face teaching to supporting learners online.

The Changing Role of the Teacher

In recent years new approaches to teaching, based on constructivist theories of learning, have come to the fore. From this perspective, the teacher's role is to provide learning experiences that fulfil students' intellectual and social needs, and help develop a positive and open attitude to learning. The focus has moved towards support for learning, and away from delivery of content. This is consistent with ideas discussed in Chapter 2, *Theories of Learning in Online Communities*, such as scaffolding learners' development.

The availability of online communication has also contributed to this change in the teacher's role. Rather than being the single source of information, instruction and assessment, the teacher can now act as a guide to students in learning from online resources and from each other. The teacher can help students to:

- find, evaluate and use suitable learning resources;
- learn via discussion and collaborative work;
- take part in peer feedback and assessment.

Chapter 2 introduced the community of inquiry framework for online learning communities (Garrison & Anderson, 2003), which is based on three elements: social presence; cognitive presence and teaching presence. The present chapter is mainly concerned with teaching presence, which the community of inquiry framework further divides into design, facilitation and instruction. For much of this chapter I will look at the issues that need to be considered when designing settings and activities for online collaborative learning.

From the course-design point of view, imagine that a teacher has taught a particular course face-to-face and would now like to teach it online, or as a blend of online and face-to-face activities. How might they go about moving the course into the online domain, and planning collaborative activities for students? When considering this question, the following aspects, among others, need to be considered:

- the learners;
- the course topic;
- the available technologies;
- the teacher or teachers.

Each aspect here will influence how the online elements of a course are designed. In the sections that follow I will discuss each of the above aspects in turn.

The Learners

In my imaginary design scenario of transferring a face-to-face course to an online environment, there are several questions to consider relating to the learners. I suggest they are:

- What is the learner's context (for example, distance or college-based, part-time or full-time)?
- What is the learner's age and experience (of learning and of technology)?
- What is the learner's attitude to studying (for example, why are they studying the course and what is their approach to learning)?

I will use this set of questions as the framework for thinking further about the learners' needs in an online setting.

The Learner's Context

In considering the learner's context, we are concerned with such things as: whether the student is campus-based or studying at a distance; or whether full-time or part-time. Students who are full-time and campus-based should have little difficulty attending face-to-face classes, getting together with other students, and contacting their teachers. However, we are moving into an era when full-time, campus-based study may no longer be the norm. Some students may live at a considerable distance from their place of study, and find it difficult to travel. Many will have part-time jobs that they need to fit in with their studies. Others will be working full-time, and studying in the evenings and at weekends.

If students are mainly on campus, they will expect regular face-to-face classes. However, these classes do not need to be lectures; they can be more like workshops or seminars. If the teacher provides online access to learning resources, students can study and discuss these online, as preparation and follow-up to face-to-face sessions. This leaves time in face-to-face classes to discuss the issues raised by the course materials in more detail, and resolve any problems or misunderstandings.

For students studying mainly at a distance, online communication can be a vital support mechanism. It allows students to gain help, check their understanding and feel more in touch with each other. Distance learners typically have limited time available for study, and are subject to pressures associated with their jobs, as well as the day-to-day pressures of family life. For these reasons flexibility of time can be as important to distance learners as flexibility of location.

Asynchronous technologies such as forums, blogs and wikis are particularly helpful for distance learners because they can be used anywhere and at any time. However, even when using asynchronous communication, there is a risk of designing in too many time restrictions. For example, if an online group project has several closely spaced milestones, this could cause difficulties. Activities using synchronous communication, such as chat or video-conferencing, are beneficial for building community, but there may be difficulties arranging times that suit all the students. Careful thought therefore needs to be given to when the benefits of a synchronous activity outweigh this disadvantage (Finkelstein, 2006).

The Learner's Age and Experience

My second question relating to the learner concerned their age and experience – of technology and of learning. There has been much discussion in recent years of the concept of 'digital natives' (Prensky, 2001). The idea is that today's young people have spent their lives surrounded by digital technologies, and the use of these technologies therefore comes naturally to them. 'Digital natives' are contrasted with 'digital immigrants' – older people who have learned to use technology later in life, and for whom its use may be far from ingrained. Other terms have also been used to express this idea of young people's familiarity with new technologies, for example 'the net generation' (Oblinger & Oblinger, 2005).

The concept of the digital native is often used to argue for a more rapid adoption of technologies in education. In particular, it is argued that young people's use of social networking tools and mobile technologies should be extended into the sphere of learning. If this can be achieved without problems for students or teachers, then there could be significant benefits. However, recent research suggests that a cautious approach is needed, because the level of familiarity with technology varies considerably, even among the young (Kennedy et al., 2008; Ryberg et al., 2010). Although most young people in the developed world have had considerable exposure to technology, not all are competent and confident users in a learning context. For example, students may be skilled at searching the web using Google, but they are not necessarily skilled at sifting and evaluating the resources they find. They may be very familiar with communicating via instant messaging and texting, but they may not have the interpersonal communication skills that are needed for effective online collaboration.

When using communication technologies in a course, it is important to realize that students will have varying degrees of confidence in using technologies for learning, and that this is not necessarily dependent on age. Some students may be very competent technically, but may not have well-developed communication or learning skills. For others, the reverse may be true. In either case, teachers need to be prepared to provide training and support as required.

The Learner's Attitude to Studying

I suggested above that we need to think about why learners are studying the course and about their attitude to learning. Some learners study purely from interest, so for them enjoying the experience is important. They may consider their studies to be part of their leisure and social lives. Others study because they are expected or required to, or to gain a qualification. They may adopt strategies that reduce the amount of time they need to spend, while still ensuring that they pass the course. These two examples illustrate opposite ends of a spectrum, but most students will lie somewhere in between, and may be at different places in the spectrum for different subjects they are studying.

Differences in students' attitudes to learning have been characterized as 'deep' and 'surface' approaches (Marton & Saljo, 1976; Entwistle & Ramsden, 1983). In the deep approach, the student aims to gain a personal understanding of the subject. This approach is associated with intrinsic motivation for learning – a desire to learn for its own sake. In the surface approach, the student's aim is to pass the course, and their focus may be on memorizing course material. In this case, the student's motivation is extrinsic – a desire to gain the necessary marks – so their activities will be strongly influenced by the course assessment. A third 'strategic' approach has also been identified, where the student skillfully adopts a combination of deep and surface approaches, according to the tasks they are being asked to carry out (Hartley, 1998).

Students' learning practices will be strongly influenced by their beliefs about what it means to learn, and the purpose of learning. This takes us back to the theories of learning discussed in Chapter 2. Some students may believe that learning is primarily a process of absorbing and remembering new material, and may therefore adopt a surface approach. They will focus on the content of the course, and on the teacher's presentation of this content. Other students will believe that learning is primarily the development of understanding, and will tend to adopt a deep approach. They will want opportunities to explore their understanding with the teacher and with other students. Cultural aspects may also have an influence on students' attitudes. In some cultures the teacher is held in great esteem, and students might be unwilling to question anything the teacher presents to them. These students might feel uncomfortable, at least initially, in an educational context that is more learner-centred.

Differences in students' approaches to learning need to be taken into account when designing online learning activities. This is particularly important for gaining the desired participation from students. For those students who are intrinsically motivated, it is important that online activities contribute significantly to their learning and understanding, without taking excessive amounts of time. For students who are extrinsically motivated, it is helpful (and may be essential) to link online activities to the course assessment. This will encourage active participation, which will benefit all the students. However, as discussed in Chapter 8, *Assessment for Learning in Online Communities*, this needs to be thought through carefully to ensure that the assessment criteria are aligned with the learning activities and intended learning outcomes.

The Course Topic

In my imaginary design scenario of transferring a face-to-face course to an online environment, I suggested that another aspect to consider was the course topic. The inherent characteristics of the subject will influence the choice of activities and online facilities. For example:

- Do students need access to particular subject-specific learning resources?
- Is the subject discursive, with a basis in debates and discussion?
- Is there a practical side, where the focus is on developing skills?

In many cases, the answer to all three questions will be 'yes'. For example, when studying a language, students need to learn the vocabulary and grammar particular to the language; they need to discuss the cultures of the countries where that language is spoken; they need to practice speaking, reading and writing the language. Similarly, when studying science, students need to learn about particular theories, experiments and findings; they need to discuss the interpretation of experiments, and the role of science in society; and they need to develop skills in designing and carrying out experiments and working with data. Nevertheless, although the answer to the above questions is likely to be 'yes' for many subjects, the questions have different implications for different subjects. I will therefore use these questions as a framework for my comments on how the course topic affects the design of an online course.

Subject-specific Resources

When transferring an existing course to online form, it may be necessary to convert existing subject-specific teaching materials to digital form, or to create new resources that can be delivered online. An alternative to transferring or creating resources is to use content that is available on the open web, or via a university library. There is a vast amount of material on the web that can be used for learning, but care needs to be taken when using it. Locating resources that are suitable for a particular learning context can be time consuming. In addition, there is risk of websites changing or disappearing. This can be a problem for a course that uses a lot of web sources. The teacher therefore needs to keep a watchful eye on the availability of online materials, or use a facility for automatically checking web links.

In recent years there have been significant developments in providing open educational resources (OERs) via the web. These are learning materials that are freely available for teachers or learners. Examples of OER initiatives include MIT's OpenCourseWare (ocw.mit.edu) and the UK Open University's OpenLearn (www.open.ac.uk/openlearn). OER repositories can be searched to identify resources that are suitable for specific subjects, students or purposes. These repositories therefore provide a rich source of online learning materials for teachers to explore.

Once suitable sources of learning materials have been identified, the teacher needs to draw them together for learners to use. This can be done in a number of ways – for example, via a virtual learning environment, a bespoke website, a blog or a social bookmarking service. An alternative approach is for the teacher to provide the support for learners to gather and share suitable resources. For example, the teacher could direct students to a few key resources, and then ask them to find and share others. This sharing could be done via a number of online tools, for example a forum, a wiki or a social bookmarking facility. Using social bookmarking, students could tag resources, rate them and comment on them.

Discussion and Debate

Another question I raised regarding the subject matter of an online course was whether the topic was discursive. The usual online tool for supporting the more discursive aspects of a course is a discussion forum. Discussion forums support a conversational model of learning (Laurillard, 2002), while allowing students to reflect on the contributions, and engage at their own pace. If a faster-paced discussion is desirable, this can be enabled using a synchronous technology such as a chat room or videoconference.

Blogs and wikis can also be used for the discursive aspect of a course, but these tools move away somewhat from a conversational metaphor for learning. If each student has their own blog, the postings are centred on that individual's perspective, although other students can add comments. A group blog moves the ownership of the discussion back to the group, much like a forum. A wiki could be used for discussion, but wikis are more suited to creating shared products than exchanging views on a topic.

Developing Skills

My third question related to skills development. To develop skills, students, need to undertake relevant activities. If the activities are carried out collaboratively using online communication tools, students can gain feedback and ideas from each other. For example, students learning a language could improve their skills by posting short pieces of writing to a forum or wiki for review by their peers. Students learning computer networking could work together in a shared simulation environment, communicating via instant messaging or Internet telephony.

The teacher can be online supporting students as they carry out their activities (either synchronously or asynchronously). However, this is not essential, as students can learn a considerable amount from each other without the constant intervention of a teacher. What is essential is that the teacher designs the online activities carefully, so that they are suited to the course context and make a significant contribution to students' learning.

The Available Technologies

In our imaginary transfer from face-to-face to online course presentation, we need to consider what online tools are available, and how they relate to the teaching institution or organization. Chapter 3, *Tools for Online Learning Communities*, introduced the large palette of tools that are now available for teachers and students to choose from. Many of these are provided within virtual learning environments, and others are freely available on the web. However, some institutions stipulate the use of certain resources, for example a particular VLE. This is something the teacher needs to be aware of.

Virtual Learning Environments

There are many ways in which a VLE can be used to support learners. The examples given in 'Three short VLE case studies' are from three teachers at different universities, using different VLEs. The perspectives of these teachers, and others, are presented in more detail later in the chapter.

THREE SHORT VLE CASE STUDIES

Studying Health Online

In this first example, the VLE is used to facilitate group work and mutual support among students. The teacher uses the VLE in this way with health students who are studying entirely online. The course has several hundred students, and they are required to do group work and peer review through the VLE. In this case, despite the large size of the class, the teacher only uses small groups in his teaching because he has found that 'anarchy' is often a problem in large online forums.

Blended Learning of History

Where classes are not so large, and students not so widely dispersed, online and face-to-face modes can be successfully combined. In this second example, the VLE is a place where history students post their work and provide feedback to each other. To encourage students to take part, their posted work is assessed by the teacher, and feedback given online. Longer course discussions, however, take place off line, in face-to-face sessions. These face-to-face classes are improved through shared preparation by students in the VLE. By monitoring online activity, the teacher can see where students need help.

Group Projects for Art Students

A somewhat different approach is taken by a third teacher working with art students. Here the emphasis is more on stimulating creativity in groups. The students work on group projects, and the online system allows for time-flexible discussion among students. As with the history students, the VLE is a place where students can prepare for face-to-face sessions, which can then be more like workshops. The teacher has endeavoured to make the online spaces look interesting and inviting, even though this was difficult and time consuming. Her aim is for students to explore ideas and resources, and initiate activities for themselves.

As shown in 'Three short VLE case studies', using the facilities of a VLE has many benefits in terms of learning and teaching. In addition, a practical benefit of using an institutional VLE is technical support for teachers and students. In particular, there will be access to training resources – courses, online material or personal contact with support staff. The local support team may have considerable skills in the educational aspects of using online tools as well as the technical aspects, and it is worth tapping into their ideas and experience. Teachers who have made the transition into online teaching, via a VLE or other institutionally supported environment, often comment that the local support team were invaluable in the process.

Because a VLE provides a choice of applications, teachers should be able to select the tools needed for particular learning activities. However, VLEs can lack flexibility. They are fairly standardized, and teachers may find that certain things cannot be done in the way they intended. This is frustrating, and leads some teachers to reject VLEs. Creative teachers do not want to be locked into fixed ways of designing their courses.

Web-based Social Software

For the reasons mentioned above, online teachers are increasingly turning to the public web for tools to offer to students. A wide range of social software is available on the web, and many of these products are free to use. Teachers who are sufficiently confident can make their choice from various web-based forums, blog hosting facilities, wiki tools and so on. The suite of tools offered by Google (www.google.com) is one possibility. Google has tools for collaborating on documents, online discussion and a number of other shared activities.

When considering the use of open, web-based tools with students, there are a number of issues that need to be borne in mind. First there is the question of support and training, as mentioned above. When using third-party tools selected by an individual teacher, support for students will be the teacher's responsibility. Other issues for which the teacher will be responsible include accessibility, reliability and privacy. I will discuss each of these briefly below.

Facilities used as part of a course must be accessible to all the students, including those with disabilities or other special requirements. For example, learners with visual impairment may need to use a screen reader, which reads aloud text from the screen. Other learners may be unable to use a mouse. Not all public websites meet the standards needed to ensure accessibility, and for educational institutions these are often a legal requirement.

The reliability of the web service also needs to be considered. The service must be reliable, so that it is virtually certain to be available when students need it (such as the evening before an assignment deadline). It is also vital that students' work is held safely, and backed up properly. Some institutions will not allow students' work for assessment to be held on external servers. This is not an insurmountable problem, as some web services can be hosted on local servers, but this requires a level of institutional support.

Finally, the issue that is foremost in the minds of many web users is privacy. If students are required to use a web service as part of a course, it is important that their privacy is protected. The boundaries between students' educational identities and their social identities need to be considered, particularly in relation to web services that students may already be using for their own purposes (for example social network sites).

The issue of privacy is explored in the following case study, written by a teacher who used a public instant messaging tool with her teenage students. This case study is also pertinent to the question, discussed earlier in this chapter, of whether young people are 'digital natives', and if so, what are the implications for education. Unlike the earlier case studies in the book, this account is written in the first person, giving the reader a more personal sense of the teacher's perspective.

CASE STUDY

USING ONLINE COMMUNICATION TO SUPPORT YOUNG LEARNERS OF ENGLISH

Christa Hamilton, Berufsbildende Schulen, Germany

From August 2008 to July 2009, I was teaching English as a foreign language in a further education college in a semi-rural area of Northern Germany. The college, called Berufsbildende Schulen (BBS) Walsrode, has approximately 2,000 students. It has four major departments: food technology; economics; metal work; and social and health care. I was teaching English to students of all levels in all departments, and I enjoyed the different backgrounds of students and teachers. English is one of the core subjects, having equal status with mathematics and German. In addition, considerable efforts are made to teach ICT (information and communication technology) at different levels throughout the college.

Adopting Online Communication Tools

I knew that students often used online tools to exchange subject-related information, so I offered them the option of sending homework to me via email, or contacting me via email if they had any queries. From this developed the idea of using a real-time communication tool (ICQ) to enable students to practise their language skills, in the context of an English project.

The project was part of the English 'A' level topic 'Science and Technology'. In the project, year 12 and 13 students are required, in small groups, to investigate a science and technology topic, placing the emphasis on information technology. Some of the students investigated the pros and cons of online games, and others chose communication tools like ICQ. As most of the students in Germany use ICQ, my students and I agreed that we would use this facility to support their learning of English.

Learning with ICQ

ICQ is similar to Skype. It allows different kinds of real-time communication, for example instant messaging and spoken conversations. Between 3 November and 7 December 2008, we used ICQ communication to support the project tasks. Students mainly contacted me to clarify set tasks or receive encouragement that they were on the right track.

Some of the students had difficulties using English in a spontaneous way.

English use is normally confined to the classroom, where students can prepare what they want to say, and the focus is on books or grammatical issues. In the classroom most students will answer with just one sentence, and other students will build on this. But when using ICQ, this type of social interaction did not take place, and instead students preferred one-to-one tuition. There were no spoken conversations, as most of the students did not feel confident enough to converse in English, so the ICQ interactions were all via text.

Participation

From a total of 22 students in years 12 and 13, only six participated in the online tuition, even though all the students had computers available at home. Of these six students, three felt confident enough to engage in longer text chats with me on a one-to-one basis. One student used the online facility for over an hour to organize her project topic, interacting in English all the way through. Some of the students in the two classes stated that they preferred to communicate with the teacher face-to-face. Their attitudes towards using the computer for educational purposes were rather critical, as they did not enjoy the subject of ICT in general.

After the project tasks were completed on 7 December, the communication via ICQ stopped altogether. One possible explanation is that there needs to be a set task to engage students in online learning. Once the task has been completed, the learner disconnects from the learning environment unless a further task is set. This behaviour does not differ significantly from the classroom context, which leads to me to conclude that an online learning environment needs to be treated like a virtual classroom in order to be effective. Another important factor for students was time. In the last two weeks before the Christmas holiday, students have to write a considerable number of assignments, for different subjects. They physically do not have the time to chat online, especially in English, which takes much longer for them.

Blurring Boundaries: Work Time and Personal Time

From my own perspective, using online communication for teaching was extremely time consuming. It was nearly impossible to fulfil every student's learning needs, especially when lessons for other classes needed to be prepared, or marking needed to be done. I actually had to cut short one of my student's online sessions in order to complete my assignment marking. The online tuition also led to restrictions in my private life, as I made myself available at all times. The boundaries between working and private life seemed to be more blurred than ever.

In future, I would only offer this learning opportunity if I had sufficient time, with a fixed schedule in which I would make myself available for the students. For myself, I have now re-defined clear boundaries between work and private life. It seems likely that the students and I shared similar issues in relation to time and boundaries. In a full-time occupation, whether you are a teacher or a student, it is difficult to find the time to participate in online learning, as well as fulfilling the requirements of the traditional classroom.

Blurring Boundaries: Work Life and Social Life

In Germany, ICQ is mainly used by young people for social purposes – interacting with their peers. I am therefore somewhat doubtful about using an online facility for learning that is already used for social purposes by my young learners. The students tended to keep strictly to the topic, and converse in a very polite manner, which suggests to me that they need to maintain a distance from the teacher. By engaging in ICQ conversations, I might have been seen as an intruder into their social interactions. For young learners, ICQ is simply for meeting 'friends', and having general chats about nothing and everything. Perhaps, in their view, learning languages belongs more to the traditional classroom setting.

Privacy Issues

Within the project, two students, Malte and Friedrich, presented their view about social networking using the German version of Facebook for school and college students, the Schülerverzeichnis (SVZ). Their presentation led to a lively discussion about use and abuse, and the possible loss of privacy when participating in this type of social network. In their project report they expressed considerable concern that anybody can log on to this site to retrieve information about young learners:

> using websites like 'Schüler-VZ' is full of unknown inconsiderable risks and dangers. Social networks give the possibility for unauthorized persons to get access to sensitive facts and pictures

In addition, they pointed out how privacy could be easily invaded by adding too much private information onto the website:

> Another big abuse is made by modern human resources departments, which are checking the social background of the candidates. Through the internet the manager gets uncontrolled access to disadvantageous party pictures or details about private problems of the candidate.

Malte and Friedrich's report, however, also highlighted benefits of social networking. For example:

> The most apparent advantage of 'Schüler-VZ' is the opportunity to stay in contact with people living abroad or in greater geographical distance. Users can make enquiries about former classmates or friends. . . . So, you can be somehow a part of their life without a direct and intensive contact.

The Teacher

The final aspect of my imaginary design of an online course is the teacher herself or himself. For some courses, there may be just one teacher, but a course may also be taught by a small team. In the case of large-scale distance learning, the course may be designed by a small team of staff, and presented by a much larger group of tutors. When planning online aspects of a course, the following questions need to be asked about the responsibilities of the teachers:

- What skills and experience do teachers need?
- What time commitments are required from teachers?

As in earlier sections, I will take these questions as a framework for my discussion.

Teachers' Skills and Experience

Teaching in an online context requires particular skills and experience if it is to be successful. Moving from face-to-face teaching to online teaching is not a trivial step. Although online teachers often comment that the skills and techniques for teaching online are not very different from those used in face-to-face contexts, transferring the techniques used in face-to-face contexts to the online domain calls for careful consideration. To explore this a little further, we will use two examples:

- a group project;
- a tutorial or seminar.

For group work in a face-to-face context, a teacher would keep a watchful eye on the progress and dynamics of each group. The teacher would look for an even level of participation among students, with no-one left out and no-one dominating. The teacher would try to spot if a group was in difficulties, if students were clashing with each other, or if the group had ground to a halt. Transferring these facilitating functions to the online context, the responsibilities would be much the same. However, the teacher would be 'observing' the work of the group online, for example via students' contributions in a forum. From these postings the teacher would look for development of ideas and plans, and would check that there was a reasonable number of postings from each student – not too many and not too few. The teacher would also try to pick up the 'tone' of students' contributions, in order to make sure the group was not having any serious difficulties.

For a tutorial, in a face-to-face context a teacher would think about how to present the relevant concepts and techniques, and would prepare resources to use (for example, slides and handouts with activities). During the tutorial, the teacher would check that students were following the explanations – perhaps judging from their expressions or body language. When students were carrying out activities, the teacher might walk around the room, looking over students' shoulders to see how they were getting on. Moving now to the online context, the teacher might design a tutorial to be carried out via audio-conferencing. They would plan the tutorial and prepare resources to use in the audio-conferencing environment. The teacher would design activities for students to carry out in small groups using the system's 'breakout rooms'. During the tutorial, the teacher could use the shared whiteboard to explain concepts or demonstrate techniques. They would check whether students were following, perhaps asking them to indicate this via the text chat or voting tools. When students were carrying out the activities, the teacher would 'visit' each breakout room to see how they were progressing.

These two examples have focused on the design and facilitation of online learning activities, but another key aspect of the teacher's role is to build community among the students. When communication is mainly online it is important that students enjoy the interactions, otherwise they may not be sufficiently motivated to take part. This requires attention to affective issues, and the relationships among students. The development of a sense of community will be helped by the use of 'icebreaker' activities, and by encouraging students to share their interests beyond their studies. These are considerations that good face-to-face teachers bear in mind, and they are even more important in an online setting. As discussed in Chapter 6, teachers need to create an online environment that is inviting, and which can play a social role for students as well as an educational role.

As the discussion above has shown, many important teaching skills and techniques are transferable from face-to-face to online contexts. Although some adjustments are needed, the most important skills for supporting online communities are skills in teaching, in its broadest sense. However, some technical skills are also required, so online teachers need a degree of technical confidence, and willingness to try things out. The specific skills needed will depend on the type of tools being used and the institutional context, as well as on the skills and confidence of the students. In general, online teachers need to cope with some level of technical 'troubleshooting', both for themselves and for their students.

Time Commitments for Teachers

When online learning first began to attract widespread interest, it was seen by some educational managers as a way of reducing teaching time, and hence costs. This was based on the idea that courses could simply be 'put online' and delivered to large numbers of students with little intervention from teachers. Thankfully, this view of online learning has largely disappeared. It is now accepted that teaching well online takes a considerable amount of time, although there can be time savings in the longer term.

The amount of online time needed will depend on the type of course and the particular role of the teacher. A teacher who moves their course from an entirely face-to-face context to one that is primarily online will probably need to spend several hours a day, at least initially, working online or carrying out associated tasks. For example:

- designing and planning online activities;
- setting up online environments (for example, forums or wikis for student groups);
- providing learning resources online;
- monitoring students' online activity (in forums, blogs, wikis and so on);
- answering students' queries;
- helping students with any technical problems.

This may seem a daunting prospect. However, teachers who have made the move from face-to-face to online teaching find that the time they need to spend gradually reduces as they, and their students, gain experience in working online.

A further consideration is when time needs to be spent. Teachers will need to log in regularly in order to provide adequate support for their students. It is important to make clear to students at the start of a course how often the teacher will log on, and hence how quickly students should expect to receive a response to any queries. This needs to be carefully managed, as some students can make unreasonable demands, expecting a response within a matter of hours. It is advisable to encourage students to help each other, rather than relying on interventions from the teacher. Many students' enquiries will relate to practical issues, for which they may already have access to the necessary information. In these cases, a quick pointer from another student is the most effective response. This means encouraging students to post their queries to a course forum, rather than directing their queries to the teacher.

A final consideration related to time is the use of synchronous technologies. Although these technologies have many benefits, they are less flexible in terms of the teacher's and students' time. For example, having scheduled drop-in sessions for students via a chat room will be helpful for resolving difficulties, but it requires the teacher to be online during fixed periods. Arranging online teaching activities via videoconferencing again requires specific periods online, and if the times do not suit all students the teacher may need to offer these sessions more than once.

Teachers' Views and Experiences

Having explored an imaginary transfer of a course from face-to-face to online, I want to draw these threads together by presenting the views and experiences of teachers who have used online communication in their courses. I am drawing here on the findings of a small study of educators who used virtual learning environments with students (Kear, 2007). Six teachers from UK universities were interviewed about their experiences of using the online communication tools within their university's VLE. Three of the teachers were those whose work using VLEs was presented in 'Three short VLE case studies' earlier in the chapter. The VLEs used were Moodle, Blackboard, WebCT and an in-house VLE. The main communication facilities used were discussion forums, with some use of synchronous chat rooms.

Learning and Teaching Activities

The teachers mentioned a range of learning activities that their students were required to carry out online. The tasks set for students were sometimes individual pieces of work, but usually included collaborative work such as discussion or peer review. Often this work was carried out in groups of between four and ten students. Some of the teachers required their students to write short papers or presentations and post these online for other students to comment on. Other activities included: online discussions or debates in response to questions set by the teacher; collaborative writing tasks; role play; and group projects.

The teachers also mentioned a number of different teaching and management tasks that they needed to carry out. These are summarized in Table 9.1.

The remainder of this section presents the teachers' perspectives on their experiences. The teachers gave their views on the issues arising from the use of online communication, and the benefits. I will start with the issues they identified.

Issues Raised by Teachers

One issue was students' anxiety when they were new to the online environment. Some students were nervous and some were 'technophobes', and this

Table 9.1 Teaching and Management Tasks

Teaching tasks	*Management tasks*
Marking students' online work and posting up grades;	Creating and maintaining a suitable structure for their course areas on the VLE;
Providing resources, worksheets and links to useful web sites;	
Setting quizzes;	Putting students into groups with their own forums;
Responding to questions via forums or via email;	Maintaining a course calendar with events and key dates;
Using moderating skills to motivate students;	Tracking students' participation;
Facilitating or summarising discussions;	Archiving messages in forums when they got too full;
Providing key information and updates;	Handling the transition from one year to the next.
Giving technical help to students.	

could result in low participation. Teachers mentioned several ways in which they monitored participation. For example, they looked to see when a student had last logged on, and how many messages they had read and written. In some systems it was also possible to tell which students had read which postings. To address the issue of participation, several of the teachers included online activities as part of the course assessment. The marks allocated to online tasks acted as motivation for students to use the system, then, as one teacher said, 'once they are doing it, they see, and are enthusiastic'. Another teacher reported that an early assessed activity was effective in getting students comfortable with the system and overcoming anxiety.

A significant issue discussed was the time needed for online work, and several of the teachers said that finding time was the biggest problem for them. The teachers reported that the time they spent working with the VLE varied considerably. During intensive teaching periods they might log in three or four times a day, spending up to two hours per day in total, and during quieter periods they might log in about three times a week. There were two main aspects of teachers' online work that took time:

- learning how to use the online facilities, overcoming small hurdles and helping students with technical problems;
- closer engagement with students, and having them constantly in touch, particularly students who seemed to expect instant responses.

The teachers said they had needed to spend more time when they were new to the system, and subsequently when setting up new courses. Efficiencies and some practical time-saving came later. Teachers also pointed out that their students faced similar issues in relation to the time needed for online work.

The teachers discussed specific problems that arose when using forums. These related to handling the large number of messages and discussion threads that could build up in an active course:

> it's being able to manage that wall of information that you've got, that permanency. You've got to almost be able to filter the information much more effectively. In some sense be quite ruthless, 'I'm going to reply to that but I'm not going to reply to that', and recognise that it's OK to do that. And it's those sorts of issues that students can be overwhelmed by.

Teachers explained that students had difficulties finding their way through the different discussion threads, and discussions could easily be 'lost' or 'buried':

> I find personally that the threads don't really work because students don't stick to the thread. They compose a new message but the same subject. So it is quite difficult to track, when you get a lot of messages, where the threads actually are.

One of the teachers reported that he only used forums for structured activities where students posted set pieces of work and other students commented on them. Another teacher only used discussion forums for small groups. A third teacher commented that she thought carefully about how many students to have in a forum.

The teachers also discussed technical problems and usability issues, which they described as 'quirks' which were 'irritating'. Several of the teachers mentioned that they wrote instructions to help their students. Teachers commented that good usability was important, because if students were struggling with technical problems they could became frustrated and stop using the system. A related theme that emerged was the need for flexibility. The teachers reported that the systems sometimes did not quite do what they wanted, so they needed to adjust their approach to fit the system. The teachers wanted to use system features in different ways, to suit their different teaching styles and approaches. They did not want to be restricted to a particular structure or educational model.

Teachers' Views of Benefits

Despite the issues outlined above, all the teachers were convinced of the value of using online communication with their students. They felt that this provided a richer learning environment, encouraged students to be more active and engaged, and resulted in deeper learning. The teachers said that online activities could support different learning and teaching styles and encourage an approach based on learning as a social process. Equality of participation was mentioned, both in relation to the balance among students (encouraging quieter students to take part) and the balance between teachers and students (allowing students to challenge teachers). One teacher expressed her hope that students would become more than just 'consumers of courses'.

Teachers said that having the online environment meant that face-to-face classes improved because students played a more active role:

> they're much better prepared for the seminars when they come, and consequently the tutorials are much more interactive – everybody's done something, everybody's answered a question and they're much more willing to participate.

As a result, face-to-face sessions could include deeper and broader discussions, rather than needing to provide basic information. Discussions could also be continued online after a face-to-face session.

Several of the teachers specifically mentioned the benefits of discussion forums. They reported that forums helped them to keep in touch with students and helped students to keep in touch with each other. The forums allowed students to ask questions and receive answers from the teacher or from other students. In this way, the forums built into a resource based on students' own knowledge, giving a sense of ownership. The asynchronous nature of forums was seen as valuable for reflective learning. Students had time to think about what they wanted to say, and could think about others' contributions without needing to respond straight away.

The teachers also highlighted the role of online communication in building community. The flexibility of time and place provided by forums was seen as particularly important to students who lived at a distance from the university and to those who were on placements. One teacher commented:

A few of them can meet in small local groups. But this gives a much stronger, much deeper sense of community by enabling people to communicate and get to know each other.

Several teachers mentioned the value of a VLE for providing information and notices to students. This was normally done via a course calendar for events and a 'news' area or forum for more general information. One concern was that some students did not log in often enough to pick up important items. However, in this case, the student could choose to have messages forwarded to their email account.

One of the teachers said that online communication provided a 'virtual life' for his student teachers, who spent most of their time in schools on teaching practice, and often felt isolated and lonely. For these students, knowing that others were in the same situation and facing similar problems was reassuring:

it's really nice for them to log on and just go and tell somebody else and to hear somebody else saying 'Well, yeah, you know, I had that'.

Two of the teachers were keen to extend the reach of the VLE beyond individual courses, to build a student-led online community for the department. Overall, the teachers seemed confident that it was possible to build relationships, understanding and community online.

This section has presented the views and experiences of university teachers who used online communication tools to support their students. Overall, although the teachers identified some difficulties, they were very positive about the benefits of using online communication with students. Based on their experiences, the teachers felt that there were significant gains in learning and community-building. When asked to what extent use of online communication provided educational value, they responded using expressions such as 'huge', 'tremendous'.

Online Learning in a Developing World

The teachers whose views were presented in the previous section were all based in the UK, and they and their students had access to equipment and resources provided by their universities. However, teachers in developing countries are often faced with a shortage of learning resources such as books and laboratory equipment. Even the basic infrastructure, such as reliable communication links and power supply, may be lacking. This situation presents significant challenges, but many developing countries are rapidly overcoming these difficulties.

The final case study in this book presents an inspiring example of how online communication can help address a lack of educational resources in the developing world. The case study, by a university teacher in Rwanda, describes how Open Educational Resources and a freely available learning platform were used to overcome local problems. It is a fitting example of a teacher's resourcefulness and innovation with which to close this book.

CASE STUDY

USING OPEN EDUCATIONAL RESOURCES IN A DEVELOPING COUNTRY

Rwagasana Gerard, National University of Rwanda

The teaching of science, especially physics, presents a particular problem in the universities of developing countries, such as Rwanda. At the National University of Rwanda we have found that Open Educational Resources – OERs – can contribute enormously to solving this problem. I teach the *Introductory Modern Physics* course in the third year at the department of Mathematics and Physics of the Faculty of Education. The Faculty trains students – future secondary school teachers – in all disciplines, including physics.

Teaching at secondary school is fundamentally important, as it is here that pupils gain the basic physical concepts and approaches that determine their higher studies and their careers. The quality of their learning prior to university studies depends on the skills of their teachers, so effective physics teaching in secondary school is very important. My aim is to produce teachers who understand very well physics concepts and laws, and who are skilled in teaching methodology – that is to say, teachers who can help their pupils understand the fundamental concepts and laws of physics, and who can instil a love of the subject.

The Rwandan Context

The Government of Rwanda places great importance on science and technology, for economic development and the construction of a new knowledge based society. From this perspective everything is done to promote science and technology in teaching, from primary to higher education levels. Nevertheless, despite the government's efforts, scientific infrastructure and equipment, such as laboratories and libraries, are so expensive as to be almost impossible to afford.

The Government of Rwanda has found that Information and Communication Technologies (ICTs) can help enormously in the achievement of its objectives. Measures taken include the suppression of tax on ICT products at importation, the creation of a National Commission for Information Technology in charge of ICT policy, and, at the national level, an infrastructure development plan for ICTs.

Equipping universities and secondary schools with computers and Internet connections has become a national priority for the government. Universities are installing computer labs for teachers and students. In the absence of conventional materials – labs and libraries – teachers and learners can easily access open educational resources on the web. Using Open Educational Resources, it is now possible to find the resources and tools needed for effective teaching and learning activities, particularly in blended learning mode.

Using Open Educational Resources (OERs)

In view of the almost complete lack of laboratory equipment, and of updated textbooks in the library, I have found a solution by using free resources (OERs) found on the Internet. In particular, I have made use of resources found in the MERLOT (Multimedia Educational Resources for Learning and Online Teaching) repository (www.merlot.org). This facility has the best learning objects from all disciplines intended for university teaching, and is peer reviewed by specialist teachers (see Figure 9.1).

Figure 9.1 Physics resources in the MERLOT OER repository.

Source: Reproduced with permission.

The course *Introductory Modern Physics* introduces some concepts from relativistic physics and quantum physics, such as time dilation, energy quantisation, absorption/emission of energy or radioactivity, etc. These concepts are difficult to explain because they do not correspond to the conceptions, or 'preconceptions', familiar from our environment. They are also difficult to show in the classroom or traditional laboratories.

The course is organized in three stages. First, I meet my students face to face in the classroom. I introduce new concepts, and this is followed by discussion, questions and answers.

Second, students work in small groups of 4–6, on projects provided by me, using the Dokeos learning platform (www.dokeos.com). On the platform the students find all the documentation that I have chosen and deposited. These are links to various resources on the web: essentially, texts, simulations and virtual laboratories. Students' work on the Dokeos platform is enriched by exchanges between students themselves and between students and teacher. These discussions take place using forums, chat and email.

Finally we have a further meeting in the classroom, where each group presents its project to the class, followed by discussions, questions and answers.

Findings

Assessment results at the end of the training period have been significantly better than those from classes where the teaching has been organized on the classic model. Students have expressed their satisfaction with the hybrid mode and with collaborative work. Relations between students, and between students and teacher, have improved, creating a climate of confidence among the students. Moreover, students have acquired new knowledge and skills in the use of ICTs for their communication and learning.

The only difficulties have been technical ones. There were a few problems owing to power failures during learning sessions when students were using the online platform. There have also been some problems because of the slow speed of the Internet connection.

Further Developments

The National University of Rwanda has now adopted e-learning as a solution to the lack of premises and equipment and for improving the quality of teaching and learning. The University's Centre for Instructional Technology initially planned to train all teachers in the use of the Dokeos platform, so that they could put their courses online. However, in January 2009, the university adopted the open source platform Moodle (moodle.org) as its institutional Learning Management System.

As yet, there are not many lecturers using Moodle because there are few connected computers for the large numbers of students (approximately 13,000 students in 2010). However the University plans to install wireless connectivity across the whole campus so that students and staff can use their own laptops. Once this has been achieved, the University can gain the full benefits of open source developments and Open Educational Resources.

References

Adam, R. (2002) 'Is e-mail addictive?', *Aslib Proceedings*, 54(2), pp. 85–94.

Ahern, T.C. (1993) 'The effect of a graphic interface on participation, interaction and student achievement in a computer-mediated small-group discussion', *Journal of Educational Computing Research*, 9(4), pp. 535–548.

Ahern, T.C. (1994) 'The effect of interface on the structure of interaction in computer-mediated small-group discussion', *Journal of Educational Computing Research*, 11(3), pp. 235–250.

Alexander, B. (2006) 'Web 2.0: A new wave of innovation for teaching and learning?' *Educause Review* 41, 33–44. Available from http://www.educause.edu/ir/library/pdf/ERM0621.pdf (accessed 29 December 2009).

Alexander, G. (2000) 'Extract from a communications guide'. Available from http://sustainability.open.ac.uk/gary/netique.htm (accessed 26 January 2010).

Asay, M. (2009) 'Shirky: problem is filter failure, not info overload', *The open road: the business and politics of open source*, CNET. Available from http://news.cnet.com/8301-13505_3-10142298-16.html (accessed 6 January 2010).

Aspden, E.J. and Thorpe, L.P. (2009) 'Where do you learn? Tweeting to inform learning space development', *Educause Quarterly* 32(1). Available from www.educause.edu/EDUCAUSE+Quarterly/EDUCAUSEQuarterlyMagazineVolum/WhereDoYouLearnTweetingtoInfor/163852 (accessed 20 November 2009).

Barab, S.A., MaKinster, J.G., Moore, J.A., Cunningham, D.J. and The ILF Design Team (2001) 'Designing and building an on-line community: the struggle to support sociability in the Inquiry Learning Forum', *Educational Technology Research and Development*, 49(4), pp. 71–96.

Barab, S.A., MaKinster, J.G. and Scheckler, R. (2003) 'Designing system dualities: characterizing a web-supported professional development community', *The Information Society*, 19, pp. 237–256.

Baron, N.S. (2004) 'See you online: gender issues in college student use of instant messaging', *Journal of Language and Social Psychology*, 23(4), pp. 397–423.

Barrett, H. (2004) 'Electronic portfolios as digital stories of deep learning: emerging digital tools to support reflection in learner-centered portfolios'. Available from http://electronicportfolios.org/digistory/epstory.html (accessed 3 January 2010).

Bartle, R. (2003) *Designing virtual worlds*, Indianapolis, NJ: New Riders.

Bates, T. (1995) *Technology, open learning and distance education*, London: Routledge.

Baym, N.K. (1997) 'Interpreting soap operas and creating community: inside an electronic fan culture', in Kiesler, S. (ed.), *Culture of the internet*, Mahwah, NJ: Lawrence Erlbaum Associates, pp. 103–120.

Berge, Z. (2008) 'Multi-user virtual environments for education and training? A critical review of *Second Life*', *Educational Technology* 48(3), pp. 27–31.

Biggs, J. and Tang, C. (2007) *Teaching for quality learning at university*, Maidenhead: McGraw-Hill.

Bonk, C.J., Kirkley, J., Hara, N. and Nennan, V.P. (2001) 'Finding the instructor in post-secondary online learning: pedagogical, social, managerial and technological locations', in Stephenson, J., *Teaching and learning online: pedagogies for new technologies*, London: Kogan Page, pp. 76–97.

Boulos, M.N.K. and Wheeler, S. (2007) 'The emerging Web 2.0 social software: an enabling suite of sociable technologies in health and health care education', *Health Information and Libraries Journal*, 24, pp. 2–23.

Bowie, C., Joughin, G., Taylor, P., Young, B. and Zimitat, C. (2002) 'Portfolios from Cyberia', in Schwartz, P. and Webb, G. (eds), *Assessment: case studies, experience and practice from higher education*, London: Kogan Page, pp. 54–61.

boyd, d.m. and Ellison, N.B. (2007) 'Social network sites: definition, history, and scholarship', *Journal of Computer-Mediated Communication*, 13(1), Article 11. Available from http://jcmc.indiana.edu/vol13/issue1/boyd.ellison.html (accessed 5 February 2010).

Brown, J.S., Collins, A. and Duguid, P. (1989) 'Situated cognition and the culture of learning', *Educational Researcher*, 18(1), pp. 32–42.

Brown, R.E. (2001) 'The process of community building in distance learning classes', *Journal of Asynchronous Learning Networks* 5(2). Available from http://www.sloan-c.org/publications/jaln/v5n2/v5n2_brown.asp (accessed 25 September 2009).

Browne, E. (2003) 'Conversations in cyberspace: a study of online learning', *Open Learning*, 18(3), pp. 245–259.

Bruner, J. (1975) 'The ontogenesis of speech acts', *Journal of Child Language*, 2, pp. 1–19.

Bruner, J. (1984) 'Vygotsky's zone of proximal development: the hidden agenda', in Rogoff, B. and Wertsh, J. (eds), *Children's learning in the 'zone of proximal development'*, San Francisco: Jossey-Bass, pp. 93–97.

Bryan, C. (2006) 'Developing group learning through assessment', in Bryan, C. and Clegg, K., *Innovative assessment in higher education*, Abingdon: Routledge, pp. 150–157.

Castronova, E. (2005) *Synthetic worlds: the business and culture of online games*, Chicago: University of Chicago Press.

Clausen, S.K. and Jacobsen, M.K. (2008) *Læringspotentialer i social software*. Unpublished Master Thesis, Aalborg University, Aalborg. Available from http://projekter.aau.dk/projekter/research/laeringspotentialer_i_social_software%2814633983%29/ (accessed 14 June 2010).

Conrad, D. (2002) 'Deep in the heart of learners: insights into the nature of online community', *Journal of Distance Education*, 17(1). Available from http://www.jofde.ca/index.php/jde/article/view/133/114 (accessed 16 June 2010).

Contreras-Castillo, J., Favela, J., Perez-Fragoso, C. and Santamaria-del-Angel, E. (2004) 'Informal interactions and their implications for online courses', *Computers and Education*, 42, pp. 149–168.

Coppola, N.W., Hiltz, S.R. and Rotter, N.G. (2002) 'Becoming a virtual professor: pedagogical roles and asynchronous learning networks', *Journal of Management Information Systems*, 18(4), pp. 169–189.

Cotterill, S., Bradley, P. and Hammond, G. (2006) 'ePortfolios: supporting assessment in complex educational environments', in Bryan, C. and Clegg, K., *Innovative assessment in higher education*, Abingdon: Routledge, pp. 123–131.

Cox, G., Carr, T. and Hall, M. (2004) 'Evaluating the use of synchronous communication in two blended courses', *Journal of Computer Assisted Learning*, 20, pp. 183–193.

Cress, U. (2005) 'Ambivalent effects of member portraits in virtual groups', *Journal of Computer Assisted Learning*, 21, pp. 281–291.

Curtis, P. (1997) 'Mudding: social phenomena in text-based virtual realities', in Kiesler, S. (ed.), *Culture of the Internet*, Mahwah, NJ: Carnegie Mellon University, Lawrence Erlbaum.

Daft, R.L. and Lengel, R.H. (1986) 'Organisational information requirements, media richness and structural design', *Management Science*, 32, pp. 554–571.

Dalsgaard, C. (2006) 'Social software: E-learning beyond learning management systems', *European Journal of Open and Distance Learning*, 2006(II). Available from http://www.eurodl.org/?p=archives&year=2006&halfyear=2&article=228 (accessed 15 June 2010).

Daniel, J. (2010) *Mega-schools, technology and teachers*, New York: Routledge.

de Freitas, S. (2008) 'Serious virtual worlds: a scoping study', JISC, UK. Available from http://www.jisc.ac.uk/media/documents/publications/seriousvirtualworldsv1.pdf (accessed 26 January 2010).

de Freitas, S. and Neumann, T. (2009) 'Pedagogic strategies supporting the use of Synchronous Audio Conferencing: a review of the literature', *British Journal of Educational Technology*, 40(6), pp. 980–998.

Denning, P.J. (1982) 'Electronic junk', *Communications of the ACM*, 25(3), pp. 163–165.

Dewey, J. (1933) *How we think: a restatement of the relation of reflective thinking to the educative process* (Revised edn), Boston: D.C. Heath.

Dickey, M.D. (2005) 'Three-dimensional virtual worlds and distance learning: two case studies of Active Worlds as a medium for distance education', *British Journal of Educational Technology*, 36(3), pp. 439–451.

Dirckinck-Holmfeld, L. (2002) 'Designing virtual learning environments based on problem oriented project pedagogy', in Dirckinck-Holmfeld, L. and Fibiger, B. (eds), *Learning in virtual environments*, Frederiksberg C: Samfundslitteratur Press, pp. 31–54.

Donelan, H., Kear, K. and Ramage, M. (2010) *Online communication and collaboration: a reader*, Abingdon: Routledge.

Dron, J. (2007) *Control and constraint in e-learning: choosing when to choose*, London and Hershey, PA: Idea Group Publishing.

Dron, J. and Anderson, T. (2007) 'Collectives, networks and groups in social software for e-learning', in Richards, G. (ed.), *World conference on e-learning in corporate, government, healthcare, and higher education 2007*, Quebec City, Canada: AACE, pp. 2460–2467.

Dron, J. and Anderson, T. (2009) 'Lost in social space: information retrieval issues in web 1.5', *Journal of Digital Information*, 10(2). Available from http://journals.tdl.org/jodi/article/view/443/280 (accessed 13 June 2010).

Durkee, D., Brant, S., Nevin, P., Odell, A., Williams, G., Melomey, D., Roberts, H., Imafidon, C., Perryman, R. and Lopes, A. (2009) 'Implementing e-learning and web 2.0 innovation: didactical scenarios and practical implications', *Industry and Higher Education*, 23(4), pp. 293–300.

Edirisingha, P., Nie, M., Pluciennik, M. and Young, R. (2009) 'Socialisation for learning at a distance in a 3-D multi-user virtual environment', *British Journal of Educational Technology*, 40(3), pp. 458–479.

Educause Learning Initiative (2009) '7 things you should know about … Microblogging', Educause. Available from http://net.educause.edu/ir/library/pdf/ELI7051.pdf (accessed 26 January 2010).

Ellis, C.A., Gibbs, S.J. and Rein, G.L. (1991) 'Groupware: some issues and experiences', *Communications of the ACM*, 34(1), pp. 38–58.

Ellis, R. and Goodyear, P. (2010) *Students' experiences of e-learning in higher education*, New York: Routledge.

Entwistle, N.J. and Ramsden, P. (1983) *Understanding student learning*, London: Croom Helm.

Falchikov, N. (2002) ' "Unpacking" peer assessment', in Schwartz, P. and Webb, G. (eds), *Assessment: case studies, experience and practice from higher education*, London: Kogan Page, pp. 70–77.

Finkelstein, J. (2006) *Learning in real time*, San Francisco: Jossey Bass.

Fox, B. (2001) 'Teaching online … reluctantly', in Murphy, D., Walker, R. and Webb, G. (eds), *Online learning and teaching with technology: case studies, experience and practice*, London: Kogan Page, pp. 55–62.

Gagne, R. (1985) *The conditions of learning*, New York: Holt, Rinehart and Winston.

Garrison, D.R., and Anderson, T. (2003) *E-learning in the 21st century*, Abingdon and New York: Routledge-Falmer.

Garrison, D.R. and Arbaugh, J.B. (2007) 'Researching the community of inquiry framework: review, issues, and future directions', *The Internet and Higher Education*, 10(3), pp. 157–172.

Garrison, D.R., Anderson, T. and Archer, W. (2000) 'Critical inquiry in a text-based environment: computer conferencing in higher education', *The Internet and Higher Education*, 2(2–3), pp. 87–105.

Gibbs, G. (2006) 'Why assessment is changing', in Bryan, C. and Clegg, K., *Innovative assessment in higher education*, Abingdon: Routledge, pp. 11–22.

Gibbs, G. and Simpson, C. (2004–5) 'Conditions under which assessment supports students' learning', *Learning and Teaching in Higher Education*, 1, pp. 3–31.

Godwin, P. (2007) 'Information literacy meets web 2.0: how the new tools affect our own training and our teaching', *New Review of Information Networking*, 13(2), pp. 101–112.

Goldberg, D., Nichols, D., Oki, B.M. and Terry, D. (1992) 'Using collaborative filtering to weave an information tapestry', *Communications of the ACM*, 35(12), pp. 61–70.

Goodfellow, R. (2001) 'Credit where it's due', in Murphy, D., Walker, R. and Webb, G. (eds), *Online learning and teaching with technology: case studies, experience and practice*, London: Kogan Page, pp. 73–80.

Greenhow, C. and Robelia, B. (2009) 'Informal learning and identity formation in online social networks', *Learning, Media and Technology*, 34(2), pp. 119–140.

Gunawardena, C. and Zittle, F. (1997) 'Social presence as a predictor of satisfaction within a computer-mediated conferencing environment', *American Journal of Distance Education*, 11(3), pp. 8–26.

Gunawardena, C., Plass, J. and Salisbury, M. (2001) 'Do we really need an online discussion group?', in Murphy, D., Walker, R. and Webb, G. (eds), *Online learning and teaching with technology: case studies, experience and practice*, London: Kogan Page, pp. 36–43.

Guy, M. and Tonkin, E. (2006) 'Folksonomies: tidying up tags?', *D-Lib Magazine* 12(1). Available from http://www.dlib.org/dlib/january06/guy/01guy.html (accessed 6 January 2010).

Hammond, T., Hannay, T., Lund, B. and Scott, J. (2005) 'Social bookmarking tools (I) a general review', *D-Lib Magazine* 11(4). Available from http://www.dlib.org/dlib/april05/hammond/04hammond.html (accessed 22 January 2010).

Hampel, R. (2003) 'Theoretical perspectives and new practices in audio-graphic conferencing for language learning', *ReCALL*, 15(1), pp. 21–36.

Harasim, L. (ed.) (1990) *Online education: perspectives on a new environment*, New York: Praeger.

Harasim, L. (1999) 'A framework for online learning: the Virtual-U', *Computer*, 32(9), pp. 44–49.

Harasim, L., Hiltz, S., Teles, L. and Turoff, M. (1995) *Learning networks: a field guide to teaching and learning online*, Cambridge, MA: MIT Press.

Hartley, J. (1998) *Learning and studying: a research perspective*, London: Routledge.

Haythornthwaite, C. (2007) 'Social networks and online community', in Joinson, A., McKenna, K., Postmes, T. and Reips, U. (eds), *The Oxford handbook of internet psychology*, Oxford: Oxford University Press, pp. 121–137.

Haythornthwaite, C., Kazmer, M.M., Robins, J. and Shoemaker, S. (2000) 'Community development among distance learners: temporal and technological dimensions', *Journal of Computer Mediated Communication*, 6(1).

Heap, N.W., Kear, K.L. and Bissell, C.C. (2004) 'An overview of ICT-based assessment for engineering education', *European Journal of Engineering Education*, 29(2), pp. 241–250.

Hemmi, A., Bayne, S. and Land, R. (2009) 'The appropriation and repurposing of social technologies in higher education', *Journal of Computer Assisted Learning*, 25, pp. 19–30.

Hemp, P. (2009) 'Death by information overload', *Harvard Business Review*, September 2009, pp. 83–89.

Henri, F. (1995) 'Distance learning and computer mediated communication: interactive, quasi-interactive or monologue?', in O'Malley, C. (ed.), *Computer-supported collaborative learning*, Berlin: Springer-Verlag, pp. 145–161.

Herrington, A., Herrington, J., Kervin, L., and Ferry, B. (2006) 'The design of an online community of practice for beginning teachers', *Contemporary Issues in Technology and Teacher Education*, 6(1), pp. 120–132.

Herrington, J., and Oliver, R. (2000) 'An instructional design framework for authentic learning environments', *Educational Technology Research and Development*, 48(3), pp. 23–48.

Hewitt, J. (2001) 'Beyond threaded discourse', *International Journal of Educational Telecommunications*, 7(3), pp. 207–221.

Hiltz, S.R. (1994) *The virtual classroom: learning without limits via computer networks*, Norwood, NJ: Ablex.

Hiltz, S.R. and Turoff, M. (1985) 'Structuring computer-mediated communication systems to avoid information overload', *Communications of the ACM*, 28(7), pp. 680–689.

Hiltz, S.R. and Turoff, M. (1993) *The network nation: human communication via computer* (2nd edition), Cambridge, MA MIT Press.

Honeycutt, L. (2001) 'Comparing e-mail and synchronous conferencing in online peer response', *Written Communication*, 18(1), pp. 26–60.

Hrastinski, S. (2006) 'Introducing an informal synchronous medium in a distance learning course: how is participation affected?', *The Internet and Higher Education*, 9, pp. 117–131.

Hudson, K. and deGast-Kennedy, K. (2009) 'Canadian border simulation at Loyalist College', *Journal of Virtual Worlds Research*, 2(1). Available at https://journals.tdl.org/jvwr/article/view/374/449 (accessed 14 June 2010).

Hudson, K. and Nowosielski, L. (2009, April) *Canadian border simulation*. Poster session presented at the Federal Consortium on Virtual Worlds Conference, National Defense University, Washington DC.

Jarmon, L., Traphagan, T., Mayrath, M. and Trivedi, A. (2009) 'Virtual world teaching, experiential learning and assessment: an interdisciplinary communication course in Second Life', *Computers and Education*, 53, pp. 169–182.

Jonassen, D., Davidson, M., Collins, M., Campbell, J. and Haag, B.B. (1995) 'Constructivism and computer-mediated communication in distance education', *American Journal of Distance Education*, 9(2), pp. 7–26.

Jones, S.G. (1995) 'Understanding community in the information age', in Jones, S.G. (ed.), *Cyber-Society: computer-mediated communication and community*, Thousand Oaks, CA: Sage, pp. 10–35.

Jordan, S. and Mitchell, T. (2009) 'E-assessment for learning? The potential of short-answer free-text questions with tailored feedback', *British Journal of Educational Technology*, 40(2), pp. 371–385.

Kaye, A. (1992) 'Learning together apart', in *Collaborative learning through computer conferencing*, Berlin and Hedelberg: Springer-Verlag.

Kear, K. (2001) 'Following the thread in computer conferences', *Computers and Education*, 37, pp. 81–99.

Kear, K. (2004) 'Peer learning using asynchronous discussion systems in distance education', *Open Learning*, 19(2), pp. 151–164.

Kear, K. (2007) *Investigating design features of a computer-mediated communication system*, unpublished PhD thesis, The Open University, Milton Keynes, UK.

Kear, K. (2010) 'Collaboration via online discussion forums: issues and approaches', in Donelan, H., Kear, K. and Ramage, M. (eds), *Online communication and collaboration: a reader*, Abingdon: Routledge, pp. 30–33.

Kear, K. and Heap, N. (1999) 'Technology-supported group work in distance learning', *Active Learning*, 10, pp. 2126.

Kear, K. and Heap, N. (2007) ' "Sorting the wheat from the chaff": investigating overload in educational discussion systems', *Journal of Computer Assisted Learning*, 23(3), pp. 235–247.

Kear, K., Williams, J., Seaton, R. and Einon, G. (2004) 'Using information and communication technology in a modular distance learning course', *European Journal of Engineering Education*, 29(1), pp. 17–25.

Kennedy, G.E., Judd, T.S., Churchward, A., Gray, K. and Krause, K. (2008) 'First year students' experiences with technology: are they really digital natives?', *Australasian Journal of Educational Technology*, 24(1), pp. 108–122. Available from http://www.ascilite.org.au/ajet/ajet24/kennedy.html (accessed 1 February 2010).

Kerawalla, L., Minocha, S., Kirkup, G. and Conole, G. (2009) 'An empirically grounded framework to guide blogging in higher education', *Journal of Computer Assisted Learning*, 25, pp. 31–42.

Kervin, L., Mantei, J. and Herrington, A. (2010) 'Blogs as a social networking tool to build community', in Dumova, T. and Fiordo, R. (eds), *Handbook of research on social interaction technologies and collaboration software: concepts and trends*, Hershey, PA: Information Science Reference (IGI Global), pp. 685–700.

Kim, A.J. (2000) *Building communities on the web*, Berkeley, CA: Peachpit Press.

Kim, J. and Shaw, E. (2009) 'Pedagogical discourse: connecting students to past discussions and peer mentors within an online discussion board', *The 21st Innovative Applications of Artificial Intelligence Conference (IAAI-2009)*. Available from http://www.isi.edu/~jihie/papers/PedDiscourse-IAAI-09.pdf (accessed 8 February 2010).

Kim, J., Shaw, E., Ravi, S., Tavano, E., Arromratana, A. and Sarda, P. (2008) 'Scaffolding of on-line discussions with past discussions: an analysis and pilot study of PedaBot', in *Proceedings of the 9th International Conference on Intelligent Tutoring Systems (ITS'08)*. Available from http://www.isi.edu/~jihie/papers/Kim-ITS08.pdf (accessed 8 February 2010).

Kimble, C. and Hildreth, P. (2004) 'Communities of practice: going one step too far?', *Proceedings of the 9th Colloque de l'AIM*, Evry, France. Available from http://papers.ssrn.com/sol3/papers.cfm?abstract_id=634642 (accessed 7 February 2010).

Kirkpatrick, G. (2005) 'Online "chat" facilities as pedagogic tools', *Active Learning in Higher Education*, 6(2), pp. 145–159.

Kolb, D.A. (1984) *Experiential learning: experience as the source of learning and development*, Englewood Cliffs NJ: Prentice-Hall.

Konstan, J., Miller, B.N., Maltz, D., Herlocker, J.L., Gordon, L.R. and Riedl, R. (1997) 'GroupLens: applying collaborative filtering to Usenet News', *Communications of the ACM*, 40(3), pp. 77–87.

Kress, G. and van Leeuwen, T. (2001) *Multimodal discourse: the modes and media of contemporary communication*, London: Arnold.

Lamy, M.N. and Hampel, R. (2007) *Online communication in language learning and teaching*, Houndmills: Palgrave Macmillan.

Latchem, C. and Jung, I. (2010) *Distance and blended learning in Asia*, New York: Routledge.

Laurillard, D. (2002) *Rethinking university teaching: a conversational framework for the effective use of learning technologies*, London: Routledge Falmer.

Laurillard, D. (2009) 'The pedagogical challenges to collaborative technologies', *International Journal of Computer-Supported Collaborative Learning*, 4(1), pp. 5–20.

Lave, J. and Wenger, E. (1991) *Situated learning: legitimate peripheral participation*, Cambridge: Cambridge University Press.

Loch, B. and McDonald, C. (2007) 'Synchronous chat and electronic ink for distance support in mathematics', *Innovate*, 3(3). Available at http://innovateonline.info/pdf/vol3_issue3/ Synchronous_Chat_and_Electronic_Ink_for_Distance_Support_in_Mathematics.pdf (accessed 16 June 2010).

Loch, B. and Reushle, S. (2008) 'The practice of web conferencing: where are we now?', in *Hello! Where are we now in the landscape of educational technology?* Proceedings of Ascilite Melbourne 2008, 30 November–3 December, pp. 562–571.

McConnell, D. (2006) *E-learning groups and communities*, Maidenhead: Open University Press.

Macdonald, J. (2006) *Blended learning and online tutoring: a good practice guide*, Aldershot: Gower.

McDonald, C. and Loch, B. (2008) 'Adjusting the community of inquiry approach to a synchronous mathematical context', Poster presentation, in *Hello! Where are we now in the landscape of educational technology?* Proceedings of Ascilite Melbourne 2008, 30 November–3 December, pp. 603–606.

McInnerney, J.M. and Roberts, T.S. (2004) 'Online learning: social interaction and the creation of a sense of community', *Educational Technology and Society*, 7(3), pp. 73–81.

McLoughlin, C. and Lee, M.J.W. (2010) 'Educational podcasting: a taxonomy of pedagogical applications', in Dumova, T. and Fiordo, R. (eds), *Handbook of research on social interaction technologies and collaboration software: concepts and trends*, Hershey, PA: Information Science Reference (IGI Global), pp. 194–208.

McLoughlin, C. and Luca, J. (2001) 'Houston, we have a problem!', in Murphy, D., Walker, R. and Webb, G. (eds), *Online learning and teaching with technology: case studies, experience and practice*, London: Kogan Page, pp. 13–20.

Marton, F. and Saljo, R. (1976) 'On qualitative differences in student learning: 1. outcome and process', *British Journal of Educational Psychology*, 46(1), pp. 4–11.

Mason, R. and Bacsich, P. (1998) 'Embedding computer conferencing into university teaching', *Computers in Education*, 30(3/4), pp. 249–258.

Mason, R. and Kaye, A. (eds) (1989) *Mindweave: communication, computers and distance education*, Oxford: Pergamon Press.

Mason, R. and Rennie, F. (2008) *E-learning and social networking handbook: resources for higher education*, New York: Routledge.

Matthews, D. and Scrum, L. (2003) 'High-speed internet use and academic gratifications in the college residence', *The Internet and Higher Education*, 6, pp. 125–144.

Maturazzo, G. and Sellen, A. (2000) 'The value of video in work at a distance: addition or distraction?', *Behaviour and Information Technology*, 19(5), pp. 339–348.

Mayes, T. and de Freitas, S. (2007) 'Learning and e-learning: the role of theory', in Beetham, H. and Sharpe, R. (eds), *Rethinking pedagogy for a digital age*, London: Routledge, pp. 13–25.

Mazer, J.P., Murphy, R.E. and Simonds, C.J. (2007) 'I'll see you on "Facebook": the effects of computer-mediated teacher self-disclosure on student motivation, affective learning, and classroom climate', *Communication Education*, 56(1), pp. 1–17.

Miller, A.H., Imrie, B.W. and Cox, K. (1998) *Student assessment in higher education: a handbook for assessing performance*, London: Kogan Page.

Minocha, S. (2009) *Effective use of social software in UK further and higher education*, JISC. Available from http://www.jisc.ac.uk/whatwedo/projects/socialsoftware08.aspx (accessed 8 February 2010).

Moore, G. (1995) *Inside the tornado*, New York: HarperBusiness.

Morgan, C. and O'Reilly, M. (1999) *Assessing open and distance learners*, London: Kogan Page.

Moshell, J.M. and Hughes, C.E. (2002) 'Virtual environments as a tool for academic learning', in Stanney, K.M. (ed.) *Handbook of virtual environments: design, implementation and applications*, Mahwah, NJ: Lawrence Erlbaum, pp. 893–910.

Murphy, D., Walker, R. and Webb, G. (2001) *Online learning and teaching with technology: case studies, experience and practice*, London: Kogan Page.

Nardi, B.A., Whittaker, S. and Bradner, E. (2000) 'Interaction and outeraction: instant messaging in action', *Proceedings of the 2000 ACM Conference on Computer Supported Cooperative Work*, Philadelphia, USA, pp. 79–88.

Nicholson, S. (2002) 'Socialisation in the "virtual hallway": instant messaging in the asynchronous web-based distance education classroom', *The Internet and Higher Education*, 5(4), pp. 363–372.

Nicol, D. and Milligan, C. (2006) 'Rethinking technology-supported assessment practices in relation to the seven principles of good feedback practice', in Bryan, C. and Clegg, K., *Innovative assessment in higher education*, Abingdon: Routledge, pp. 64–77.

Nicol, D.J. and Macfarlane-Dick, D. (2006) 'Formative assessment and self-regulated learning: a model and seven principles of good feedback practice', *Studies in Higher Education*, 31(2), pp. 199–218.

Nicol, D.J., Minty, I. and Sinclair, C. (2003), 'The social dimensions of online learning', *Innovations in Education and Teaching International*, 40(3), pp. 270–280.

Nicosia, L.M. (2009) 'Virtual constructivism: avatars in action', Dumova, T. and Fiordo, R. (eds), *Handbook of research on social interaction technologies and collaboration software: concepts and trends*, Hershey, PA: Information Science Reference (IGI Global), pp. 623–638.

O'Reilly (2005) 'What Is Web 2.0?' Available at http://www.oreillynet.com/pub/a/oreilly/tim/news/2005/09/30/what-is-web-20.html (accessed 20 January 2010).

O'Reilly, M. and Morgan, C. (1999) 'Online assessment: creating communities and opportunities', in Brown, S., Bull, J. and Race, P., *Computer-assisted assessment in higher education*, London: Kogan Page, pp. 149–162.

Oblinger, D.G. and Oblinger, J.L. (2005) *Educating the net generation*, Educause. Available from http://www.educause.edu/educatingthenetgen (accessed 1 February 2010).

Palloff, R.M. and Pratt, K. (1999) *Building learning communities in cyberspace: effective strategies for the online classroom*, San Francisco: Jossey-Bass.

Palloff, R.M. and Pratt, K. (2007) 'Online learning communities in perspective', in Luppicini, R. (ed.), *Online learning communities*, Charlotte, NC: Information Age Publishing, pp. 3–15.

Palme, J., Karlgren, F. and Pargman, D. (1996) 'Issues when designing filters in messaging systems', *Computer Communications*, 19, pp. 95–101.

Piaget, J. (1952) *The origins of intelligence in children*, London: Routledge and Kegan Paul.

Pilkington, R., Bennett, C. and Vaughan, S. (2000) 'An evaluation of computer mediated communication to support group discussion in continuing education', *Educational Technology and Society*, 3(3), pp. 349–360.

Preece, J. (2000) *Online communities: designing usability, supporting sociability*, Chichester: John Wiley & Sons.

Preece, J. (2001) 'Sociability and usability in online communities: determining and measuring success', *Behaviour and Information Technology*, 20(5), pp. 347–356.

Preece, J. (2004) 'Etiquette online: from nice to necessary', *Communications of the ACM*, 47(4), pp. 56–61.

Prensky, M. (2001) 'Digital natives, digital immigrants', *On the Horizon*, 9(5), pp. 1–6.

Quan-Haase, A. and Collins, J.L. (2008) 'I'm there, but I might not want to talk to you', *Information, Communication and Society*, 11(4), pp. 526–543.

Ramage, M. (2010) 'Communities of practice – real and virtual', in Donelan, H., Kear, K. and Ramage, M. (eds), *Online communication and collaboration: a reader*, Abingdon: Routledge, pp. 176–178.

Ramsden, P. (1992) *Learning to teach in higher education*, London: Routledge.

Rapaport, M. (1991) *Computer mediated communications: bulletin boards, computer conferencing, electronic mail, and information retrieval*, New York: John Wiley and Sons.

Redecker, C. (2009) *Review of learning 2.0 practice: study on the impact of web 2.0 innovations in education and training in Europe*, Seville: European Commission Joint Research Centre Institute for Prospective Technological Studies. Available from http://ipts.jrc.ec.europa.eu/publications/pub.cfm?id=2059 (accessed 8 February 2010).

Rennie, F. and Mason, R. (2004) *The Connecticon: learning for the connected generation*, Greenwich, CT: Information Age Publishing.

Renninger, K.A. and Shumar, W. (eds) (2002) *Building virtual communities: learning and change in cyberspace*, Cambridge: Cambridge University Press.

Resnick, P. and Varian, H.R. (1997) 'Recommender systems', *Communications of the ACM*, 40(3), pp. 56–58.

Resnick, P., Iacovou, N., Suchak, M., Bergstrom, P. and Riedl, J. (1994) 'GroupLens: an open architecture for collaborative filtering of Netnews', *Proceedings of the ACM 1994 conference on computer-supported cooperative work*, Chapel Hill, NC: ACM, pp. 175–186.

Rheingold, H. (1993) *The virtual community: homesteading on the electronic frontier*, Reading MA: Addison Wesley.

Richardson, W. (2006) *Blogs, wikis, podcasts and other powerful web tools for classrooms*, Thousand Oaks, CA: Corwin Press.

Robertshaw, M. (2001) 'Flame war', in Murphy, D., Walker, R. and Webb, G. (eds), *Online learning and teaching with technology: case studies, experience and practice*, London: Kogan Page, pp. 13–20.

Robinson, J.M. (1999) 'Computer-assisted peer review', in Brown, S., Bull, J. and Race, P., *Computer-assisted assessment in higher education*, London: Kogan Page, pp. 95–102.

Rosedale, P. (2009) 'Train for success lecture'. Available from http://www.gronstedtgroup.com/MP3s/Philip_Rosedale_Linden_Lab.mp3 (accessed 16 June 2009).

Rosell-Aguilar, F. (2005) 'Task design for audiographic conferencing: promoting beginner oral interaction in distance language learning', *Computer Assisted Language Learning*, 18(5), pp. 417–442.

Ross, S., Jordan, S. and Butcher, P. (2006) 'Online instantaneous and target feedback for remote learners', in Bryan, C. and Clegg, K., *Innovative assessment in higher education*, Abingdon: Routledge, pp. 123–131.

Rourke, L., Anderson, T., Garrison, R. and Archer, W. (1999) 'Assessing social presence in asynchronous text-based computer conferencing', *Journal of Distance Education*, 14(2). Available from http://www.jofde.ca/index.php/jde/article/view/153 (accessed 5 February 2010).

Rowntree, D. (1995) 'Teaching and learning online: a correspondence education for the 21st century?', *British Journal of Educational Technology*, 26(3), pp. 205–215.

Ruberg, L., Moore, D.M. and Taylor, C.D. (1996) 'Student participation, interaction and regulation in a computer-mediated communication environment: a qualitative study', *Journal of Educational Computing Research*, 14(3), pp. 243–268.

Rutter, M. (2009) 'Messenger in the barn: networking in a learning environment', *ALT-J, Research in Learning Technology*, 17(1), pp. 33–47.

Ryberg, T., Dirckinck-Holmfeld, L. and Jones, C. (2010) 'Catering to the needs of the "digital natives" or educating the "net generation"?', in Lee, M.J.W. and McLoughlin, C. (eds), *Web 2.0-based e-learning: applying social informatics for tertiary teaching*, Hershey PA: IGI Global.

Sadler, D.R. (2002) 'Aha! . . . so *that's* "quality" ', in Schwartz, P. and Webb, G. (eds), *Assessment: case studies, experience and practice from higher education*, London: Kogan Page, pp. 13–20.

Salmon, G. (2002) *E-tivities: the key to active online learning*, Abingdon: Taylor & Francis.

Salmon, G. (2004) *E-moderating: the key to teaching and learning online*, 2nd edition, Abingdon: Taylor & Francis.

Scardamalia, M. and Bereiter, C. (1996a) 'Student communities for the advancement of knowledge', *Communications of the ACM*, 39(4), pp. 36–37.

Scardamalia, M. and Bereiter, C. (1996b) 'Computer support for knowledge building communities', in Koschmann, T. (ed.), *CSCL: theory and practice of an emerging paradigm*, Mahwah, NJ: Erlbaum.

Scardamalia, M., Bereiter, C., McClean, R., Swallow, J. and Woodruff, E. (1989) 'Computer-supported intentional learning environments', *Journal of Educational Computer Research*, 5(1), pp. 51–68.

Schroeder, J. and Greenbowe, T.J. (2009) 'The chemistry of Facebook: using social networking to create an online community for the organic chemistry laboratory', *Innovate* 5(4). Available from http://www.innovateonline.info/ (accessed 26 January 2010).

Schueth, M. (2008) 'Using ning.com in an English course for social networking', University of Nebraska-Lincoln. Available from http://eeando.unl.edu/facultyPortfolio/public/display_portfolio.php?search=port&portfolio_id=37 (accessed 26 February 2010).

Schwan, S., Straub, D. and Hesse, F.W. (2002) 'Information management and learning in computer conferences: coping with irrelevant and unconnected messages', *Instructional Science*, 30, pp. 269–289.

Schwartz, P. (2002) 'Gain without pain?', in Schwartz, P. and Webb, G. (eds), *Assessment: case studies, experience and practice from higher education*, Kogan Page, London, pp. 25–31.

Shaw, E., Kim, J. and Supanakoon, P. (2009) 'Mentor match: using student mentors to scaffold participation and learning within an online discussion board', *Proceedings of the AI in Education Conference, 2009*. Available from http://www.isi.edu/~jihie/papers/MentorMatch-AIED2009.pdf (accessed 8 February 2010).

Shaw, J. and Woodthorpe, J. (2009) 'fOUndIt? Sharing online resources to support subject communities', in *7th international conference on education and information systems, technologies and applications: EISTA 2009*, 10–13 July 2009, Orlando, Florida, USA.

Shirky, C. (2008a) *Here comes everybody: the power of organizing without organizations*, London: Allen Lane.

Shirky, C. (2008b) 'It's not information overload. It's filter failure', *Web 2.0 expo* New York, available from Asay, M. (2009) 'Shirky: problem is filter failure, not info overload', *The open road: the business and politics of open source*, CNET. Available from http://news.cnet.com/8301-13505_3-10142298-16.html (accessed 6 January 2010).

Short, J., Williams, E. and Christie, B. (1976) *The social psychology of telecommunications*, London: John Wiley & Sons.

Skiba, D.J. (2008) 'Nursing education 2.0: Twitter & tweets', *Nursing Education Perspectives*, 29(2), pp. 110–112. Available from http://nln.allenpress.com/pdfserv/i1536-5026-029-02-0110.pdf (accessed 26 January 2010).

Skinner, E. (2007) 'Building knowledge and community through online discussion', *Journal of Geography in Higher Education*, 31(3), pp. 381–391.

Skinner, E. (2009) 'Using community development theory to improve student engagement in online discussion: a case study', *ALT-J, Research in Learning Technology*, 17(2), pp. 89–100.

Skinner, E. and Derounian, J. (2008) 'Building community through online discussion', *Teaching and Learning in Higher Education*, 2, pp. 57–70.

Skinner, R.F. (1954) 'The science of learning and the art of teaching', *Harvard Educational Review*, 24(1), pp. 86–97.

Smith, G.G. and Ferguson, D. (2004) 'Diagrams and math notation in e-learning: growing pains of a new generation', *International Journal of Mathematics Education in Science and Technology*, 35(5), pp. 681–695.

Song, L., Singleton, E.S., Hill, J.R. and Koh, M.H. (2004) 'Improving online learning: student perceptions of useful and challenging characteristics', *The Internet and Higher Education*, 7(1), pp. 59–70.

Sproull, L. and Kiesler, S. (1991) *Connections: new ways of working in the networked organisation*, Cambridge, MA: MIT Press.

Surowiecki, J. (2005) *The wisdom of crowds*, London: Abacus.

Swan, K. (2002) 'Building learning communities in online courses: the importance of interaction', *Education, Communication & Information*, 2(1), pp. 23–49.

Sweller, J. and Chandler, P. (1994) 'Why some material is difficult to learn', *Cognition and Instruction*, 12(3), pp. 185–233.

Tanis, M. and Postmes, T. (2007) 'Two faces of anonymity: paradoxical effects of cues to identity in CMC', *Computers in Human Behavior*, 23, pp. 955–970.

Tarbin, S. and Trevitt, C. (2001) 'Try, try again!', in Murphy, D., Walker, R. and Webb, G. (eds) *Online learning and teaching with technology: case studies, experience and practice*, London: Kogan Page, pp. 13–20.

Thorpe, M. (1998) 'Assessment and "third generation" distance education', *Distance Education*, 19(2), pp. 265–286.

Trentin, G. (2009) 'Using a wiki to evaluate individual contribution to a collaborative learning project', *Journal of Computer Assisted Learning*, 25, pp. 43–55.

Tuckman, B. (1965), 'Developmental sequences in small groups', *Psychological Bulletin*, 63, pp. 384–399.

Twining, P. (2009) 'Exploring the educational potential of virtual worlds – some reflections from the SPP', *British Journal of Educational Technology*, 40(3), pp. 496–514.

Virtual Worlds Review (n.d.) http://www.virtualworldsreview.com/index.shtml (accessed 6 February 2010).

Vonderwell, S. (2003) 'An examination of asynchronous communication experiences and perspectives of students in an online course: a case study', *The Internet and Higher Education*, 6(1), pp. 77–90.

Vygotsky, L.S. (1962) *Thought and language*, Cambridge, MA: MIT Press.

Vygotsky, L.S. (1978) *Mind in society: the development of higher psychological processes*, Cambridge, MA: Harvard University Press.

Walker, M. (2009) 'An investigation into written comments on assignments: do students find them usable?', *Assessment & Evaluation in Higher Education*, 34(1), pp. 67–78.

Wang, Y. (2004) 'Web-based eportfolios system in elearning environment', *Open Education Research*, 51(5), pp. 56–58.

Wang, Y. (2008) 'ePortfolios: A new peer assessment technology in educational context', *2008 International Symposiums on Information Processing*, IEEE Computer Society, pp. 360–363.

Wang, Y. and Chen, N.S. (2009) 'Criteria for evaluating synchronous learning management systems: arguments from the distance language classroom', *Computer Assisted Language Learning*, 22(1), pp. 1–18.

Warren, K.J. and Rada, R. (1998) 'Sustaining computer-mediated communication in university courses', *Journal of Computer Assisted Learning*, 14, pp. 71–80.

Wegerif, R. (1998) 'The social dimension of asynchronous learning networks', *Journal of Asynchronous Learning Networks*, 2(1).

Weller, M. (2007) *Virtual learning environments: using, choosing and developing your VLE*, Abingdon: Routledge.

Weller, M. and Robinson, L. (2001) 'Scaling up an online course to deal with 12000 students', *Education, Communication & Information*, 1(3), pp. 307–323.

Wellman, B. (1999) 'The network community: an introduction', in Wellman, B. (ed.), *Networks in the global village: life in contemporary communities*, Boulder, CO: Westview Press, pp. 1–47.

Wellman, B. (2001) 'Physical place and cyberplace: the rise of personalized networking', *International Journal of Urban and Regional Research*, 25(2), pp. 227–252.

Wellman, B. and Gulia, M. (1999) 'Virtual communities as communities: net surfers don't ride alone', in Kollock, P. and Smith, M. (eds), *Communities in cyberspace*, London: Routledge.

Wenger, E. (1998) *Communities of practice: learning, meaning and identity*, Cambridge: Cambridge University Press.

Wenger, E., McDermott, R. and Snyder, W. (2002) *Cultivating communities of practice: a guide to managing knowledge*, Cambridge MA: Harvard Business School Press.

West, J.A. and West, M.L. (2009) *Using wikis for online collaboration: the power of the read-write web*, San Francisco: Jossey-Bass.

Wheeler, S., Yeomans, P. and Wheeler, D. (2008) 'The good, the bad and the wiki: evaluating student-generated content for collaborative learning', *British Journal of Educational Technology*, 39(6), pp. 987–995.

Whittaker, S. and Sidner, C. (1997) 'Email overload: exploring personal information management of email', in Kiesler, S. (ed.), *Culture of the internet*, Mahwah, NJ: Lawrence Erlbaum Associates, pp. 277–295.

Wiley, D. (2007) 'Online self-organising social systems: four years later', in Luppicini, R. (ed.), *Online learning communities*, Charlotte, NC: Information Age Publishing, pp. 289–298.

Wilson, T. and Whitelock, D. (1998) 'What are the perceived benefits of participating in a computer-mediated communication (CMC) environment for distance learning computer science students?', *Computers and Education*, 30(3/4), pp. 259–269.

Wood, D., Bruner, J. and Ross, G. (1976) 'The role of tutoring in problem solving', *Journal of Child Psychology and Psychiatry*, 17, pp. 89–100.

Zhao, Y. (1998) 'The effects of anonymity on computer-mediated peer review', *International Journal of Educational Telecommunications*, 4(4), pp. 311–345.

Zimmer, R. and Alexander, G. (1996) 'The Rogerian interface: for open, warm empathy in computer mediated collaborative learning', *Innovations in Education and Training International*, 33(1), pp. 13–21.

Zimmer, R., Harris, R. and Muirhead, B. (2000) 'Building an online learning community', in Higgison, C. (ed.), *Online tutoring e-book*. Available from http://web.archive.org/web/20040625185806/otis.scotcit.ac.uk/onlinebook/t3-06.pdf (accessed 14 June 2010).

Index